Roadside Baseball

Uncovering hidden treasures from our national pastime

By Chris Epting

Photo credits

All photos appear courtesy of The Sporting News Archives unless noted below:

Author's collection, p. 7 top, p. 8, p. 15, p. 17, p. 22, p. 25, p. 26, p. 52. p. 60, p. 61. p. 62, p. 63 right, p. 65, p. 67. p. 70, p. 77, p. 82, p. 89, p. 92, p. 100, p. 114, p. 159, p. 177, p. 205. P. 220, p. 225 bottom, p. 234 top, p. 246, p. 247, p. 248, p. 250, p. 255, p. 256, p. 258, p. 259, p. 264, p. 266, p. 267, p. 286.

Fred Willard, p. 7, bottom; Jim Lytle, p. 9; Cal Ripken Museum, p. 20; David McAleer, p. 34, p. 36. p. 37, p. 51. p. 69; Dennis LeBeau, p. 40; Becker College, p. 43; Yogi Berra Museum and Learning Center, p. 53; William Gill, p. 78; Peter J. McGovern Little League Museum, p. 96; Virginia Sports Hall of Fame and Museum, p. 102; Alabama Sports Hall of Fame, p. 107; David Brewer, p. 108, p. 109; Arkansas Travelers, p. 112; Eric and Wendy Pastore/www.digitalballparks.com, p. 116, p. 142, p. 149; Ivan Allen Jr. Braves Museum and Hall of Fame, p. 124; Dr. Linda Walden, p. 125; Ed Jackson, p. 126, p. 129; Georgia Sports Hall of Fame, p. 128; Ty Cobb Healthcare System, p. 130; Savannah Sand Gnats, p. 131; Louisville Slugger Museum, p. 133; City of Delhi, p. 137; City of Gretna/Virgie Ott, p. 138 top; Jim Lytle, p. 139; Tony Farlow, p. 141; John Byrne/Fuquay Mineral Spring Inn & Garden, p. 143; Harriet Woodard, p. 145; Charleston RiverDogs, p. 148; ©2003 by Grand Slam Enterprises, Inc. Appeared in BASEBALLPARKS.COM website. Used by permission of photographer Joe Mock and Grand Slam Enterprises, p. 152; The Legends of the Game Museum, p. 154; Sandra McIntosh/News Editor, Ennis Daily News, p. 156; Fort Worth Cats, p. 157; Milton Babb, p. 158; Terry Stembridge, p. 162; Texas Sports Hall of Fame, p. 163; Jeannine Hedges, p. 167 right; Todd Olsen, p. 171, p. 173; BRS Museum, p. 174; Courtesy Billy Sunday Historic Site Museum, Winona Lake, Indiana, p. 182 top; Quad City River Bandits, p. 184; Bob Feller Museum, p. 185; Dick Davis, p. 188, p. 189, p. 190, p. 191; Matt Rogers, Wichita Baseball, Inc., p. 194, p. 195 top; Baseball Hall of Fame Museum Minnesota, p. 203; Stew Thornley, p. 204; Jesse Frazer/KCMO Parks and Recreation, p. 207; Andrew G. Clem, p. 208; Negro Leagues Baseball Museum, p. 209, p. 210; Roger Maris Museum, p. 218; Indian Hill Historical Society, p. 225 top; Terry Hembree, p. 230; Oklahoma Sports Museum, p. 231; Oklahoma Red Hawks, p. 233 top & bottom; Sioux Falls Stadium, p. 236; Clear Lake Area Historical Museum, p. 237; Johnson Monument, p. 238; Lee Gibbs, p. 240; Big League Dreams Sportsparks, p. 252; Courtesy Point Loma Nazarene University, p. 261; Eydie Fenton, p. 273; Courtesy Portland Parks and Recreation, p. 276; John Scherich, p. 278; Kevin Kalal/Tacoma Rainiers, p. 279; Fairbanks Alaska Goldpanners, p. 283.

ISBN: 0-89204-714-3   10 9 8 7 6 5 4 3 2 1

The book is dedicated to my "home team:" wife, Jean, son, Charlie and daughter, Claire. Perennial all-stars are they; no man is luckier than I.

To Richard "Dick" Davis of Chanute, Kansas. Dick's tremendous heart and dedication toward recognizing and establishing the historic sites in Humboldt, Kansas, for Walter Johnson and George Sweatt only begin to tell the story. His passion for the history and glory of the game is matched only by his courage and sparkling optimism, and it is because of people like Dick (and his wife Gloria) that a book like this can exist in the first place.

Thank you, my friend. The game is better for having you here.

And to the real MVPs, the men and women of the United States military, whose bravery and unselfish dedication during these tumultuous times make it possible for the rest of us to do simple things like go out to the ballpark for a baseball game.

Acknowledgements

Eternal thanks to my family, especially my wife Jean and children Charlie and Claire, my mom Louise and sisters Margaret and Lee. Also to the memory of my late grandmother, Margaret Gallo, and my dad, Lawrence Epting.

A special thanks, also, to the team at *The Sporting News*: Joe Hoppel, Ron Smith, Bob Parajon, Christen Sager, Pam Speh, Vern Kasal, Steve Romer and Steve Meyerhoff for their interest, encouragement and consummate teamwork. You guys are simply awesome and it's a privilege to work with you.

To my friends and family who share the passion of baseball, both along the side of the road and in the ballpark—Jack Riley, Thom Sharp, Fred Willard, David McAleer, Gabe Miller, Ronnie Schell, Pat McCormick, Smitty and Charlie.

To Bob Bluthhardt, Joe Mock, David Burkett and Terry Cannon, who contributed to my research. And to everyone else who so generously helped with their time, information, resources and stories, particularly John Outland, Henry Thomas (author of the exceptional *Walter Johnson, Baseball's Big Train*), Lee Gibbs, Stew Thornley, Joe Mock, David Brewer, Milton Babb, Terry Hembree, Virgie Ott, William Gill, David Brewer, Terry Stembridge, Boyce Cox, Chuck Foertmeyer, Dennis LeBeau and Dr. Linda Walden.

A salute to Mike Scioscia's 2002 champion Anaheim Angels, who reminded me how important teamwork is, and how thrilling baseball can be, and our Angels game "neighbors," Gail and Dave Vize.

And to you, the reader, for holding this book in your hands right now. Thank you for being a part of this rewarding journey.

Note: I have tried my best to include all of the baseball-related sites out there, but I know there are still some stones uncovered. If you know of a site that should be included in any future edition of *Roadside Baseball*, write me at chris@chrisepting.com. All comments are welcome.

Roadside Baseball

Foreword by Joe Buck

Even if you consider yourself the foremost authority on the history of the game, this book can't help but put a smile on your face. It put one on mine because its pages are filled with information that I thought I knew but really didn't; stories of which I was totally unaware and now am glad I know. The real treat, however, is that each piece is short, to the point, and stated in a way that gives me a chance of remembering impressive facts should I find myself at a cocktail party with, say, George Will or Bob Costas. I guess I am known as a baseball guy, but after reading through an advanced copy of this gem, I realize I have been living a lie. I dare even the most diehard fan to pick up this book and not learn something from any random page.

What Chris Epting has done is put together a travel guide, filled with landmarks and tidbits of fascinating information about the game and those who played it. You can read it in the comfort of home or take it with you as you journey far and wide learning about the game we all love. What makes this book special for me is the focus on happenings away from the famous stadiums we all know and remember. Yes, those places are detailed in the book as well, but what I love are the stories that remind us all that the game's great players were just men making a living doing what they loved. They were people who had lives away from box scores and cheering crowds, with stories that are as legendary and noteworthy as the accomplishments you can find in any baseball encyclopedia. Whether it's Hubert's Flea Market, where Grover Cleveland Alexander entertained after giving up baseball, or Dyersville, Iowa, where the movie *Field of Dreams* was filmed, there is so much detail about what has happened, and still does, on the periphery of the game. From hometown plaques dedicated to the birthplace of local legends to burial sites and

Buck grew up idolizing Gibson and Brock (left and right end), while his father, Jack, had broadcast games involving Musial and Schoendienst.

all the stories in between, there is information here that makes the game come to life in a unique way.

Baseball is a very personal game. Because of my childhood as Jack Buck's son, I can trace my life along the recent timeline of the St. Louis Cardinals' franchise. I was born in 1969, which means I missed a golden age in Cardinals history, as well as a golden age of the game itself. Timing is everything, and living in St. Louis in the 1970s meant idolizing Gibson, Brock and Simmons as individuals, but having little to cheer by way of a team. If Chris Epting and *The Sporting News* were to detail my travels with my father, the stories that would most warm my heart would be those that often took place away from the ballpark, well after the final out was recorded in the games.

In Los Angeles, a trip to Hollywood Park might mean placing bets alongside actor Walter Matthau. In San Francisco, a day at Candlestick Park often was followed by golf at the Olympic Club and a late dinner at Lefty O'Doul's restaurant and bar—named after a San Francisco baseball legend. In Chicago, it was Wrigley Field and dinner at Harry Caray's. In New York, there were tales of late nights at Toots Shor's, where press and athletes gathered for food, drink, stories and other night-time activities (to put it mildly). The stories and the people around the game who would join us from time to time were both fascinating and entertaining. And those days on the road and the different things we did all related to my concepts and impressions of baseball. These were cherished times in my childhood, the very experiences that prompted me to pick the profession I did. The games are exciting and the moments they produce are memorable, but it's the life around baseball, its people and personalities, that make it all so much fun.

The beauty is that you don't have to be a Hall of Fame announcer's son to have baseball memories that will always be a part of you. Simple recollections of walking for the first time into Crosley Field for a Reds game, or what you were doing in 1960 when Mazeroski hit the Series-clinching home run at Forbes Field to beat the Yanks, are the stories handed down from generation to generation, from grandpa to grandson, father to son, mother to daughter. Roadside Baseball brings these memories to life while providing a special historical context of where these pieces of baseball Americana actually took place. I believe people in my generation would be shocked to learn how close Yankee Stadium was to the Polo Grounds. Any baseball fan would be interested to visit the Boston hotel where Chicago players planned the infamous "Black Sox" scheme of 1919, or to know that a banyan tree planted by Babe Ruth in Hilo, Hawaii, in the 1930s is still thriving and a public landmark. But this is more than just a baseball map. It's also a storybook and I cannot think of a better way to learn the history of this great game.

And, remember, if you do use this book as a travel guide and you're driving east to west, those bugs on the grill of your car will need to be washed off. Don't worry. You can stop in Simi Valley, California, at Lenny Dykstra's car wash, a mini-baseball museum with soap and water. Just don't get the tobacco-scented air-freshener; it's not a big hit on dates.

—**Joe Buck**

"It breaks your heart. It is designed to break your heart. The game begins in the spring, when everything else begins again, and it blossoms in the summer, filling the afternoons and evenings, and then as soon as the chill rains come, it stops and leaves you to face the fall."

—*A. Bartlett Giamatti*

"The field was even greener than my boy's mind had pictured it. In later years, friends of ours visited Ireland and said the grass there was plenty green all right, but that not even the Emerald Isle itself was as green as the grass that grew in Ebbets Field."

—*Duke Snider*

"Baseball was, is and always will be to me the best game in the world."

—*Babe Ruth*

Introduction

Completing this book has satisfied a journey that began long ago. Baseball has been a wonderful tonic for me, as much in my boyhood as it is now. And a lot of that pleasure has been derived from studying its old structures—the ballparks. I remember pitching in Little League, looking off at our old bleachers at the field and thinking, "This is just like playing in the old Polo Grounds ... or League Park in Cleveland!" Taking my son to the same field years later and watching him run those bases crystallized my love for the game. It's something we hand down to our juniors as surely as the golden rule. It's the continuum of the ages. One ball, two mitts and all of a sudden life's lessons become easier to explain. Bonds are forged, and we are so much richer for the simple act of having a catch.

I think the seeds for this book were planted when I was about 11 years old. Looking through a baseball picture book, I remember seeing the famous Charles Conlon photograph of Ty Cobb sliding hard into Jimmy Austin at third base. The cap-

The park where the Giants, Yankees and Mets once roamed now is the site of the Polo Grounds Towers.

Proof you can go home again—a home plate marking Hilltop Park.

tion said the picture had been snapped at Hilltop Park in New York. We lived in New York and I was a huge baseball fan, but I had never heard of the stadium. I had heard of the Polo Grounds, torn down in the early '60s when I was about 3. I was well aware of Ebbets Field, where my mom and many relatives had grown up seeing ballgames. But not Hilltop.

After some research, I learned that Hilltop Park was the original home of the Yankees, a park that had been torn down many years earlier. I was intrigued. If I wanted to go stand on the spot where the picture was taken, to sense what it might have been like there so many years ago, would it be possible? If the ballpark was gone, what was there now? I discovered that Columbia Presbyterian Hospital had been built where the stadium once stood, but that was all I knew. It was something I knew some day I had to investigate; I had to stand where that wonderful baseball image had been captured. And I got to thinking about other famous images, of Willie Mays' World Series catch at the Polo Grounds, Jackie Robinson stealing home at Ebbets—all those ancient photos I loved to study ...

what occupied those places now?

What about all of those great ballparks of yesteryear, those longtime city landmarks that weren't around any more? I remember being in Pennsylvania in the early 1970s when the abandoned Connie Mack Stadium caught fire. It stung to watch the local news reports. I

Pittsburgh's once-splendid Forbes Field, shortly before the wrecking ball.

remember when Forbes Field was torn down. And I felt then as I do now—the ground where those ballparks were located was sacred and should, at the very least, be identified. Put up a building if you must, create another parking lot if you have to, but please, let people know what happened there, maybe even try to preserve a shred or piece of what once stood. Let the future generations know that there was once a field here with bright green grass and fresh brown dirt. A place where dreams came true and hearts were broken. Make it possible for a father to bring his child to the spot where he saw Roberto

Charlie Epting, the author's son, checks out the Reggie Jackson handprints at Edison International.

Clemente play; allow old fans to relive Enos Slaughter's Mad Dash in the 1946 World Series; help an interested young fan locate the spot and stand where one of his favorite historic pictures was taken.

Today, it seems, inspired efforts are being made throughout the country to recognize baseball history. In both huge cities and small towns around America, museums, plaques, signs, markers and memorials are popping up to identify historic baseball figures and events. When I finally made it to the site of Hilltop Park years later, I was thrilled to find a plaque, in the shape of home plate, placed near where the original one once sat. I mapped the scene of that Charles Conlon photo. It gave me peace of mind—and an idea. Why not try to document all of these sites?

Hence, this book.

Some places have not yet been marked, but hopefully they will be soon. In addition to the stadium sites, I also became interested over the years in other sites that make up the fabric of the game's history. Birthplaces ... museums ... statues ... forgotten fields ... final resting places. They all play a part in helping to define why baseball remains our National Pastime, and they all are an intimate part of *Roadside Baseball.*

And while this book is about history, it also is about the emotions encountered on the quest for baseball's past—the love, passion, dreams, courage, glory and pain, found in places like a school in Baltimore, where Babe Ruth first picked up a mitt ... at the park where he hit his first home run ... at the park where he hit his last. At a hotel lobby where Lou Gehrig told Yankees manager Joe McCarthy he was pulling himself from the lineup later that day. At the Daytona Beach park where Jackie Robinson first took the field, righting decades of terrible wrong. At the Oxnard, California, field where Hans Lobert

This plaque marking the birthplace of Negro League star Cool Papa Bell can be found in Starkville, Mississippi.

raced a horse around the bases.

This is about hometowns and local fans who refuse to let a memory die, lovingly erecting signs for such former greats as Walter Johnson, Tris Speaker, Mickey Mantle and Grover Cleveland Alexander ... and build shrines and dedicate parks in their honor.

It's about vacant lots that once mesmerized visitors with the carnival smell of hot dogs, beer and cigars ... about playing catch on a diamond where Satchel Paige, Buck O'Neil and Josh Gibson once performed their magic ... about standing where Ruth, Williams, Speaker, Hornsby, Maris, Mantle and Musial waited for their pitch.

This is a story of once-glorious places where ghosts still might play; where, in the dust and in the wind, you still might swear you can hear the distant crack of a bat and the faint echoes of a crowd.

This is about finding our own personal fields of dreams and reconnecting with the innocence of oiling a glove ... keeping score with a #2 pencil ... getting a priceless autograph ... lying awake at night, dreaming about some day playing in a World Series Game 7.

This is about Roadside Baseball. So pack up the car, grab your mitts and get ready to discover the heart and soul of the game. Are you ready?

Play ball!

—**Chris Epting**

The East

Grave of
Louis Sockalexis
Old Town, Maine

Baseball
Hall of **Fame**
Cooperstown, New York

Former site of
Shibe Park
Philadelphia,
Pennsylvania

Site of Ron Necciai's
27 strikeout game
Bristol, Virginia

Jackie Robinson Park of Fame features a life-size bronze statue of the man who broke baseball's color barrier.

Connecticut

Roberto Clemente Baseball Field Park

City: Bridgeport
Location: Iranistan Avenue
Seaside Park
A monument to Clemente stands at this youth baseball field which bears his name.

Roberto Clemente Memorial

City: Hartford
Location: Wawarme Avenue
Colt Park
This monument dedicated to the Pirates great is located behind field No. 3.

Jackie Robinson Park of Fame

City: Stamford
Location: Jackie Robinson Way
W. Main St.
For more than 20 years, Jackie Robinson lived with his family in Stamford. To honor him, the city erected a life-size bronze statue of the Brooklyn Dodgers

star with an engraved base bearing the words "COURAGE, CONFIDENCE AND PERSEVERANCE." The statue is in a park also named for the man who in 1947 broke the color barrier in modern major league baseball.

Yale Field

City: West Haven
Location: 252 Derby Ave.
Yale Field is home to the Yale University baseball team and the New Haven Ravens of the Class AA Eastern League. Renovated in 1927 after being an open field with just a few bleachers, the park has its own version of the "Green Monster"—a 35-foot-high metal scoreboard in center field. Yale's Bulldogs have played at this site since 1902. Babe Ruth once remarked that the playing surface at Yale Field was the best he had ever seen. The noted 1948 photograph of Ruth and Yale first baseman George Bush was taken here. Ruth was presenting a manuscript of *The Babe Ruth Story,* written by Bob Considine, to the Yale captain and future U.S. President for delivery to the Yale Library.

Hall of Famers buried in Connecticut

Morgan Bulkeley
Cedar Hill Cemetery
Hartford

Roger Connor
Old St. Joseph's Cemetery
Waterbury

Jim O'Rourke
St. Michael's Cemetery
Bridgeport

George Weiss
Evergreen Cemetery
New Haven

Jim O'Rourke (top) was a career .313 hitter and caught a game at age 54. As general manager of the New York Yankees, George Weiss won seven World Series titles.

Delaware

Judy Johnson House

City: Marshallton
Location: Intersection of Newport Rd. and Kiamensi St.

This is the house where William Julius "Judy" Johnson and his wife Anita lived for 55 years. During a career that ran from 1921 through 1937, Johnson was considered the best third baseman in the Negro leagues. He captained a legendary Pittsburgh Crawfords team that also featured future Hall of Famers Satchel Paige, Oscar Charleston, Josh Gibson and Cool Papa Bell. Johnson went on to serve as a major league scout and helped sign such future stars as Dick Allen (for the Philadelphia Phillies) and Bill Bruton (for the Milwaukee Braves). This residence is listed in the National Register of Historic Places.

Hall-of-Famer Judy Johnson, who is buried at Silverbrook Cemetery in Wilmington, batted over .300 most of his career and was considered the best third baseman in the Negro leagues.

Judy Johnson statue

City: Wilmington
Location: Judy Johnson Field at Daniel S. Frawley Stadium
801 S. Madison St.

No Delaware-born player has ever made the Hall of Fame, but Negro leagues star Judy Johnson made the state proud in 1975 when he was elected to Cooperstown. Johnson was born in Maryland, but he moved with his family to Delaware at an early age and developed his many skills on the sandlots of Wilmington. He died in 1989—four years before a statue of the third baseman was dedicated at Daniel S. Frawley Stadium, home of the Carolina League's

Vic Willis (left) recorded eight 20-win seasons in his career and pitched 45 complete games in 1902, a 20th century N.L. record. Bill McGowan, whose colorful antics made him a fan favorite, was known as baseball's best balls-and-strikes umpire and didn't miss an inning over a 16-year stretch.

Wilmington Blue Rocks. The field bears Johnson's name as a tribute to this soft-spoken, keen student of the game.

Judy Johnson is buried at Silverbrook Cemetery.

Other Hall of Famers buried in Delaware

Bill McGowan
Cathedral Cemetery
Wilmington

Vic Willis
St. John's Cemetery
Newark

Maine

Gravesite of Louis Sockalexis

City: Old Town
Location: Old Town Cemetery
Louis Sockalexis was the first major-leaguer known to be a Native American. He was born at Indian Island (Penobscot Indian Reservation) in Maine in 1871 and showed phenomenal athletic skill at an early age. He played baseball at Notre Dame and later was an outfielder for the Cleveland Spiders of the National League. Injuries, alcoholism and racial taunting contributed to a quick demise for Sockalexis, who batted .338 for Cleveland in 66 games in 1897 but wound up with only 367 at-bats over three major league seasons. Sockalexis spent his final years on the reservation, teaching boys how to play baseball until his death in 1913. Though for years it was suggested that the American League's Cleveland Indians chose their name in partial tribute to Sockalexis, that contention has never been substantiated.

Coombs Field

City: Waterville
Location: Colby College
4000 Mayflower Hill Drive
The baseball field at Colby College is named for righthander "Colby Jack" Coombs, who went from the Waterville campus to the Philadelphia Athletics in 1906. Coombs and Boston's Joe Harris, matched up late in the '06 season, established an American League innings-pitched record for one game when both hurled all 24 innings of a game the A's won, 4-1. Rookie Coombs, who struck out 18 Boston batters, finished with a 10-10 record that year. (Harris struggled to a 2-21 mark and was 3-30 in

Jack Coombs, who went from Colby College to the Philadelphia A's, set an A.L. record in 1910 with 13 shutouts en route to a 31-9 record.

his career.) Four years later, Coombs set an A.L. record with 13 shutouts en route to a 31-9 record. In the 1910 World Series, the Colby product defeated the Chicago Cubs three times. In 1911, Coombs compiled a 28-12 mark. After his retirement as a player, Coombs became a noted coach at Duke University, where the baseball field also is named in his honor.

Maryland

Cal Ripken Museum

The Cal Ripken Museum features a huge display from Ripken's record-breaking 2,131st game, and the gift shop has items signed by the longtime Orioles star.

City: Aberdeen
Location: Aberdeen City Hall, U.S. 40 and Bel Air Ave.
410-273-2525

The city of Aberdeen, just 30 miles from Baltimore and about 65 miles from Washington, D.C., is where the Ripken family has its roots, and this museum is the official repository for Cal's memorabilia. It's loaded with items from his record consecutive-games streak, including a huge display from game No. 2,131 and even a ball from Ripken's first game in the streak (May 30, 1982). The gift shop features items signed by the longtime Orioles star. Ripken Stadium, at 873 Long Drive, is home of the Cal Ripken-owned Aberdeen IronBirds of the New York-Penn League.

Babe Ruth Birthplace and Museum

City: Baltimore
Location: 216 Emory St.

This brick row house is where "The Sultan of Swat" was born on February 6, 1895. Designated a National Historic Site, it features rare photos, films, radio broadcasts and other Babe Ruth-related artifacts (including items excavated from the site of the bar that Ruth's father ran—a bar that stood in the area of what is now center field at Oriole Park at Camden Yards). Located just three blocks from Camden Yards, this also is the official Baltimore Orioles Museum. Plus, there are exhibits honoring long-ago greats Lou Gehrig, Wee Willie Keeler and Jimmie Foxx and modern stars like Cal Ripken, Ken Griffey Jr. and Mark McGwire.

Oriole Park at Camden Yards

City: Baltimore

Location: 333 W. Camden St.

When it opened in 1992, Camden Yards revolutionized the way ballparks looked and felt. Designed to resemble parks from the "good old days," it inspired the current trend toward "retro" parks that bring fans close to the field after years of being pushed away in multipurpose stadiums. Camden Yards features tributes to legendary local baseballers. On the Eutaw St. promenade, there is a large bronze statue of Babe Ruth. Strikingly, the lefthanded Ruth is sporting a righthanded fielder's glove. Those who created the statue contend this is not a mistake—that back when the Babe played for St. Mary's Industrial School in Baltimore, the school didn't have lefthanded gloves (thus the monument's "authenticity"). If you access the ballpark through the Eutaw entrance and walk alongside the old B & O Warehouse, you will notice brass, baseball-shaped plaques embedded in the walkway with names and dates on them. The plaques mark where tape-measure home runs landed on Eutaw. The one on the wall past the Orioles Store notes the spot where Ken Griffey Jr. hit the warehouse during the 1993 Home Run Derby competition at the All-Star Game. (No one has hit the Warehouse during a game.) If you enter from the left-field side of

The park that started the wave of retro ballparks, Camden Yards features a 60-foot promenade between it and the B&O Warehouse (left) that includes, among other amenities, culinary delights from Boog's Bar-B-Q.

the stadium, you'll see a plaza with monuments of the numbers retired by the Orioles. Cal Ripken Sr., the longtime Orioles coach and proponent of "The Oriole Way," is honored with a commemorative plaque in the Baltimore dugout. Two Camden Yards seats are specially marked. One in left field (Section 86, Row FF, Seat 10) is red and indicates where Cal Ripken Jr. hit career home run No. 278 in 1993, breaking Ernie Banks' record for a shortstop. In the right-field bleachers, an orange seat (Section 96, Row D, Seat 23) marks where Eddie Murray hit his 500th career homer on September 6, 1996, one year to the day after Cal Jr. played in his 2,131st consecutive game. The foul poles here are from Memorial Stadium, where the Orioles played from 1954 through 1991.

Cardinal Gibbons School

City: Baltimore
Location: 3225 Wilkens Ave.

This formerly was St. Mary's Industrial School for Boys, where Babe Ruth first picked up a baseball. Ruth, deemed out of control by his parents, was

The fields where Babe Ruth first picked up a baseball remain intact behind Cardinal Gibbons School, formerly a reformatory and orphanage.

placed at St. Mary's (a reformatory/orphanage) at age 7. St. Mary's was run by Jesuit missionaries, and it was Brother Matthias who made the greatest impact on Ruth. A man of discipline, guidance and support, he helped teach Ruth how to play baseball—and how to find more structure in his life. Ruth became an excellent pitcher, and he demonstrated the ability to hit a baseball distant places. By his late teens, he had developed into a major league prospect. In February 1914, at age 19, Ruth entered the pro ranks when he signed a contract with Jack Dunn's Baltimore Orioles of the International League. Although some of the school's original buildings have been destroyed by fire, the fields where Ruth first played remain intact. A marker was recently placed there in tribute to Ruth.

Babe Ruth's first professional game

City: Baltimore
Location: American League Park (former site)
Grandstand was located at 29th St. and Greenmount Ave.

This was where Babe Ruth broke into pro ball on April 22, 1914. Pitching for Baltimore, he tossed a six-hitter as the Orioles defeated Buffalo, 6-0, in an International League game. Buffalo's second baseman was Joe McCarthy, who 17 years later became Ruth's manager with the New York Yankees. An industrial park now occupies the site.

Former site of Memorial Stadium

City: Baltimore
Location: Bounded by center field (N), E. 36th St.; third base (W), Ellerslie Ave.; home plate (S), 1000 E. 33rd St.; first base (E), Ednor Rd.

Memorial Stadium opened in 1950 to serve as home of the minor league Orioles, who had played at Municipal Stadium (also called Venable Stadium and Babe Ruth Stadium) after Oriole Park was destroyed by fire in 1944. When the American League's Browns moved here from St. Louis in 1954 to become the major league Orioles, a second deck was added to the stadium, increasing the park's capacity to nearly 48,000. In the park's 38-year history as a big-league venue, only Frank Robinson hit a home run that left the confines of Memorial Stadium. He did it on May 8, 1966, connecting against Cleveland's Luis Tiant. When the Washington Senators left the nation's capital after the 1971 season, Memorial Stadium inherited the spring ritual of U.S. Presidents throwing out

A senior housing center and a YMCA are planned for the grounds where Brooks Robinson once made so many spectacular plays at third base.

Memorial Stadium was named in honor of the Baltimore veterans who died in both World Wars and the Korean War.

the first ball on opening day (although the practice has become somewhat of a rarity). The Orioles played their last game here in 1991, and the stadium was torn down in 2001. Though there is nothing at the site now, a senior housing center and a YMCA are planned for the location.

Notable moments at Memorial Stadium:

- July 8, 1958: The American League won the All-Star Game, 4-3. There were no extra-base hits in the Midsummer Classic, attended by Vice President Richard M. Nixon and a crowd of 48,829.

- September 20, 1958: Knuckleballer Hoyt Wilhelm, in one of only 52 starts in a 21-season major league career, tossed a no-hitter against the Yankees.

- June 10, 1959: Cleveland's Rocky Colavito slammed four home runs against the Orioles. Previously, no team—much less an individual—had hit more than three home runs in one game at the spacious ballpark.

- October 9, 1966: Dave McNally's four-hit shutout completed a sweep of the Dodgers, giving Baltimore its first World Series title.

- September 13, 1971: The Orioles' Frank Robinson hit his 500th career home run, connecting off Detroit's Fred Scherman.

- September 24, 1974: Detroit's Al Kaline collected his 3,000th career hit. His victim: Baltimore's McNally.

- May 30, 1982: Cal Ripken, penciled into the lineup against Toronto, began a playing streak that would reach 2,632 consecutive games.

Walter Johnson High School

City: Bethesda
Location: 6400 Rock Spring Drive
Walter Johnson, "The Big Train" pitching star of the Washington Senators, became a prominent member of the Bethesda community. His standing in the area—he once served on the Montgomery County Council—is reflected by the naming of this high school in his honor. A monument to Johnson, who won 417 major league games, stands at the front of the school, which opened in 1956.

Walter Johnson High School pays tribute to the respect the Big Train commanded in his adopted city of Bethesda.

The memorial dates to 1947, the year after Johnson died. (President Harry Truman had unveiled the granite monument and bronze tablet in the presence of Johnson's mother in a ceremony at Griffith Stadium, and the memorial remained at the ballpark through the stadium's final season, 1961, before being moved to the high school.) A school newsletter is called "The Big Train."

Walter Johnson house

City: Bethesda
Location: 9100 Old Georgetown Road
This private residence, recently designated a state landmark, was the home of Walter Johnson from 1926-1936. From 1936 until his death 10 years later,

Johnson lived and worked on a farm in Germantown, about 20 miles from here. The property where the farm sat has been developed into a shopping center and also is the site of Seneca Valley High School.

Bill "Swish" Nicholson statue

City: Chestertown
Location: Next to Town Hall on Cross St.

Bill Nicholson, a Chestertown native, was the National League home run and RBI king in 1943 and 1944 while playing with the Chicago Cubs. His stature as a slugger was evident in '44 when the New York Giants issued an intentional walk to the outfielder with the bases loaded. The strategy came late in the second game of a doubleheader in which Nicholson already had homered four times. Nicholson died in Chestertown in 1996.

Babe Ruth gets married

City: Ellicott City
Location: St. Paul the Apostle Catholic Church
3755 St. Paul Street

Babe Ruth was a 19-year-old rookie pitcher for the Boston Red Sox when he married Helen Woodford in this church in 1914.

On October 17, 1914, Babe Ruth married Helen Woodford at this church in suburban Baltimore. Ruth was just months removed from St. Mary's Industrial School for Boys when he met Helen at a Boston coffee shop in July 1914. He was 19 years old; she was 17 (there were reports she might have been even younger). The couple adopted a daughter, Dorothy, in 1921. Babe and Helen were living apart in 1929 when Helen died in a fire.

Charlie Keller's horse farm

City: Frederick
Location: Yankeeland Farms
8423 Yellow Springs Rd.

Yankeeland Farms was founded by former Yankees star Charlie Keller in 1955. Along with members of his immediate family, Keller built the 100-acre farm into a major East Coast Standardbred facility. Today, Yankeeland remains a family-run business and a leading breeding establishment. Its many success stories include trotter Fresh Yankee, who in the early 1970s exceeded $1 million in winnings.

Lefty Grove's 1931 MVP trophy

City: Lonaconing
Location: George's Creek Public Library
76 Main St.

Hall of Fame pitcher Robert Moses "Lefty" Grove, who was born in Lonaconing in 1900, won exactly 300 games in the majors. In 1931, he compiled an astonishing 31-4 record for the Philadelphia Athletics and won the A.L. Most Valuable Player award. Grove donated the trophy to the local high school, and the award has since made its way to a showcase in the public library.

Lefty Grove had seven straight 20-win seasons, and his .680 career winning percentage (300-141) ranks No. 1 all-time among 300-game winners.

Charlie Keller plaque

City: Middletown
Location: Middletown Memorial Park
Between Church (Route 17) and Franklin Sts.

Middletown native Charlie "King Kong" Keller hit .334 for the Yankees in his rookie season of 1939 and had five 100-RBI seasons for the Yankees in the 1940s. He also hit 30 or more homers five times. Keller appeared in four World Series with New York, but back problems eventually forced him into a reserve role and duty as a pinch hitter. On September 26, 1998, Middletown honored its hometown hero with a granite monument and plaque placed at the field where he played baseball as a youth.

The Eastern Shore Hall of Fame Museum

City: Salisbury
Location: U.S. 50 and Hobbs Rd.

This museum, located within Perdue Stadium (home of the Delmarva Shorebirds of the South Atlantic League), is a celebration of old-time minor league baseball. Exhibits feature uniforms, equipment, photos and other memorabilia from local low-classification minor leagues and semipro leagues of years gone by. Admission to the museum is included when you buy a Shorebirds game ticket.

Jimmie Foxx statue

City: Sudlersville
Location: Church and Main Sts.

A three-time MVP, Jimmie Foxx's 534 career home runs ranked second all-time to Babe Ruth for many years.

Slugger Jimmie Foxx was born in Sudlersville in 1907. He began his professional baseball career in 1924 with manager Frank "Home Run" Baker's Easton, Md., club of the Eastern Shore League. "Double X" was the second player in major league history to hit 500 home runs, reaching the landmark total in 1940 (11 years after Babe Ruth accomplished the feat). Foxx won American League MVP awards in 1932 and 1933 with the Philadelphia Athletics and in 1938 with the Boston Red Sox. In '33, he won the Triple Crown. He had 58- and 50-homer seasons, won three A.L. homer titles outright and shared the league lead in home runs once. Elected to the Baseball Hall of Fame in 1951, he died in 1967. The statue was dedicated on October 25, 1997. In addition to this monument, there is Foxx memorabilia on display at the Sudlersville Train Station and Museum.

Though many remember Griffith as the stadium where William Howard Taft began the Presidential tradition of throwing out the first ball, many also recall the indent in center field where the fence detoured around five duplexes (the owner wouldn't sell).

Former site of Griffith Stadium

City: Washington, D.C.

Location: Seventh St. and Florida Ave. NW

While the Washington Senators were at spring training in 1911, the club's National Park burned down. (Just the year before, William Howard Taft had begun the Presidential tradition of throwing out the first ball at the season-opening game in Washington.) On the same site of the old National Park, a new park bearing the same name was hastily constructed, with steel and concrete among the components. In 1920, National was renamed Griffith Stadium in honor of Senators owner Clark Griffith. That same year, a second deck was added to the stadium, which was known for its unusually long distance to left field (adjusted from time to time, the distance often was more than 400 feet). Although the Senators won the World Series in 1924 and repeated as A.L. champions in 1925, the club became a perennial second-division team beginning in the mid-1930s and fan support faltered. After the 1960 season, the Senators were relocated to Minnesota and Washington was awarded an expansion team. The new Senators played at Griffith Stadium in 1961, then moved into new District of Columbia Stadium (later renamed Robert F. Kennedy Stadium). Griffith was demolished in 1965. Today, Howard University Hospital occupies the site of the old ballpark. After the 1971 season, the new Senators skipped town, too, fleeing to Arlington, Texas, to become the Texas Rangers.

Notable moments at Griffith Stadium:

- July 5, 1924: The Yankees got a big scare when Babe Ruth, furiously pursuing a fly ball, crashed into the right-field wall. After several anxious moments, Ruth got up and stayed in the game. Shaken but hardly unnerved, Ruth went 3-for-3 in the game, which was the opener of a doubleheader.

- October 10, 1924: The Senators won their only World Series title, defeating the Giants in Game 7 when Earl McNeely's 12th-inning bad-hop grounder drove in the winning run.

- April 13, 1926: Walter Johnson, making his 14th and last opening-day start, outdueled Philadelphia's Ed Rommel in a 15-inning, 1-0 game in which both pitchers went the distance.

- July 7, 1937: Cardinals ace pitcher Dizzy Dean suffered a toe fracture when struck by a line drive in the All-Star Game. The Yankees' Lou Gehrig doubled, homered and drove in four runs in the A.L.'s 8-3 victory.

- April 17, 1953: Batting righthanded, New York's Mickey Mantle crushed a Chuck Stobbs pitch and sent it caroming off the side of the football scoreboard in left field. The ball, which landed in a backyard across the street, traveled an estimated 565 feet.

Hall of Famers buried in Maryland and Washington, D.C., area

Leon Day
Arbutus Memorial Park
1101 Sulphur Spring Rd.
Arbutus, Md.

Richard "Rube" Marquard
Baltimore Hebrew Cemetery
2100 Belair Rd.
Baltimore

Wilbert Robinson, Ned Hanlon, Joe Kelley, John McGraw
New Cathedral Cemetery

Pitcher Rube Marquard had a record 19-game winning streak in 1912.

4300 Old Frederick Rd.
Baltimore

Frank "Home Run" Baker
Spring Hill Cemetery of Talbot
County
Hanson and Aurora Sts.
Easton, Md.

Robert "Lefty" Grove
Frostburg Memorial Park
70 Green St.
Frostburg, Md.

Clark Griffith
Fort Lincoln Cemetery
3401 Bladensburg Rd.
Brentwood, Md.

Sam Rice
Woodside Cemetery
Haviland Mill Road
Brinklow, Md.

Walter Johnson
Rockville Union Cemetery, 1 mile
east of Highway 28 on Baltimore Rd.
Rockville, Md.

Smokey Joe Williams
Lincoln Memorial Cemetery
4001 Suitland Road
Suitland, Md.

Frank "Home Run" Baker, Clark
Griffith and Walter Johnson (top
to bottom).

White Sox players Swede Risberg (left), Buck Weaver (middle) and Happy Felsch (right) wait outside the courtroom with their attorneys during a break in the 1921 Black Sox trial.

Massachusetts

The "Black Sox" hatch their scheme

City: Boston
Location: Buckminster Hotel
645 Beacon St.

It was in this hotel near Fenway Park that Chicago White Sox players, in town to play the Red Sox, conspired to fix the 1919 World Series against the Cincinnati Reds. Bitter about the perceived greed of White Sox owner Charles Comiskey, Sox first baseman Chick Gandil invited bookie Joseph "Sport" Sullivan to his hotel room on September 18, 1919, and told him: "I think we can put it in the bag." (The Sox, comfortably in first place, were obviously Series-bound.) Gandil demanded $80,000—a figure later raised to $100,000—and then approached Chicago pitcher Eddie Cicotte to take part in the plan. Cicotte agreed, provided he got $10,000 up front. Gandil also sold the idea to teammates Lefty Williams, Swede Risberg and Fred McMullin. Sox star "Shoeless Joe" Jackson insisted that when Gandil offered him $10,000, then $20,000, he refused to join the scheme. Gandil allegedly told Jackson to take it or leave it because the fix was arranged anyway. In all, eight players and several gamblers were indicted for conspiracy to defraud the public. (The other players involved were Happy Felsch and Buck Weaver.) All were acquitted at the trial after transcripts of confessions by Cicotte and Jackson disappeared from the court files, but the eight players ultimately were banned from baseball for life by commissioner Kenesaw Mountain Landis. Landis said the players' "crookedness" was evident throughout the trial.

Ted Williams Tunnel

City: Boston

The city of Boston's third harbor tunnel is named after Ted Williams.

Williams officially became part of the Boston family in December of 1937 when the Red Sox acquired him from the San Diego Padres. From the outset, Beantown knew they had a winner. Williams hit his first home run in an exhibition game at Holy Cross College in Worcester, on April 14,1939. His last one came in his last career at-bat on September 28, 1960 at Fenway Park. In between, the fiery superstar, fisherman and patriot carved out one of the all-time great careers. "The Splendid Splinter" was the last major league player to hit for a .400 average or better for a full season. He was voted the league's most valuable player in 1946 and 1949 and won the Triple Crown in 1942 and 1947.

Ted Williams, the last major leaguer to hit .400, had a lifetime batting average of .344.

During his major league career he had a lifetime batting average of .344, batted in 1,839 runs, hit 521 home runs, and was batting champion of the American League six times (1941, 1942, 1947, 1948, 1957, 1958). In 1966 Williams was elected to the Baseball Hall of Fame. The Ted Williams Tunnel opened on December 15, 1995, and connects South Boston to East Boston and Logan Airport.

Former site of Braves Field

City: Boston
Location: Nickerson Field
Boston University
Harry Agganis Way

While only a portion of Braves Field exists today—as Nickerson Field, where Boston University plays its football and soccer games—the Gaffney Street ticket office that was located down the right-field line remains intact, as a child-care center and security office for Boston University.

Home to the Boston Braves from 1915 until their move to Milwaukee after the 1952 season, Braves Field also was home to Red Sox home games in the 1915 and 1916 World Series because the N.L. park had a larger seating capacity than the American Leaguers' new Fenway Park. Today, a portion of the ballpark remains, albeit as part of Boston University's Nickerson Field, where football and soccer are played today. The virtually unchanged Gaffney Street ticket office that was located down the right-field line is now a child-care center and security office for Boston University. Directly behind the ticket office building is a grandstand that made up the right-field bleachers at Braves Field. A plaque near the ticket office building commemorates the historical significance of this site. In addition, a crumbling, peeling portion of the original right field wall still stands.

Notable moments at Braves Field:

- June 16, 1916, Boston's Tom Hughes hurled the first no-hitter in Braves Field history, baffling the Pirates, 2-0.

- May 1, 1920: Major league baseball's longest game, a 26-inning, 1-1 tie between the Dodgers and Braves, was played here. Joe Oeschger went the distance for the Braves and Leon Cadore pitched all the way for the Dodgers.

- October 6, 1923: The third unassisted triple play in regular-season major league play was pulled off by Braves shortstop Ernie Padgett in a game against the Phillies.

- July 7, 1936: The National League won the All-Star Game here, 4-3, as Dizzy Dean beat Lefty Grove.

- June 19, 1942: The Braves' Paul Waner got his 3,000th career hit, achieving the milestone blow against Pittsburgh's Rip Sewell.

- October 11, 1948: In the third and last World Series game played at Braves Field, Boston lost to Cleveland, 4-3, in decisive Game 6 of the Fall Classic.

- Only 281,278 fans attended Braves home games in 1952, spurring relocation of the franchise to Milwaukee.

Former site of Huntington Avenue Grounds

City: Boston
Location: Left field (NW), Huntington Avenue; third base (SW), Bryant (Rogers) Street, now Forsyth Street; first base (SE) New Gravelly Pt. Rd. and New York, New Haven and Hartford Railroad tracks; right field (NE), New Gravelly Pt. Rd.

Before the 1912 opening of Fenway Park, Huntington Avenue Grounds was home to the Boston Red Sox. In fact, it was their very first ballpark. Built for $35,000 in 1901, Huntington Avenue Grounds originally seated only about 9,000 fans. However, there was room for thousands more (albeit via standing room) beyond ropes in the outfield and in the huge foul territory. With just a single entrance (and one turnstile), the simple structure was home field to the team known as the Boston Americans, who won their first game played here on May 8, 1901, defeating Connie Mack's A's, 12-4, behind the pitching of Cy Young. Nearly three years later, on May 5, 1904, Young tossed the first perfect game in American League history when he stopped the A's, 3-0, here. In use for only 11 years, Huntington Avenue Grounds is notable because of what is conveyed on a plaque that sits near the original spot of home plate: Dedicated in 1993, the inscription reads: "On October 1, 1903 the first modern World

A plaque in the shape of home plate marks the spot where modern baseball's first World Series took place. About sixty feet away stands a statue
of a hunched over Cy Young (background).

Series between the American League champion Boston Pilgrims (later known
as the Red Sox) and the National League champion Pittsburgh Pirates was
played on this site. General admission tickets were fifty cents. The Pilgrims, led
by twenty-eight game winner Cy Young, trailed the series three games to one
but then swept four consecutive victories to win the championship five games
to three." Now located on the campus of Northeastern University, there also is
a life-size statue of Cy Young located near where the pitcher's mound used to be
(in the Churchill Hall Mall). Additionally, there is a World Series Exhibit Room
in the nearby Cabot Physical Education Center with memorabilia from the
1901-1911 Red Sox teams and a plaque attached to the side of the building
marking where the left-field foul pole stood.

Former site of South End Grounds

City: Boston
Location: Columbus Ave. and Walpole St. Walpole ran behind home plate,
Columbus along the first-base side of the field. The New York, New Haven and
Hartford Railroad tracks ran along the third-base side. Behind the outfield was
a railroad roundhouse, and behind that was Gainsborough St.

In early Boston baseball, this was the home to the Doves, Red Caps and finally the Braves. And from 1871-1914, three baseball parks were located on the
site known as the "South End Grounds." Located across the street from

A parking lot now covers what was once the right field (left) and infield (right) of South End Grounds in Boston.

Huntington Avenue Grounds, the most famous of the parks that stood here was The Grand Pavilion, which was used from 1883-1894. A majestic, double-decked, six-spired masterpiece, it was destroyed by fire in 1894 and replaced with a less distinctive structure. This park served as home of the Boston Braves for 20 years, until Braves Field was built. (The Miracle Braves of 1914 played their World Series games at the larger Fenway Park before moving into their Braves Field the following season.) At the Ruggles T Station today, a plaque reads:

"South End Grounds: Professional baseball games were regularly played here from 1871-1914. Boston's only double-decked ballpark was topped with distinctive twin towers, and was regarded as the latest in sports stadiums when it opened in 1888. Also known as the Walpole Street Grounds, the park burned in 1894 during a ball game. It was rebuilt and served as the home of the National League's Boston Braves."

Fenway Park

City: Boston
Location: 4 Yawkey Way.
After two rain delays, Fenway Park finally hosted its first American League game on April 20, 1912. Coincidentally, Tiger Stadium (Navin Field) in Detroit opened the same day. On opening day, the Red Sox deafeated the New York Highlanders (later known as the Yankees) in an 11-inning thriller, 7-6. (The park's grand opening was overshadowed on the news pages because of the continuing coverage of the sinking of the Titanic in the Atlantic.) Today, Fenway Park is the oldest major league park in use and its basic configuration remains much like it was on opening day. The mythical left field wall, known as the

Young fans in Fenway Park's center field bleachers eagerly await a home run ball during batting practice at the 1999 All-Star Game.

"Green Monster," is synonymous with Boston baseball, and so is the so-called "Curse of the Bambino," which has seemingly doomed the team from winning a World Series since the Red Sox sold Babe Ruth to the Yankees in January 1920. As well, its manually operated scoreboard and peculiar shape (including the only ladder in play in the majors) make Fenway Park one of the most classic and revered landmarks in baseball history—a gem that helps connect the past with the present. Excellent tours are offered here at what some purists call "Boston's Sistine Chapel."

Some of the many memorable moments at Fenway Park:

- Site of the 1946, '61 and '99 All-Star Games.

- October 1, 1967: Jim Lonborg defeated the Twins, clinching Boston's "Impossible Dream" pennant.

- October 21, 1975: Carlton Fisk's 12-inning home run decided Game 6 of the World Series.

- September 12, 1979: Carl Yastrzemski collected his 3000th hit in a game against the Yankees.

- April 29, 1986: Roger Clemens struck out a major league-record 20 Seattle Mariners.

New England Sports Museum

City: Boston
Location: The FleetCenter
1 FleetCenter
617-624-1234

Opened in 1987, the New England Sports Museum is located on the 5th and 6th levels of the FleetCenter arena. Although it includes historic memorabilia from all major Boston sports teams, there is a good deal of emphasis on Boston baseball. (The Museum also displays artifacts loaned from private collectors and other museums, such as the Baseball Hall of Fame.) The Sports Museum was also the first museum ever to bring an outside exhibition to the Baseball Hall of Fame when it presented "Boston Braves 1876- 1952" at Cooperstown in 1990.

Mickey Cochrane monument

City: Bridgewater
Location: Legion Field at the Mickey Cochrane Sports Complex
Bridgewater State College
508-531-1200

Born here in Bridgewater April 6, 1903, Mickey Cochrane attended local public schools and played on one of the town's semi-pro baseball teams known as the Old Bridgewater Club. In 1925, he made his professional baseball debut as a catcher for the Philadelphia Athletics. He started for the A's for nine consecutive seasons, which included three World Series appearances. In 1933, Cochrane was traded to the Detroit Tigers and helped lead the team to the American League pennant in 1934. The season after that, the Tigers won the World

Mickey Cochrane was known as one of the smartest and toughest players in baseball history.

Series. Unfortunately, Cochrane's career ended after he was knocked unconscious by a Bump Hadley fastball at Yankee Stadium on May 25, 1937. Cochrane was elected to the Baseball Hall of Fame in 1947 and died in Lake Forest, Illinois, June 28, 1962, at age 59. Interestingly, Mickey Mantle was named after Cochrane—Cochrane was the favorite player of Mantle's father.

The house in the background at the end of Connie Mack Drive is where the legendary manager grew up. East Brookfield holds an annual parade in his honor.

Birthplace of Connie Mack

City: East Brookfield

Location: East Main Street

Cornelius Alexander McGillicuddy, better known as Connie Mack, was born on December 22, 1862, here in East Brookfield. A major league manager for over 50 years with the Philadelphia Athletics, the "Tall Tactician" left a huge mark in the town he still visited occasionally after becoming a legend. The house in which he lived on East Main Street is marked with a plaque. Each year the town holds a Memorial Day parade along Connie Mack Drive and July 4th celebrations end with fireworks at Connie Mack Field. As well, signs welcoming visitors into town make note of their hometown hero.

First game played under the lights

City: Hull

Location: Nantasket Bay, on the lawn behind Nantasket's Sea Foam House

On September 2, 1880, two amateur teams played a nine-inning 16-16 tie game at Nantasket Beach in Hull, Massachusetts. What made the game special is that it was played at night, under temporary lights, as staged by the newly formed Northern Electric Light Company. (Edison had invented the incandescent lightbulb just the year before.) The teams were actually representing two popular Boston department stores, Jordan Marsh and R. H. White. The *Boston Post* reported the next day that "A clear, pure, bright light was produced, very strong and yet very pleasant to the sight" by the 12 carbon-arc electric lamps. More specifically, 36 lamps were placed on three 100-foot wooden towers. They were powered by two engines and three generators, emitting just 30,000 candlepower of light. For the next 50 years, the night game experiments continued. While several promoters used the gimmick of portable lighting to illuminate the field as their exhibition teams traveled around the country, the first "official" major league game played under the lights happened at Cincinnati on

May 24, 1935 (with President Franklin Roosevelt throwing the light switch from the White House six hundred miles from old Crosley Field).

Jack Chesbro plaque at the Joe Wolfe Baseball Field

City: North Adams
Location: Noel Field Complex State Street

Born here on June 5, 1874, Hall of Famer "Happy Jack" Chesbro was one of baseball's early spitball aces. Among his career highlights was his 1904 performance with the New York Highlanders. The numbers almost defy logic. He started 51 games, completed 48 of them. In all, he was the victor in 41 of those games and tossed a total of $454\frac{2}{3}$ innings. And from 1901 to 1906, Chesbro won 153 games—an average of more than 25 per season. He played for pennant winners in

Jack Chesbro won 41 games in 1904—the most single-season wins in the 20th century.

Pittsburgh and New York, and led the league in winning percentage three times. After retiring in 1909, Chesbro returned to North Adams to start a career as a merchant, running both a saw mill and lumber yard in town. North Adams honored him with a plaque at Joe Wolfe field, named for a former local minor league ballplayer who revived the North Adams Babe Ruth League in addition to working in other local youth-related baseball groups.

Babe Ruth's farmhouse

City: Sudbury
Location: 558 Dutton Rd.

Babe Ruth bought this then-80-acre farm in 1916 for $12,000, using his $4,000 World Series check as the down payment. It was Ruth's primary residence while he was a member of the Boston Red Sox. Today, most of the

Babe Ruth, shown here with his first wife, Helen, rented a cottage near Willis Pond in 1917 and 1918.

acreage has been developed into other homes, but the former Ruth house remains as a private residence.

Babe Ruth's piano

City: Sudbury
Location: Willis Pond

The legend of Babe Ruth's piano finding its way into this pond lives on. While Ruth definitely spent off-season time at a cabin here, the facts about the piano are difficult to nail down. One story is that Ruth, "under the influence" during one of his many parties, pushed the piano onto the frozen pond to show off his strength. Another version is that Ruth shoved the piano onto the pond to entertain youngsters at a singalong he was hosting. After the kids left, he supposedly forgot about the piano, which eventually sank once the ice gave way. Whatever the case, there has been enough interest in the goings-on to compel divers to survey the murky bottom of the pond with high-tech sonar equipment. So far, the missions have proved fruitless.

Christy Mathewson gets his start

City: Taunton
Location: Whittenton Athletic Grounds
Pleadwell Street and 4th Avenue

In 1899, Christy Mathewson was a budding college superstar at Bucknell University in Pennsylvania. After his freshman year, he joined his first professional baseball team, the minor league Taunton Herrings (of the New England League). Taunton's home field was called the Whittenton Athletic Grounds, today known simply as the Whittenton ball field. Mathewson first pitched here on July 24th, 1899, and was shelled by the Brockton Shoemakers, losing 13-4. By the next season, Mathewson had moved over to play for Norfolk in the Virginia League where he had a 20-2 record. In 1901, he was pitching for the New York Giants, going 20-17 in his first full major league season. In 1994, a plaque was placed at the Whittenton field, used today by Little Leaguers and softball players. It states that this is where Christy Mathewson spent his first season in professional baseball.

Site of baseball's first perfect game

City: Worcester
Location: Current site of Becker College
61 Sever St.

In 1880, the Worcester Agricultural Fairgrounds was located here, and the fairgrounds field was home to the National League's Worcester team. On June 12, 1880, it was here that Worcester's Lee Richmond tossed the first perfect game in major league history. In the last season in which the pitching distance was 45

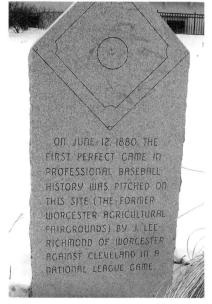

This marker sits where fans entered the park at Worcester Agricultural Fairgrounds, home of the N.L.'s Worcester team.

feet, Richmond mowed down Cleveland, 1-0. Just five days later, Providence's John Montgomery Ward pitched a perfect game against Buffalo. Incredibly, the third perfect game in National League history did not occur until 1964, when the Phillies' Jim Bunning accomplished the feat against the Mets. The spot where the Worcester marker sits today—in front of Becker's Main Academic Building—is where fans entered the park.

Hall of Famers buried in the Boston Metropolitan Area

George Wright
Holyhood Cemetery
Heath Street, Brookline

Tim Keefe and John Clarkson
Cambridge Cemetery, 76 Coolidge Avenue
Cambridge
617-349-4890
Mike "King" Kelly

John Clarkson, Hugh Duffy and
Tommy Connolly (top to bottom).

Mount Hope Cemetery
355 Walk Hill Street
Mattapan
617-635-7361

Hugh Duffy and Tommy McCarthy
Mount Calvary Cemetery
Harvard Street and Cummins
Highway
Mattapan
617-296-2339

Frank Selee
Wyoming Cemetery
205 Sylvan Street
Melrose
Pine Banks Section, Lot 200
781-665-0405

Tommy Connolly
St. Patrick's Cemetery
Pond Street
Natick

Eddie Collins
Linwood Cemetery
U. S. Hwy. 20 and Linwood Avenue
Weston
781-893-8695

Other areas:
Joe Cronin
St. Francis Xavier Cemetery
Pine Street (one half mile off Strawberry Hill Road)
Centerville

Jack Chesbro
Howland Cemetery
Shelburne Falls Road

Conway

Billy Hamilton
Eastwood Cemetery
Old Common Road
Lancaster

Walter "Rabbit" Maranville
St. Michael's Cemetery
1601 State Street
Springfield
413-733-0659

Candy Cummings
Aspen Grove Cemetery
95 Pleasant Street
Ware
413-967-9626

Jesse Burkett
St. John's Cemetery
260 Cambridge Street
Worcester
508-757-7415

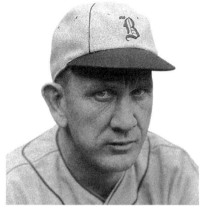

Rabbit Maranville (top) played more games at shortstop than any other N.L. player. Jesse Burkett had a .338 career batting average.

Roy Campanella (left) and Don Newcombe integrated modern minor league baseball in 1946 by starting for the Brooklyn Dodgers' Class B team in Nashua, N.H. Jackie Robinson starred that season for their AAA club in Montreal.

New Hampshire

Sunset baseball

City: Concord
Location: Red Eastman Field
White Park
Washington St.

New Hampshire sandlots and youth programs have produced such well-known major leaguers as Carlton Fisk, Mike Flanagan and Bob Tewksbury. But there's more distant baseball history to be found in this park. It's the site of the Sunset League, known as the "oldest after-supper amateur baseball league in the United States." Organized in 1909 at this very park, the league was the training ground for the likes of Red Rolfe, a New York Yankees standout in the late 1930s. Today, the league consists of five teams—four from Concord and one from Manchester. Players are at least 17 years old, teams are locally sponsored and a 16-game schedule is played. A marker was placed in the park in 1984, and the field was recently rededicated in honor of Red Eastman, the man who ran the league for three decades.

Holman Stadium

City: Nashua
Location: Amherst St.
(From Route 3, take exit 7E onto Amherst St. Holman Stadium is approximately one mile on the left.)

Opened in 1937, Holman Stadium is now home to the Nashua Pride of the independent Atlantic League. Unquestionably, though, the park's claim to fame dates to 1946 when it was home field for Roy Campanella and Don Newcombe, who played for the Nashua club of the New England League. The '46 season marked the integration of modern minor league baseball, and the Brooklyn Dodgers led the way with Jackie Robinson starring for their Class AAA affiliate in Montreal and Campanella and Newcombe standing out for Brooklyn's Class B Nashua team (which, under manager Walter Alston, won the New England League playoffs). Campanella drove in 96 runs in 113 games for Nashua; Newcombe compiled a 14-4 record and finished with a 2.21 ERA.

Red Rolfe Field

City: Hanover
Location: Dartmouth College

This playing site, formally named Red Rolfe Field in 1971, has been home to Dartmouth baseball for almost 100 years. It honors Robert A. "Red" Rolfe, a former Dartmouth star who was a key player on Yankees team that won four consecutive World Series titles beginning in 1936 and captured five Series crowns and six American League pennants in a seven-year span. Third baseman Rolfe led

Red Rolfe batted .300 or better four times and scored 100 or more runs in seven of his 10 seasons with the New York Yankees.

the A.L. in hits, doubles and runs scored in 1939. He later managed Detroit for 3½ seasons, guiding the club to a 95-59 record and a second-place finish in 1950. He then served as Dartmouth athletic director from 1954-67.

Babe Ruth slept here

City: North Conway
Location: Cranmore Mountain Lodge
859 Kearsarge Rd.

In the 1940s, this bed-and-breakfast inn was owned by Babe Ruth's daughter and son-in-law. The Bambino spent many vacation days here after his baseball career ended. His favorite room, No. 2, has been maintained with the original furnishings from Ruth's days at the ski-country lodge.

After his playing days were over, Babe Ruth was a frequent visitor to the inn owned by his daughter and son-in-law.

New Jersey

Former site of Bacharach Park

City: Atlantic City

Location: 500 N South Carolina Avenue

In the mid-1920s, this was home of the Bacharach Giants of the Eastern Colored League. The Mayor of Atlantic City, Henry Bacharach, had been to Jacksonville, Florida, and was so enamored with the black baseball team he saw play there that he brought it home and built a park to showcase its talents. The park was home to Game 2 of the 1926 Negro League World Series. Today, it's the site of the Carver Hall housing development.

John Henry Lloyd Park

City: Atlantic City

Location: Martin Luther King, Jr. Boulevard at US Route 30

John Henry Lloyd was one of the best black players of the dead-ball era. A soft-spoken gentleman off the field, Lloyd was a ferocious competitor on it, drawing glowing comparisons to legendary Pittsburgh shortstop Honus Wagner. Lloyd's career spanned many teams from 1905-1931, including the New York Lincoln Giants, Brooklyn Royal Giants, New York Bacharach

John Henry Lloyd Park is a tribute to the Hall of Fame player considered by many the finest shortstop in Negro leagues history. After retiring as a player, Lloyd organized and managed many youth leagues in the Atlantic City area.

A plaque honoring "Pop" Lloyd stands outside the stadium that bears his name.

Giants, Atlantic City Bacharach Giants, Columbus Buckeyes, Hilldale Daisies and the Harlem Stars. Over the course of a 27-year career, Lloyd was one of the Negro leagues' most prolific hitters. After retiring as a player, Lloyd helped organize and manage youth leagues here in the Atlantic City area, often serving as commissioner of the city's youth baseball leagues. For his rich contribution to the area, John Henry Lloyd Park was dedicated in his honor in 1949. Lloyd was elected to the Hall of Fame by the Special Committee on Negro Leagues in 1977, and died in Atlantic City in 1965. There is an inscribed plaque at the stadium honoring Pop Lloyd.

Lloyd is buried at:

Atlantic City Cemetery

South side of Washington Avenue between Doughty Road and New Road

Pleasantville

609-646-2260

Sports Hall of Fame of New Jersey

City: East Rutherford

Location: Continental Airlines Arena

50 Route 120

201-935-8500

More than 30 inductees have been enshrined here in the New Jersey Sports Hall of Fame since May, 1993, when the first class was inducted. The list includes baseball players Yogi Berra and Phil Rizzuto, plus such other Jersey legends as Franco Harris, Bill Bradley, Althea Gibson, Paul Robeson, Vince Lombardi and Bill Parcells. Plaques honoring the inductees are on permanent display in the box office lobby of the Continental Airlines Arena at the Meadowlands Sports Complex.

The birth of baseball?

City: Hoboken

Location: Elysian Fields (former site)

Corner of 11th and Washington Streets

It's a fact that Frank Sinatra was born in Hoboken…but was baseball? Perhaps. We know several games similar to baseball had been played in Europe and America as far back as the 1600s, but it wasn't until the 1800s that baseball's closer cousin, "Town Ball," began to take shape. But certain facts do appear clear. In 1842, several men, including Alexander Cartwright and Daniel "Doc" Adams, began drafting rules for a game called "baseball." In 1845, they formed the first actual baseball "club", the Knickerbocker Baseball Club, and adopted 20 rules not previously included in earlier editions of the game, including three strikes per batter, three outs per inning, tags and force-outs in lieu of trying to hit the batter with the ball and the inclusion of an umpire. On June 19, 1846, the Knickerbocker Baseball Club, under these new rules, played the first ever organized game versus the New York Nine. With Cartwright umpiring, the Knicker-

Some consider an 1846 game at Elysian Fields the start of organized baseball. Soon after, the sport took off.

bockers lost the four-inning game, 23-1. Soon after, with these rules, the sport caught on. In 1869, the first professional team, Cincinnati's Red Stockings, was formed and in 1871 the first nationwide professional league was founded. Was this the first game ever; the so-called birth of baseball? It's hard to say for sure. But until something displaces the seminal games that took place here, it is hard to dispute.

The lineup from the 1846 game:

New York Knickerbocker Club vs. New York Nine
June 19, 1846
Elysian Fields
Hoboken, N.J.

Knickerbockers	New York Nine
Turney	Davis
Adams	Winslow
Tucker	Ransom
Birney	Murphy
Avery	Case
H. Anthony	Johnson
D. Anthony	Thompson
Tryon	Trenchard
Paulding	Lalor

Final Score: New York Nine 23, Knickerbockers 1 (4 innings)
Umpire: Alexander Cartwright

Jackie Robinson Statue

Jackie Robinson made his minor league debut at the now defunct Roosevelt Stadium in Jersey City.

City: Jersey City
Location: Journal Square Transportation Center
2815 Kennedy Boulevard
201-659-8823

This monument to Jackie Robinson commemorates his professional debut game at nearby Roosevelt Stadium (no longer standing) on April 18, 1946. In arguably the most important minor league game in baseball history, Jackie Robinson's Montreal Royals defeated the Jersey City Giants to mark the beginning of the racial integration of baseball. Robinson's first pro game was impressive: He hit a three-run homer, singled three times, stole two bases and drove in four runs. One year later, Robinson shattered major league baseball's color line as a member of the Brooklyn Dodgers, earning distinction as the National League's Rookie of the Year.

Former site of Roosevelt Stadium

City: Jersey City
Location: Society Hill Apartments
Area bounded by Danforth Avenue (first base side), Route 440 (right field), Hackensack River (third base).

This was where Jackie Robinson made his professional debut in April of 1946 as a member of the minor league Montreal Royals. Built in 1936, it was once home of the minor league "Jersey City Giants" and "Jerseys." The Brooklyn Dodgers played 15 games here in 1956 and 1957 and Willie Mays hit the only ball ever to sail completely out of the park in 1956 to beat the Dodgers 1-0. Roosevelt Stadium was torn down in 1984 and today is the site of an apartment complex.

The Yogi Berra Museum & Learning Center

City: Little Falls
Location: On the campus of Montclair State University
8 Quarry Road
973-655-2377

Yogi Berra remains one of baseball's great characters, gentlemen and ambassadors for the game. A resident of Montclair for more than 40 years, he has received an honorary doctorate from Montclair State University and a baseball stadium has been named in his honor on campus. His museum is located next to the stadium. The Yogi Berra Museum & Learning Center's mission is "to educate and inspire all people, especially children, with culturally diverse, inclu-

The Yogi Berra Museum features permanent and rotating exhibits about baseball, Yankees history and the storied career of Yogi Berra.

sive sports-based educational programming. The Museum's programs foster literacy, as well as a better understanding of social justice, mathematical and scientific principles and the history and contemporary role of sports in our society." There are permanent exhibits as well as special, rotating exhibits featuring memorabilia from Yogi's storied career, lots of Yankee history and a celebration of baseball the way it used to be played. Admission to the Yogi Berra Museum and Learning Center is $4 for adults; $2 for children and students. Programs are free with admission (unless otherwise noted). Hours are Wednesday-Sunday, noon to 5 p.m. As Yogi might say, one visit to the museum is like deja vu all over again.

Michelin Field

City: Milltown
Location: Sheridan Avenue and Lafayette
In 1907, the Michelin Tire Company of France set up shop in this small New Jersey borough, changing it forever. By 1919, the company had not only erected more than 200 houses for its employees, it had also built a small stadium called Michelin Field where it fielded its own local team. Made up of both employees and local athletes, the team took on all comers, including teams featuring Casey Stengel and Babe Ruth and even the legendary House of David squad. In 1930, Michelin closed down and returned to France, leaving such street names as Lafayette, Joffre, Foch and Our Lady of Lourdes Church, which all recall when Milltown was predominantly French in population. It also left Michelin Field, which sits today where it always did and is used more than ever by the community.

Lou Costello Park

City: Patterson
Location: At Cianci & Ellison Streets
Famous comedian Lou Costello hailed from Patterson, New Jersey, growing up near the current location of a life-size statue dedicated to him. It's called "Lou's On First," a play upon the brilliant "Who's on First" comedy routine Costello performed for years with partner Bud Abbott.

Clarke Field

City: Princeton
Location: Princeton University
609-258-3000

Patterson native Lou Costello (right), shown with his "Who's on First" comedy partner Bud Abbott, was honored with a park and a life-size statue in his hometown.

The diamond used by the Princeton Tigers baseball team is named in honor of Bill "Boileryard" Clarke, who went to school and later coached here. Clarke shared catching duties with Wilbert Robinson on three consecutive first-place Baltimore (National League) teams (1894-96). In 1901, the American League's first season, he was the Senators' first baseman. Clarke Field is one of the finest fields in Northeast collegiate circles, and has been the site of NCAA regional tournament games as well as the host of New Jersey state high school playoff and all-star games.

Goose Goslin batted .300 or better 11 times.

Hall of Famers buried in New Jersey

Leon "Goose" Goslin
Baptist Cemetery
Yorke Street
Salem

New York

Former site of War Memorial Stadium

City: Buffalo
Location: Johnnie B. Wiley Sports Pavilion
1100 Jefferson Avenue

Though primarily a football stadium, War Memorial (referred to locally as "The Rockpile") was also used by Buffalo's Class AAA Bisons team. It was built in the 1930s and torn down in the 1980s, but what secures War Memorial Stadium's place in baseball history was its transformation into a vintage 1939 park for the 1984 filming of Bernard Malamud's novel *The Natural* starring Robert Redford. Though the stadium is gone, the pillars at the entranceway were preserved at what is now a public park facility. The flagpole from War Memorial Stadium also was moved and now sits alongside a plaque outside the right-field bleachers at the new home of the Bisons, Dunn Tire Park, at 275 Washington Street.

Greater Buffalo Sports Hall of Fame

City: Buffalo
Location: HSBC Arena
One Seymour H. Knox III Plaza

The Greater Buffalo Sports Hall of Fame honors many local athletes, including baseball legends Luke Easter, Sal Maglie and Warren Spahn. The museum is free and located on the lower level of the HSBC Arena atrium in downtown Buffalo. Memorabilia, information, interactive computer kiosks and video presentations are displayed in honor of these athletes.

Doubleday Field

City: Cooperstown
Location: The Baseball Hall of Fame
25 Main Street

Abner Doubleday probably was nowhere near Cooperstown during the summer of 1839 when he allegedly laid out the first baseball diamond and limited the number of players per side to nine. But enough baseball has been played on this field to give it a special history, Doubleday or no Doubleday. Here, at the "mythical" birthplace of baseball, a former cow pasture called Phinney's Farm, two professional baseball games are played

Two pro games, one by major league teams and another by minor leaguers, are played during each Hall of Fame induction weekend at Doubleday Field.

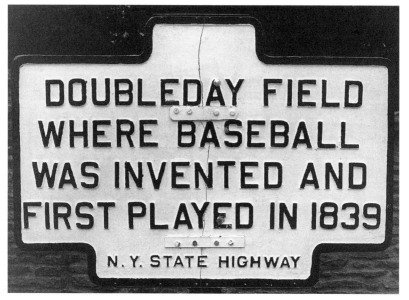

Located just a block from baseball's Hall of Fame, Doubleday Field sits on a former cow pasture called Phinney's Farm.

during each Hall of Fame induction weekend. The annual Hall of Fame game is the feature presentation; the other is hosted by the Oneonta Tigers, who play their New York-Pennsylvania League home games at nearby Damaschke Field.

The field is just a block from the Baseball Hall of Fame, the granddaddy of all sports museums and the ultimate baseball shrine. The Baseball Writers' Association of America elected its charter class in 1936: Ty Cobb, Babe Ruth, Honus Wagner, Christy Mathewson and Walter Johnson. Three years later, on June 12, 1939, the Hall of Fame officially was dedicated. Of the 26 players who had been elected to that point, 11 were still alive and all but Cobb visited Cooperstown for the spectacular celebration. Today, annual attendance at the Hall of Fame and Museum approaches 350,000 and twice has topped 400,000. The shrine is open year round. The busiest months are July and August, when the annual induction weekends take place.

Eddie Collins Park

    City: Millerton
    Location: Route 22

There's a ballfield named for him here because Hall of Fame second baseman Eddie Collins was born in this small Dutchess County town on May 2, 1887. He signed his first major league contract in 1906 and then went on to play 25 seasons after that. Part of the renowned $100,000 infield for the Philadelphia Athletics, he also played for the Chicago White Sox. Collins, a member of the 3,000-hit club, was elected to the Hall of Fame in 1939.

Former site of the Polo Grounds

City: New York
Location: Polo Grounds Towers
West 157th Street and Eighth Avenue
Washington Heights

The horseshoe-shaped Polo Grounds was the site of many of baseball's most memorable moments.

The New York Giants originally played baseball at a city polo field on 110th Street and Sixth Avenue. When owner John Brush moved the team to Coogan's Bluff in 1891, he kept the name "Polo Grounds." In April 1911, the wooden Polo Grounds burned to the ground. The stadium was quickly rebuilt with steel and concrete in time to host the Philadelphia Athletics in the 1911 World Series. An odd "bathtub-shaped" ballpark, the Polo Grounds was home to some of the greatest legends in baseball history. Mel Ott, Willie Mays, Christy Mathewson and Carl Hubbell are just a few of the famous Giants who carved out history here. (The Polo Grounds was even home to the Yankees for 10 seasons until Yankee Stadium opened in 1923.)

In 1957, Giants owner Horace Stoneham devastated the city when he announced that he was moving the Giants to San Francisco. The Polo Grounds remained for seven more years, serving as home to the New York Mets for the 1962 and 1963 seasons. In 1964 the stadium was demolished and now the Polo Grounds Towers, a housing project, occupies the site. All that is left of the

This view from Coogan's Bluff shows Polo Grounds Towers covering the grounds where the legendary stadium once stood.

original Polo Grounds is an old staircase on the side of the cliff that once led to the ticket booth. On one of the landings of the stairway is a marker that states; THE JOHN T. BRUSH STAIRWAY PRESENTED BY THE NEW YORK GIANTS. The stairway was used by fans to get to the ticket booth behind home plate. A plaque marks the approximate site where homeplate once sat.

Some memorable moments at the Polo Grounds:

- September 23, 1908: Fred Merkle neglected to touch second base on an apparent game-ending hit against Chicago, triggering a controversy that eventually cost the Giants a 1908 pennant.

- August 16, 1920: Cleveland Indians shortstop Ray Chapman was killed by a pitch thrown by Yankee Carl Mays. Chapman remains the only major leaguer ever to die after being struck by a pitched ball.

- July 10, 1934: Pitching in the All Star Game, Giants screwballer Carl Hubbell struck out Babe Ruth, Lou Gehrig, Jimmie Foxx, Al Simmons and Joe Cronin consecutively.

- August 1, 1945: Giants slugger Mel Ott became the third

A plaque (left) marks the former location of the Polo Grounds' home plate; the yard (right) shows the area a catcher might patrol for a foul ball.

member of baseball's 500-homer club with a shot off Boston's Johnny Hutchings.

- October 3, 1951: Bobby Thomson fired the "Shot Heard 'round the World"—the legendary homer that beat the Dodgers, 5-4, to give the Giants a dramatic National League pennant.

- September 29, 1954: Giants center fielder Willie Mays hauled in a 460-foot blast by Cleveland's Vic Wertz, one of the most memorable catches in World Series history.

Former site of Hilltop Park

City: New York
Location: Columbia-Presbyterian Medical Center
622 West 168th Street
Washington Heights

Opened in 1903, Hilltop Park was the New York Yankees' first home. Originally called American League Park, the stadium was renamed because it sat on high ground and the New Yorkers were called, appropriately, the Highlanders. From this perch, when seated behind home plate, spectators could enjoy scenic views of the Hudson River. Hilltop was shared by the Giants for a short period in 1911 when their Polo Grounds home was destroyed by fire. After the 1912 season, the Giants reciprocated, allowing the Yankees to become tenants of their rebuilt Polo Grounds. Hilltop Park, now empty, was razed in 1914 and the Columbia-Presbyterian Medical Center opened on the site in 1928. Today, a plaque marks the spot where home plate once sat.

A home plate plaque is the only visible reminder of the early century baseball played by the New York Highlanders at Hilltop Park.

Some memorable moments at Hilltop Park

- June 28, 1907: The Washington Senators stole 13 bases off Yankees catcher Branch Rickey and posted a 16-5 victory over the New Yorkers.

- June 30, 1908: Cy Young, at age 41, hurled his third career no-hitter, defeating Boston, 8-0.

- September 7, 1908: Washington's Walter Johnson pitched his third shutout against the New York Giants in a four-day span.

- May 15, 1912: Detroit's Ty Cobb jumped into the Hilltop stands and began punching a handicapped fan who had been insulting him. Cobb was suspended for the ugly incident.

Babe Ruth gets married

City: New York
Location: St. Gregory the Great
144 West 90th Street
Manhattan

In the mid-1920s, Babe Ruth met and became seriously interested in a young widow, Claire Hodgson. Claire had come to New York from Georgia with her young daughter, Julia, in 1920 to work as a model and actress. On April 17, 1929, Ruth and Hodgson were married at St. Gregory the Great Catholic church in New York, scheduling the ceremony at 6 a.m. to keep it private. Word leaked out, however, and hundreds of well-wishers waited on the street for a glimpse of the couple.

Babe Ruth's apartment

City: New York

An impressive monument at Gate of Heaven Cemetery marks the gravesite of former Yankees slugger Babe Ruth and wife Claire Hodgson (left) in New York.

Location: 110 Riverside Drive and West 83rd Street
Manhattan
This is the Upper West Side building where Babe Ruth lived with wife Claire in an 11-room apartment from 1942 until his death in 1948. Claire remained at the apartment for another 28 years after the Babe died. When the couple got married in 1929 (Ruth had been separated from his first wife, who later died in a fire), Babe and Claire resided at 345 West 88th Street, occupying the entire seventh floor. A plaque on the side of that building honors Ruth. After several years there, they moved to 173 Riverside Drive, at the corner of 89th Street, and eventually to the 110 Riverside Drive address.

The Babe dies

City: New York
Location: Memorial Sloan-Kettering Hospital
424 East 68th Street
Manhattan
This was where Ruth died on August 16, 1948, at 8:01 p.m. Diagnosed with throat cancer about two years earlier, doctors attributed the disease to Ruth's heavy smoking and tobacco chewing. Ruth's body laid in state for two days at Yankee Stadium while thousands of mourners gathered to pay their respects.

Babe Ruth is buried (with wife, Claire) at Gate of Heaven Cemetery, 10

W. Stevens Avenue, Hawthorne. (Billy Martin is buried just behind Ruth's grave.)

Former site of Huberts Flea Circus and Museum

City: New York
Location: 228 West 42nd Street (in Times Square)
Manhattan

This was where Hall of Fame pitcher Grover Cleveland Alexander ended up after his career ended in 1930. Home to various sideshow acts like Lydia the Contortionist and Waldo the Sword Swallower, Alexander joined the circus and regaled customers with tales of his life and baseball feats. All it cost was 25 cents to hear the legend speak for a while and Alexander was good for 10 or more "shows" per day.

Lou Gehrig's birthplace

City: New York
Location: 1994 Second Avenue and East 103rd Street

Lou Gehrig, who went on to fame as the New York Yankees' Iron Horse, was born in the Yorkville section of Manhattan.

Upper East Side
Manhattan

Lou Gehrig was born in the Yorkville section of New York on June 19, 1903. Gehrig's parents were poor German immigrants and Lou's mother, Christina, provided the bulk of the family's income, working as a cook, maid and laundress. After a brilliant college baseball career at Columbia University, Gehrig joined the Yankees and gained legendary status for his iron-man feat of playing in 2,130 consecutive games, a long-standing major league record surpassed in 1995 by Cal Ripken Jr. Gehrig also led the American League in RBIs five times and home runs three times; drove in 100 or more runs in 13 consecutive years; batted .340 and hit 493 home runs over 17 seasons, and helped the

Yankees win six World Series titles. Tragically, Gehrig died at age 37 of Amyotrophic Lateral Sclerosis (ALS), a rare and incurable disease known today as Lou Gehrig disease. The building of Gehrig's youth was torn down and the site is currently occupied by a nursery.

Joe DiMaggio Highway

City: New York
Location: From Battery Park Place to West 72nd Street
In 1999, Mayor Rudolph Giuliani was present to rename the West Side Highway in honor of Yankees legend Joe DiMaggio. Adorned with crossed bats and baseballs, new green-and-white signs were posted on the southbound side of the West Side Highway at 70th Street and on the northbound side at West Street between Morris and Thames near the Brooklyn Battery Park Tunnel in tribute to the "Yankee Clipper."

Monument Park at Yankee Stadium

City: New York
Location: 161st Street and River Avenue
The Bronx

Plaques honoring Babe Ruth and Joe DiMaggio are among the many memorials and retired-number tributes at Monument Park, located beyond the left-center field fence at Yankee Stadium.

When Yankee owner Jacob Ruppert was asked by the Giants to vacate the Polo Grounds, he didn't blink. The Yankees were outdrawing their tenants and he expected fans to relocate with them. At a site just across the Harlem River from the Polo Grounds, Ruppert built a massive, state-of-the-art stadium that would become one of the most legendary sports venues in the world. Yankee Stadium, opened in 1923, still exists along with the memories of the most successful and decorated team in baseball history. Monument Park, located behind the left-center field fence, is a reflection of that success. It is filled with monuments and plaques honoring former Yankee greats and a special area is dedicated to uniform numbers retired by the Yankees. The park is open to the public 45 minutes before every game and it can be visited as part of Yankee Stadium tours. Access is gained to Monument Park via the staircase at the end of the aisle in Section 36. For many years, beginning in the early 1930s, monuments to Miller Huggins, Babe Ruth and Lou Gehrig stood in center-field fair territory, obstacles to outfielders chasing down balls to that distant area of Yankee Stadium. When Yankee Stadium was refurbished in 1974 and 1975, the monuments were moved to the Monument Park area in left-center.

Parish of the Yankees

City: New York
Location: St. Angela Merici Church
917 Morris Avenue
The Bronx
Babe Ruth and Joe DiMaggio were parishioners at this church during their playing days with the Yankees. Ruth, his wife and daughter, in fact, donated the church's marble altar, explaining why their names appear on a plaque in the church.

Edward Grant Memorial Highway

City: New York
Location: From Jerome Avenue to Martin Luther King Boulevard (about six blocks north of Yankee Stadium)
The Bronx
This stretch of road was named in 1945 for former New York Giants player Eddie Grant, who holds the sad distinction of being the first major league player killed in wartime action. The former third baseman led a mission in the Argonne Forest offensive to rescue the "Lost Battalion" trapped behind German lines during World War I. He was killed by machine gun fire and was subsequently honored at the Polo Grounds with a plaque and monument in center

field. Every Memorial Day, the Giants held a wreath-laying ceremony at the plaque, which mysteriously disappeared after the Giants left the Polo Grounds. Grant, a Harvard graduate, had retired from baseball in 1915 to practice law in New York City before the war.

Jackie Robinson School / Public JHS 320

City: New York
Location: 46 McKeever Place
Brooklyn

Though a number of schools around the country are named for Jackie Robinson, this one is located closest to where he actually made history. It is in Brooklyn, at the point where the third base foul line at Ebbets Field used to be. The school, built in the late 1960s, features a large mural of Robinson on its outside facade.

Former site of Ebbets Field

City: New York
Location: Bedford Avenue and Montgomery Street
Ebbets Field Apartments
Crown Heights
Brooklyn

The Ebbets Field apartments now dominate the Bedford Avenue and Montgomery Street location once occupied by Ebbets Field.

Ebbets Field, once a spectacular centerpiece in baseball-crazy Brooklyn, is gone, but not forgotten by the still-passionate Dodgers faithful.

One of the most storied, romanticized venues in baseball history was opened by Dodgers owner Charles Ebbets in 1913. It was a raucous, sometimes-zany ballpark that became known for its colorful fans, interesting characters and unusual, always offbeat atmosphere. It was a place of the heart for legions of neighborhood fans, who loved their Dodgers with unrelenting passion. Among its trademark fans and memories were Hilda Chester, the cowbell-ringing bleacher regular; the right and left field walls, plastered with such advertisements as the memorable Schaefer Beer sign atop the right field scoreboard that gave fans the official scorer's ruling on hits and errors and the bottom-of-scoreboard Abe Stark ad that challenged batters to "Hit sign, win suit." ; the Dodgers Sym-Phony band, a collection of "Brooklyn Bum" musicians who wandered the stadium, entertaining fans while pounding out off-key music. But all of the characters, the local color and the teams that won nine National League pennants and one World Series couldn't keep owner Walter O'Malley from seeking greener pastures. After the 1957 season, O'Malley relocated the beloved Bums to sunny Los Angeles. Just 6,673 fans attended the final game at Ebbets Field and the park was torn down in 1960. Today, the Ebbets Field apartments occu-

Only a cornerstone marker (left) remains at the former site of Ebbets Field, but other reminders are visible throughout the borough.

py the site, with only a cornerstone left to salute the former location of a once-proud ballpark.

Some memorable moments at Ebbets Field

- June 15, 1938: Cincinnati's Johnny Vander Meer pitched his second consecutive no-hitter, defeating the Dodgers, 6-0, in the first night game at Ebbets Field.

- October 5, 1941: Catcher Mickey Owen's passed ball on what would have been the final pitch of a Dodgers' Game 4 World Series victory over the Yankees allowed the Bronx Bombers to pull out a shocking 7-4 win over Brooklyn.

- April 15, 1947: Jackie Robinson made this an opening day for the ages as he became the 20th century's first black player while contributing to a 5-3 victory over Boston.

- August 31, 1950: Dodgers first baseman Gil Hodges hit four home runs and a single in a 19-3 rout of the Boston Braves.

The location of the Ebbets Field flagpole

City: New York
Location: Corner of Utica Avenue and Farragut Road, Brooklyn
The original Ebbets Field center field flagpole still stands at this former VFW Hall (now a casket company). Though there was some talk of moving it to the new Brooklyn minor league stadium, Keyspan Park (home of the Cyclones),

During the Civil War era, the Excelsiors taught the game of baseball to soldiers from various states, thus spreading the popularity of the game.

that plan has been put on hold. A plaque at the base of the flag-pole identifies it as being from Ebbets Field.

Home of the Brooklyn Excelsiors

City: New York
Location: 133 Clinton Street Brooklyn Heights

A plaque on the building at this address commemorates it as former home of the Brooklyn Excelsiors, Brooklyn's first professional baseball team. The Excelsiors, according to the plaque, helped spread the game throughout the country in the post-Civil War years.

Jackie Robinson Parkway

City: New York
Location: Queens and Brooklyn
On April 14, 1997, the Interborough Parkway was renamed after Jackie Robinson to commemorate the 50th anniversary of him breaking the major league color barrier with the Brooklyn Dodgers. Over his 11 seasons, Robinson helped the Dodgers win six National League pennants and one World Series—a seven-game 1955 thriller against the hated Yankees. Robinson was inducted into the Hall of Fame in 1962. The Parkway serves as a link between the Kew Gardens (Grand Central Parkway-Van Wyck Expressway) interchange in central Queens and Pennsylvania Avenue in East New York, Brooklyn. It also passes the cemetery in Cypress Hills where Robinson was buried in 1972.

Former site of Washington Park

City: New York
Location: Left field (NW), 3rd Avenue; third base (SW), 3rd Street; first base (SE), 4th Avenue; right field (NW), 1st Street.
Brooklyn
This was the location for the original home of the Brooklyn Dodgers, the first ballpark erected by Charles Ebbets. Opened in 1898 when the team was called the Superbas, they played here until 1912, at which point they moved

into their new home, Ebbets Field. (Casey Stengel made his professional debut at Washington as a member of the 1912 Dodgers.) After the Dodgers vacated Washington Park, it was used by the Brooklyn entry in the Federal League in 1914 and 1915. Soon after the Federal League folded, the stadium was torn down. Amazingly, part of Washington Park's clubhouse wall still stands. It is now the 3rd Avenue wall to the Con Edison yard at 222 1st Street in Brooklyn. This is thought to be the oldest remaining piece of any major league stadium still standing and preservationists are battling to keep the ballpark relic from being demolished.

Parade Grounds

City: New York
Location: Prospect Park (southern end)
Bounded by Parkside Avenue on the north, Parade Place on the east, Caton Avenue on the south and Coney Island Avenue on the west.
Brooklyn
When Caton Avenue was constructed in 1926, Brooklyn added a small triangular section of its unused land to the project. By the late 1930s, the Parade Grounds' baseball diamonds attracted an average crowd of 20,000 daily to watch such soon-to-be-discovered players as Sandy Koufax. In the 1950s, a new recreation building was added to the Parade Grounds. In addition to housing Parks Department offices, a comfort station, a concession area and several indoor tennis courts, the Grounds also provided space for Brooklyn's 74th Police Precinct. As the loosely-formed baseball "leagues" continued to develop (becoming a breeding ground for professional and semi-pro ballplayers), the *Brooklyn Daily Eagle* covered Parade Grounds games, ran box scores and even provided highlights of the more important games. A peak of 140 teams were once registered to play at the Parade Grounds. Although some baseball is still played today on the site, tennis courts, soccer fields and football fields now take up a good portion of the real estate.

Jackie Robinson signs—Brooklyn Dodgers Headquarters

City: New York
Location: 215 Montague Street
Brooklyn
It was in August of 1945 (three weeks after the atomic bomb was dropped on Hiroshima) that Jackie Robinson secretly sat down in an office once located at this address and signed a contract to play baseball with for the 1946 Class AAA

The historic meeting between Jackie Robinson and Branch Rickey, where Robinson signed his contract to play pro ball, occurred at the former headquarters of the Brooklyn Dodgers. A plaque marks the site of the meeting.

Montreal Royals. For integration to work, Dodgers boss Branch Rickey knew Robinson would have to turn the other cheek—ignore the ugly comments he'd surely hear and not be confrontational in the face of certain cruelty. Rickey insisted that, no matter how foul the treatment Robinson got from fans or opposing players, he could not retaliate for two years. "What I'm looking for is more than a great player," Rickey told Robinson. "I'm looking for a man that will take insults, take abuse—and have the guts not to fight back." With grace, honor and courage, Robinson honored the agreement and thus changed baseball. A plaque identifies this as the former headquarters of the Brooklyn Dodgers—and salutes the historic meeting that occurred here.

Roy Campanella Occupational Training Center

City: New York
Location: 64 Avenue X
Brooklyn

Gil Hodges Way

City: New York

Location: On Bedford Avenue between Avenues L, M and N, three blocks

Brooklyn

In April, 2001, just a couple of miles from where Ebbets Field used to sit, then-New York Mayor Rudy Giuliani was on hand to rename Bedford Avenue, between Avenues L and M (the street on which Gil Hodges and his family lived), "Gil Hodges Way." Hodges' widow, Joan, was there for the ceremony. Hodges came to New York in 1943 as a 19-year-old rookie catcher for the Brooklyn Dodgers and, like many players of his generation, saw his career interrupted by service in World War II. He returned to the

Former Dodgers first baseman Gil Hodges was always a fan favorite in Brooklyn.

Dodgers in 1947 and became a staple at first base, hitting 370 career home runs and driving in 1,274 runs. His lifetime batting average of .273 was forged around 1,921 career hits. Hodges also was an outstanding fielder, earning three Gold Gloves, and he represented the National League at first base in eight All-Star Games. Nearing the end of his playing career, Hodges played for the New York Mets and gained distinction as the first Mets player to hit a home run in their expansion season of 1962. In 1968, he became Mets manager and led the team to its first World Series—the "miracle" championship of 1969.

Some other Gil Hodges-related landmarks in Brooklyn

- PS 193 is called the Gil Hodges School, located at 2515 Avenue L 7.

- There is a Gil Hodges Little League Field on Knapp Street between Avenues V and W.

- The Marine Parkway-Gil Hodges Memorial Bridge connects Floyd Bennett Field in Brooklyn with Fort Tilden in the Rockaways. A sign and bust of Hodges are at the entrance to the bridge.

First baseball game ever televised

City: New York
Location: Columbia University
Andy Coakley Field
Broadway and West 218th Street
Columbia University

The first televised game was broadcast from Columbia University's Baker Field by New York experimental NBC station W2XBS on May 17, 1939. The second game of a college doubleheader between the Princeton Tigers and Columbia Lions was shot with one camera standing on a platform behind home plate. (Approximately 400 people watched the game at home.) Three months later, on August 26, W2XBS broadcast its first major league game, the first game of a doubleheader between the Brooklyn Dodgers and Cincinnati Reds from Ebbets Field. Broadcasting legend Red Barber handled the first play-by-play and interviewed rival managers Leo Durocher (Dodgers) and Bill McKechnie (Reds) in the first post-game show.

Mickey Mantle's restaurant

City: New York
Location: 42 Central Park South

When he was still living in New York, this is where you might have found "The Mick," hanging out with old pals and teammates, relaxing in his favorite booth. Today, the restaurant continues to dazzle patrons with memorabilia, a well-supplied gift shop and classic American fare. Mickey Mantle's is to today's diner what it once was to a great sports hero: a place to relive baseball's past, to hang out and to have fun.

Former site of Dexter Park

City: New York
Location: North side of Jamaica Avenue between Dexter Court and 76th Street
Woodhaven
Queens

In the first half of the 20th century, Dexter Park played host to many of the top baseball stars of the majors and Negro leagues. (Babe Ruth even played here in 1928, after promoting a rodeo with Lou Gehrig.) But it primarily served as home for a team called the Bushwicks, which hired players on their way up or down from the major leagues. The Bushwicks were among the best semi-pro teams in America for 40 years, and their legendary Sunday afternoon games against the top Negro League teams often outdrew the Brooklyn Dodgers at Ebbets Field. Dexter Park was torn down in the mid-1950s and the site is now occupied by two-family homes. There is no marker to commemorate what happened here.

Ansonia Hotel

City: New York

Location: 2109 Broadway, between 73rd and 74th Streets
(Now a co-op apartment)

Babe Ruth spent most of the 1920s at this one-time grand hotel—an ornate, Beaux Arts-style masterpiece that catered to stars from all walks of life. Famed tenor Enrico Caruso lived here, as did boxer Jack Dempsey, composer Igor Stravinsky and many other notables. But it also was here in 1919 that

The restaurant opened by former Yankees star Mickey Mantle remains a popular New York hangout.

eight members of the Chicago White Sox (the so-called "Black Sox") plotted among themselves to throw the 1919 World Series to the Cincinnati Reds. The Ansonia was the first air-conditioned building in New York.

The birth of the National League

City: New York

Location: Grand Central Hotel (former site)
673 Broadway, just south of West 3rd Street
Lower Manhattan

It was at this site in 1876 that a small group of men led by Chicago businessman William Hulbert and pitching star Albert Spalding met to form the National League. As a result, eight teams were created to start the 1876 season. In 1952, a plaque was placed on the hotel stating that it was the "Birthplace of major league baseball. On this site the National League of Professional Baseball Clubs was organized on February 2, 1876." In 1973 the hotel collapsed after years of weakening and the plaque was lost. Today, a New York University law school dorm is located on the site.

The lights from Ebbets Field

City: New York
Location: Downing Stadium (former site)
Randalls Island
Recently torn down, this one-time track stadium (also used for Negro League baseball) attained some degree of notoriety when it was learned that some of the Ebbets Field lights were put to use here after the fabled Brooklyn park was torn down in 1960. Originally opened as the Triborough Stadium (to coincide with the 1936 completion of the Triborough Bridge), the stadium was renamed Downing Stadium in 1955. Over the years, the stadium hosted baseball and concerts and served as home to the New York Cosmos, a professional soccer team, during the 1970s. In 1991, the United States National Track and Field Championships returned to the stadium after a 25-year absence. It is not known today what has become of the Ebbets Field lights.

Damaschke Field

City: Oneonta
Location: Main Street and Neahwa Place (Exit 15 off I-88)
607-432-6041
Damaschke Field, a legendary minor league park, is the current home of the Oneonta Tigers in the New York-Pennsylvania League. Since opening in 1940, this cozy, unpretentious stadium, formerly home of the Oneonta Yankees, has played host to such greats as Babe Ruth, Lou Gehrig, Joe DiMaggio, Mickey Mantle, Don Mattingly, Bernie Williams and many more. Called Neahwa Park Field when it opened in 1940, it was renovated and renamed Damaschke Field in 1968, after Ernest Damaschke, the longtime chairman of the Oneonta Parks & Recreation Commission.

Troy baseball monument—birth of the Giants

City: Troy

The lights from Ebbets Field (right) were later put to good use at Downing Stadium, the one-time home of professional soccer's New York Cosmos,

Location: Knickerbacker Park
Lansingburgh

Many people don't realize that the origin of the San Francisco Giants baseball club lies here in upstate New York, where the legendary Troy Haymakers played in the late 19th century. In 1871, the National Association of Professional Base Ball Players (the first organized professional baseball league) was founded in New York City, and the Troy Haymakers were one of its original nine teams. Playing its first game here on May 9, Troy lost to the Boston Red Stockings, 9-5. That year, the Haymakers ended up a mediocre sixth place, going 13-15. The Haymakers disbanded, primarily for financial reasons, before the next season was over, but from 1879-82, the National League's Troy Trojans were part of the major league scenery. Voted out of the league after the 1882 season, Troy left quite a professional baseball legacy. Five future Hall of Famers played there: Dan Brouthers, Roger Connor, William "Buck" Ewing, Tim Keefe and Mickey Welch. After the Troy Trojans were kicked out of the league, the franchise was moved to New York City and was renamed the "New York Gothams." The nickname was eventually changed to "Giants" and the franchise prospered in New York through 1957, at which point Horace Stoneham relocated to San Francisco. The Troy

The five Hall of Famers who played for Troy in its brief major league history have been memorialized by a town monument.

Baseball Monument, erected in 1992, honors Troy baseball history as well as such local major league products as George Davis and Leo Durocher. The monument is located in the northern section of Troy, an area called Lansingburgh. To get there, enter Knickerbacker Park at 103rd Street and drive straight into the parking lot. The monument is about 200 yards straight ahead. The park, once the playing field for the Troy Haymakers, is now a recreation area.

Statue of John McGraw

City: Truxton
Location: Center of town at the four corners on Route 13
John J. McGraw, the longtime czar of New York baseball, hailed from this small upstate town about 20 miles from Syracuse. Born April 7, 1873, the fiery baseball legend always kept a spot in his heart for his hometown, even paying in the 1920s to build a grandstand at what became known as John J. McGraw Field. That park, which still stands, was the site of a 1938 game between the New York Giants and the local Truxton team. Four years after McGraw's death, his former team came to town to play an exhibition game that would raise

money for a statue that was erected in 1942. Interestingly, the location of the marker in the center of town is where McGraw learned to play baseball as a child.

Dan Brouthers monument

City: Wappingers Falls
Location: North Mesier Avenue, about two blocks off East Main Street

Dan Brouthers' career touched four decades, 1879-1904. Over that period, he won more major league batting crowns (five) than any other 19th century player. Playing for teams in Boston, Brooklyn, Baltimore, Detroit, Philadelphia and New York, Brouthers led his leagues in slugging seven times and was one of a handful of players to hit 100 or more homers before the 20th century. His lifetime batting average of .342 ranks among the all-time leaders and he was elected to the Hall of Fame by the Committee on Old-Timers in 1945. A monument was erected to Brouthers, a native son, in 1971.

Managerial giant John McGraw never lost connections with his hometown in Truxton, N.Y.

Dan Brouthers is buried at St. Mary's Cemetery, on Convent Avenue, in Wappingers Falls.

Other Hall of Famers buried in New York

Joe McCarthy
Mount Olivet Cemetery
4000 Elmwood Avenue
Tonawanda

John Evers
St. Mary's Cemetery
54 Brunswick Road

Joe McCarthy (top) is considered by many as the greatest manager of all time. Frank Frisch had a lifetime batting average of .316.

Troy

Jimmy Collins
Holy Cross Cemetery
2900 S. Park Avenue
Lackawanna

New York City Metropolitan Area
Frank Frisch
Woodlawn Cemetery
Webster Avenue and East 233rd Street
The Bronx

Ford Frick
Christ Church Columbarium
17 Sagamore Road
Bronxville

Jackie Robinson
Cypress Hills Cemetery
833 Jamaica Avenue
Brooklyn

Henry Chadwick
Green-Wood Cemetery
500 25th Avenue
Brooklyn

Mickey Welch and Willie Keeler
Calvary Cemetery
49-02 Laurel Hill Boulevard,
Queens, New York

John Montgomery Ward
Greenfield Cemetery
650 Nassau Road

Uniondale

Lou Gehrig and Ed Barrow
Kensico Cemetery
Commerce and Lakeview Avenue
Valhalla

Ford Frick (top) was a sports-writer, N.L. president and baseball commissioner. Henry Chadwick invented the box score and wrote the first rule book.

Pennsylvania

Former home of John Montgomery Ward

JOHN MONTGOMERY WARD
(1860-1925)

Baseball pioneer, born in
Bellefonte, grew up here.
Played for Providence,
N.Y. Giants, Brooklyn,
1878-94. Pitched profes-
sional baseball's 2nd per-
fect game, 1880. Formed
first players' union, 1885,
& Players' League, 1890.
In Baseball Hall of Fame.

PENNSYLVANIA HISTORICAL AND MUSEUM COMMISSION   2000

A plaque at Bellefonte, Pa., honors the
considerable accomplishments of Hall of
Fame native John Montgomery Ward.

City: Bellefonte
Location: 236 E. Lamb St.

John Montgomery Ward was a trailblazer. In addition to being a star pitcher/infielder (150-plus victories, more than 2,000 hits), he also was an attorney and union activist who fought the game's reserve clause and helped form the Brotherhood of Professional Baseball Players. The brotherhood brought the short-lived Players League into existence. Ward also was a golf star and authored one of the first books on baseball. A marker reads: "Baseball pioneer, born in Bellefonte, grew up here. Played for Providence, N.Y. Giants, Brooklyn, 1878-94. Pitched professional baseball's 2nd perfect game, 1880. Formed first players' union, 1885, & Players League, 1890. In Baseball Hall of Fame."

The birthplace of Honus Wagner

City: Carnegie
Location: Mansfield Blvd. and Chartiers Ave.

Like Christy Mathewson, Honus Wagner was a member of the first class of Hall of Fame inductees. Over a 21-year career, the gritty, fearless, barrel-shaped shortstop batted .329, stole 720 bases and amassed 3,430 hits (sixth on the all-time list). In 1905, Wagner became the first player to have his signature burned into a Louisville Slugger bat. In the first decade of the 20th Century, he was a superstar on Pirates teams that won four pennants and one World Series title.

A marker reads: "The 'Flying Dutchman' was hailed as baseball's greatest shortstop and one of its finest all-around players. A lifelong Carnegie resident, born to German immigrants. Played for Louisville Colonels, 1897-99, and Pittsburgh Pirates, 1900-17; a Pirates coach, 1933-51. He set many National League records, including one for eight seasonal batting titles. Known for his modesty and sportsmanship. Charter member, Baseball Hall of Fame, 1936."

Wagner is buried at Jefferson Memorial Park in Pittsburgh.

Former Pirates shortstop Honus Wagner was one of baseball's premier talents in the early 1900s.

Former home of John K. Tener

City: Charleroi
Location: 6th & Fallowfield Sts.

A marker here honors John K. Tener, who pitched in 61 major league games and had a 15-15 record for Cap Anson's 1889 Chicago N.L. club. It reads: "Governor of Pennsylvania, 1911-1915. Highlights of his administration included creation of statewide primary elections and a state highway system; establishment of the Department of Labor and Industry and Pennsylvania Historical Commission. Member of Congress, 1909-11. Professional baseball player, 1885-90; president, National League, 1913-18. Born in Ireland, he came to the U.S. at age 9. Resident of Charleroi after 1891."

The hometown of Christy Mathewson

City: Factoryville
Location: Marker at U.S. 6 and U.S. 11 in front of Keystone College (in the adjoining town of La Plume)

Christy Mathewson won 373 major league games. Only Cy Young and Walter Johnson posted more victories. A popular and highly respected player, Mathewson used his fadeaway pitch to win 22 or more games for 12 consecutive years. He reached 30 or more wins in three straight seasons. In

one of the greatest pitching performances of all time, he tossed three shutouts over six days in the 1905 World Series. He later managed the Reds and was president of the Braves. Mathewson died of tuberculosis at 45, having possibly contracted the disease as the result of being gassed during a World War I training exercise. The marker reads: "The famed baseball pitcher was born in Factoryville. Attended Keystone Academy, 1895-98; Bucknell University, 1898-1901. He was with the New York Giants, 1900-16, and Cincinnati Reds, 1916-18; pitched 373 winning games, achieving a National League record. Served overseas in World War I. One of the first five players in the Hall of Fame (1936), he was seen as a gentleman in a rough-and-tumble baseball era."

Christy Mathewson, befitting the 'Factoryville' city in which he was born, was a workhorse for John McGraw's New York Giants.

Other Mathewson-related sites:

At Bucknell University in Lewisburg, Pa., a monument called the Christy Mathewson Gateway sits across a field from Christy Mathewson-Memorial Stadium, which houses a plaque that honors the Hall of Famer.

Mathewson is buried at Lewisburg Cemetery.

The birthplace of Eddie Plank

City: Gettysburg
Location: Carlisle St. and W. Lincoln Ave.

Eddie Plank pitched more shutouts (64) and completed more games (387) than any other lefthander in history. Plank, who played little baseball as a youth, joined the Athletics after graduating from Gettysburg College. He spent 14 seasons with the A's, one with the St. Louis club of the Federal League and two with the St. Louis Browns. A marker here reads: "Baseball great. One of the most dominant pitchers of the 20th Century. 'Gettysburg Eddie' compiled a record of 326-194 throughout his career (1901-17), mostly with the Philadelphia Athletics. He won 20 games or more eight times and helped the A's win six pennants and three world championships. Plank was born here, attended Gettysburg Academy. He retired and died in Gettysburg. Elected to Baseball Hall of Fame, 1946."

Eddie Plank is buried at Evergreen Cemetery.

Philadelphia Athletics Historical Society

City: Hatboro
Location: 6 N. York Road
This organization is dedicated to preserving the legacy of the Philadelphia Athletics (and keeping alive other baseball history throughout the area). There is a terrific museum here and a gift shop loaded with books, jerseys, hats and more.

Plaque honoring the Homestead Grays

City: Homestead
Location: West St. and E. Eighth Ave.
A marker sits on the former site of the Andrew Carnegie Homestead Steel Works, where more than a century ago a group of black mill workers formed a sandlot baseball team called the Blue Ribbon. A little more than a decade later, the Blue Ribbon club became the Homestead Grays. The Grays and the Pittsburgh Crawfords, their metropolitan-area rivals, became forces among the great black teams that were formed in the days before the integration of modern major league baseball. The marker reads: "Legendary baseball team that dominated the Negro Baseball Leagues during the first half of the 20th Century. Founded by steelworkers in 1900, the Grays inspired African Americans locally and across the nation. Led by Cumberland Posey Jr., they won 12 national titles, including nine in a row, 1937-45. Players included Hall of Famers Josh Gibson, Buck Leonard and Smokey Joe Williams. Disbanded in 1950."

Bernice Gera marker

City: Indiana
Location: Blue Spruce Park
1128 Blue Spruce Road
724-463-8636
An historical marker honoring Bernice (Shiner) Gera is located here near this

beautiful park's ball field. A native of nearby Ernest, Gera made history as baseball's first female umpire. Barred by minor league baseball for five years, Gera won a landmark lawsuit allowing her to work as an umpire. Her one and only game as a professional umpire took place June 24, 1972, in a New York-Pennsylvania League game in Geneva, New York. At the Baseball Hall of Fame in Cooperstown, New York, Gera's photograph, pink whisk broom and complete umpire uniform are on display.

Bernice Gera, an Indiana, Pa., product, made history as baseball's first female professional umpire.

Roy Campanella's high school

City: Philadelphia
Location: Simon Gratz High, 18th St. and Hunting Park Ave.
Roy Campanella was one of the most beloved players of the modern era. A three-time MVP in the National League, he helped Brooklyn to its only World Series title in 1955 and was a mainstay on five pennant-winning Dodgers teams. In 1953, Campanella set a major league record (since broken) for home runs in a season by a catcher, 40, and he led the league with 142 RBIs. (He hit another homer that season as a pinch hitter.) His career ended in 1958 when he was paralyzed in a car accident just months before the Dodgers were to begin their first season in Los Angeles. Campanella remained a part of the Dodgers' organization until his death on June 26, 1993.

Philadelphia-born Roy Campanella was an offensive and defensive backbone for Brooklyn teams that won five pennants and the 1955 World Series.

A historic marker at the school reads: "A record-breaking catcher with Brooklyn Dodgers, 1948-

57. He began his professional baseball career while in high school here. In Negro League, 1937-42, '44-45. MVP, National League, 1951, '53, '55. All-Star, '49-'56. Baseball Hall of Fame, 1969.

Former site of Baker Bowl

City: Philadelphia
Location: Broad St. and Lehigh Ave.

Opened for the Phillies in 1887, 18,000-seat Baker Bowl was a simple wooden grandstand with a 40-foot-high right-field wall (later increased to 60 feet). The park was heavily damaged in an 1894 fire. Fans were seated in temporary stands for the rest of the '94 season and only a small portion of the exterior outfield wall remained (the wall was incorporated into a newly constructed stadium). The next version of Baker Bowl opened on May 2, 1895. It seated 18,800 and is generally regarded as the first "modern" park built for baseball. Misfortune struck again at Baker Bowl in August 1903 when a section of stands collapsed, killing 12 people. As years passed, the park became obsolete as steel and concrete facilities such as Shibe Park and Yankee Stadium went up. The Phillies played here until 1938, at which point the park had become dilapidated. They joined the Athletics at Shibe Park in July of that season. Recently, a marker was placed at the site (which is now home to an industrial park): "The Phillies' baseball park from its opening in 1887 until 1938. Rebuilt 1895; hailed as nation's finest stadium. Site of first World Series attended by U.S. President, 1915; Negro League World Series, 1924-26; Babe Ruth's last major league game, 1935. Razed 1950."

Baker Bowl, home of Phillies baseball from 1897-1938, was generally regarded as the game's first 'modern' ballpark.

Notable moments at Baker Bowl:

- June 9, 1914: Pittsburgh's Honus Wagner became the second member of the 3,000-hit club (Cap Anson was the first) when he doubled off the Phillies' Erskine Mayer. (Cleveland's Nap Lajoie joined the club later that season.)

- May 14, 1927: During a game between the Phils and Cardinals, 10 rows of stands collapsed and hundreds of fans fell on those sitting below. There was one death—and it was caused by a stampeding crowd.

- May 30, 1935: Babe Ruth, then with the Boston Braves, played only the first inning of the opening game of a double-header against the Phillies and went 0 for 1. It was his final major league appearance.

- June 30, 1938: The Phillies played their final game at the old park and lost to the Giants, 14-1.

Former site of Shibe Park/Connie Mack Stadium

City: Philadelphia
Location: 21st St. and Lehigh Ave.

Shibe Park opened in 1909, replacing Columbia Park as the home of the Athletics. A's owner Ben Shibe built the structure entirely of steel and concrete—an architectural first for a ballpark. Shibe Park originally had a capacity of 23,000, which could be increased significantly by allowing fans to stand in an area in deep center field. Shibe featured an ornate French Renaissance facade, complete with a Beaux Arts tower, at its main entrance, giving the park the appearance of a European church. A mezzanine level was added in 1930, bringing the capacity to 35,000. There was a 12-foot wall in right field, but buildings across the street enabled fans to watch games for free if they could gain access to a rooftop. Until 1935, fans on the roofs still had a bird's-eye view, but A's management—tired of fans beating the system—raised the wall to 50 feet. (The barrier was known locally as the "Spite Fence.") Lights were added, and the first night game was played on May 16, 1939. Shibe Park was renamed Connie Mack Stadium in 1953 in honor of the legendary manager of the A's. When the A's moved to Kansas City after the 1954 season, the Phillies bought the stadium and played there (as they had done since mid-1938) until Veterans Stadium opened in 1971. A fire destroyed much of the interior of Connie Mack

A church, fittingly, now stands at the former site of Shibe Park, which enjoyed a long, religious-like relationship with Philadelphia fans.

Stadium in '71, and the park rotted for five years. A marker at the site (where a church now stands) reads: "Early major league baseball park opened here, 1909. Renamed, 1953. Home to Athletics, 1909-1954; Phillies, 1938-1970. Site of three Negro League World Series; five A's World Series victories. Among first to host night games. Razed, 1976."

Notable moments at Shibe Park:

- May 18, 1912: Detroit players went on strike to protest the suspension of Ty Cobb, who recently had gone into the stands in New York in pursuit of a heckler. To avoid a forfeit and a fine, the Tigers recruited Philadelphia-area sandlot players to take on the Athletics. The A's won, 24-2.

- October 12, 1929: With the Cubs breezing, 8-0, in Game 4 of the World Series and on the brink of tying the Fall Classic at two victories apiece, the Athletics stunned the National League champions with a 10-run seventh inning and seized a three games-to-one advantage. The Cubs wound up losing to the A's in five games.

- June 3, 1932: The Yankees' Lou Gehrig became the first American League player to hit four home runs in one game. The Yanks outslugged the A's, 20-13.

- April 8, 1934: The Phillies and Athletics squared off in a "City Series" exhibition game—the first legal Sunday baseball game played in Philadelphia.

- May 24, 1936: Another Yankee, Tony Lazzeri, teed off against the Athletics. Lazzeri connected for three home runs—two of them grand slams—and drove in an American League-record 11 runs in New York's 25-2 rout of the A's.

- September 28, 1941: On the last day of the season, Boston's Ted Williams had a .39955 batting average—rounded off, it was .400—heading into a doubleheader against the A's. He could have sat out the two games and protected his .400 mark. Instead, he played both games and went 6 for 8. His final average: .406.

- July 13, 1943: The American League defeated the N.L., 5-3, in the first All-Star Game played at night.

Former home of Connie Mack

Scorecard-waving A's manager Connie Mack was a staple of Philadelphia baseball for more than a half century.

City: Philadelphia
Location: 604 Cliveden St.

Although he began his career as a catcher, Connie Mack made his mark as a manager. After heading up the Pirates for a brief time, Mack took over the Athletics of the fledgling American League in 1901 and managed the team for an unfathomable half-century. "The Tall Tactician," who retired at age 88, guided the A's to five World Series titles and helped craft two dynasties. He led the A's to four pennants in one five-year stretch (1910 through 1914) and to three consecutive A.L. flags beginning in 1929. A marker reads: "'Grand Old Man of Baseball.' He started as a catcher in New England, 1883. As manager of the Philadelphia Athletics, 1901-1950—a record 50 years—he led the team to nine American League pennants, 1902-31, and five World Series championships, 1910-30. In baseball's first All-Star Game, he managed the victorious American League team, 1933. Elected to the Baseball Hall of Fame, 1937. He lived on Cliveden Street here."

Connie Mack is buried at Holy Sepulchre Cemetery.

Former home of baseball pioneer Jacob C. White Jr.

City: Philadelphia
Location: 1032 Lombard St.

In tribute to White, one of the city's most notable citizens of the 19th Century, a marker reads: "A black educator who lived here, White was the principal of the Robert Vaux School for 40 years. He was a founder of the city's first black baseball club, the Pythians, and the first president of the Frederick Douglass Memorial Hospital."

Former site of Forbes Field

City: Pittsburgh
Location: 230 S. Bouquet St.

From mid-1909 through June 1970, Forbes Field was the home of the Pittsburgh Pirates. (It also was the occasional home of the Homestead Grays

Forbes Field, one of baseball's first steel-and-concrete stadiums, enjoyed a long, gloried history as home of the Pittsburgh Pirates.

and Pittsburgh Crawfords of the Negro leagues.) The classic park featured a huge foul territory behind home plate, and a spacious outfield that featured ivy-covered brick walls. A left-field bullpen area was added in 1947 to reduce the daunting home run distance faced by Pirates acquisition Hank Greenberg. The slugging Greenberg benefited from "Greenberg Gardens" for just one season before he retired, but the shortened barrier was a big help to Ralph Kiner during the rest of his stay with the Pirates. After Kiner was traded to the Cubs in 1953, "Kiner Korner," as it became known, came down and the bullpens were returned to foul territory.

Though the field is gone, remnants of Forbes Field are still around. A sizable part of the outfield wall still stands, as does the flagpole. A sidewalk plaque marks the spot where Bill Mazeroski's World Series-winning home run in 1960 cleared the wall. Also, the last home plate used at Forbes remains on display near its final location—only now it is under glass at the University of Pittsburgh's Posvar Hall (formerly the Forbes Quadrangle Building).

Notable moments at Forbes Field:

- October 8, 1909: In the first World Series game played at the park, rookie Babe Adams pitched the Pirates past Ty Cobb and the Tigers, 4-1. Adams won three times in that Series as Pittsburgh won the Fall Classic for the first time.

Remnants of Forbes Field still can be found at its former Schenley Park location, now part of the University of Pittsburgh campus.

- October 2, 1920: In the only tripleheader in modern big-league history, the Pirates managed to win only the third game against Cincinnati.

- May 25, 1935: Babe Ruth, playing for the Boston Braves, slugged the final three homers of his career. The last one, No. 714, was the first smash ever hit over the right-field roof.

- July 10, 1936: The Phillies' Chuck Klein hit four homers against Pittsburgh.

- May 28, 1956: Pirates first baseman Dale Long, connecting off Brooklyn's Carl Erskine, became the first major leaguer to hit home runs in eight consecutive games.

- October 13, 1960: Bottom of the ninth inning, Game 7 of the World Series against the Yankees, Mazeroski delivered the knockout punch with his home run off Ralph Terry. The Pirates' 10-9 triumph gave the club its first Series crown in 35 years.

A notable non-moment:

No one ever pitched a no-hitter at Forbes Field.

PNC Park is a jewel on the Allegheny River, in the shadow of Pittsburgh's impressive downtown skyline.

PNC Park

City: Pittsburgh
Location: 115 Federal St.
For tours, call: 412-325-4700

The Pirates' glittering new home (it opened in 2001), which features a remarkable view of the Pittsburgh skyline, pays tribute to past stars with a series of statues and monuments. The old Honus Wagner statue, originally placed at Forbes Field and then moved to Three Rivers Stadium, stands out front. The Roberto Clemente statue from Three Rivers is positioned outside the right-field wall; in its base, under glass, is dirt from Forbes Field. A statue honoring Willie Stargell was unveiled at PNC two days before the Pirates played their first official game at the park (Stargell died the very day the Pirates played their opener), and the Barney Dreyfuss monument from Forbes Field has been relocated here. (Dreyfuss, former owner of Louisville's National League team, bought controlling interest of the Pirates in 1900 and brought such Louisville stars as Honus Wagner and Fred Clarke to Pittsburgh. Dreyfuss owned the Pirates for more than three decades.) Around PNC, the "Roberto Clemente Bridge" (formerly known as the Sixth Street Bridge) can be used as an entrance to the park, and the street that runs down the right-field line has been renamed "Mazeroski Way."

Former site of Ammons Field/ tribute to Josh Gibson

City: Pittsburgh
Location: 2217 Bedford Ave.

Considered the "Babe Ruth of the Negro leagues," catcher Josh Gibson was one of the game's greatest power hitters. He also was a noted battery-mate of Satchel Paige. Gibson, known for his distant home runs, died at age 35, just three months before Jackie Robinson integrated modern major league baseball. The marker here reads: "Hailed as Negro leagues' greatest slugger, he hit some

A marker is all that's left of Ammons Field, where Hall of Famer and Negro League star Josh Gibson pounded out his first home runs.

800 home runs in a baseball career that began here at Ammons Field in 1929. Played for Homestead Grays and Pittsburgh Crawfords, 1930-46. Elected to the Baseball Hall of Fame, '72."

Josh Gibson is buried at Allegheny Cemetery in Pittsburgh.

Former site of Greenlee Field

City: Pittsburgh
Location: 2500 Bedford Avenue, between Chauncy and Duff
Greenlee Field was the first black-owned and black-built major baseball field in the United States. It was built thanks to Gus Greenlee, owner of the Pittsburgh Crawfords. Greenlee was irritated that his team and others in the league could not use the dressing rooms at white-owned parks like Forbes Field or Ammons Field, so he did something about it. By 1932 when the park opened, Satchel Paige, Josh Gibson and Oscar Charleston all played for the mighty Crawfords. In 1933, permanent lights were added. Given that the Cincinnati Reds didn't do this at Crosley until 1935, many consider this to be the first permanent lighting system in a ballpark. However, toward the end of the decade, interest in the Crawfords waned, and the park was demolished in December of 1938. There is nothing here to hint of its existence, though a group is involved currently in trying get a marker placed in honor of it.

Monument honoring Stan Coveleski

City: Shamokin
Location: Market Street
Upon Stan Coveleski's election to the Baseball Hall of Fame in 1969, the twin communities of Shamokin and Coal Township honored their native son with a monument. The highlight of Coveleski's career came in the 1920 World Series against the Brooklyn Dodgers, when he tossed a shutout for Cleveland in the clinching game and won three times overall. He pitched nine shutouts in 1917 and had five 20-victory seasons in the majors.

Stan Coveleski was a hero of the 1920 World Series.

Boyhood home of Jacob Nelson "Nellie" Fox

City: St. Thomas
Location: 7417 Lincoln Highway (U.S. 30) W.
Nellie Fox was a sparkplug on the "Go-Go" White Sox teams of the late 1950s and early 1960s. He was the American League's MVP in 1959, helping

A must-see attraction near the Williamsport home of Little League baseball is the Peter J. McGovern Museum, which features pictures, displays, films and various interactive exhibits.

the Sox to their first World Series appearance in 40 years. He hit .306 in '59, drove in 70 runs and led A.L. second basemen in fielding percentage. He punched out 2,663 career hits and batted .368 in All-Star Game competition. He was a master bunter and bat handler. A marker near the home reads: "1997 Baseball Hall of Fame inductee. Second baseman for the Chicago White Sox (1950-1963). Known for his passion and work ethic, Fox was an AL MVP (1959), a three-time Gold Glove Award winner and a 12-time All-Star. His boyhood home stands nearby."

Nellie Fox is buried at St. Thomas Cemetery.

Birthplace of Little League baseball

City: Williamsport
Location: Lycoming County Courthouse
48 W. Third St.

A plaque conveys the county's history—and the impact that Little League baseball has had on the area. It reads: "Formed April 13, 1795 out of Northumberland County. The name (from a Delaware Indian word) honors Lycoming Creek. Williamsport, the county seat, became a borough, 1806, and a city, 1866. Once a great lumbering center. Birthplace of Little League baseball."

Peter J. McGovern Little League Baseball Museum

City: Williamsport
Location: Route 15, South Williamsport

Located just minutes from where the Little League World Series is played, the Peter J. McGovern Little League Baseball Museum celebrates Little League baseball and softball, past and present. It features pictures, displays and films about the players, equipment, history, rules and games. Plus, there are interactive exhibits.

The original Little League Field

City: Williamsport
Location: W. Fourth St.
Founded in Williamsport in 1939 by Carl Stotz, Little League baseball has become the largest youth sports program in the world. It is played by approximately three million children in 103 countries. In '39, a $30 donation was enough to purchase uniforms for each of the first three teams, named after their sponsors: Lycoming Dairy, Lundy Lumber and Jumbo Pretzel. A plaque honoring Stotz reads: "Founder of Little League baseball and commissioner through 1955. Stotz developed the Little League idea in 1938; in the next year three teams played 24 games. It was at this site that Stotz established field distances for the pre-teenage players. The first 12 Little League World Series were played on this field, 1947-1958, and during these years the number of teams grew from 60 to thousands in many nations."

Bowman Field

City: Williamsport
Location: 1700 W. Fourth St.
This quaint 1920s-era park plays host to the Williamsport Crosscutters of the Class A New York-Penn League. A marker reads: "Bowman Field, one of the nation's oldest operating parks. Built 1926. Long noted as Pennsylvania's oldest operating minor league baseball park and the nation's second oldest. The first professional game here was played April 27, 1926, between the Williamsport Grays and the Negro League Harrisburg Giants. Over the years this park became home to successive Williamsport teams and hosted many major league teams for exhibition games. Originally Memorial Field; renamed 1929 for J. Walton Bowman."

Hall of Famers buried in Pennsylvania

Richie Ashburn
Gladwyne Methodist Church Cemetery
Gladwyne

Chief Bender
Hillside Cemetery
Roslyn

Nestor Chylak
St. Cyril and Methodist Church Cemetery
Peckville

George Davis
Fernwood Cemetery
Philadelphia

Pud Galvin
Calvary Cemetery
Pittsburgh

Bucky Harris
St. Peter's Lutheran Church Cemetery
Hughestown

Hugh Jennings
St. Catherine's Cemetery
Moscow

Herb Pennock
Union Hill Cemetery
Kennett Square

Pie Traynor
Homewood Cemetery
Pittsburgh

Harry Wright
West Laurel Hills Cemetery
Bala Cynwyd

(From top) Chief Bender,
George Davis and Herb
Pennock.

Rhode Island

McCoy Stadium

City: Pawtucket
Location: One Ben Mondor Way

This cozy minor league park, built in 1942 and renovated in 1998-1999, is home to the Class AAA Pawtucket Red Sox. Many great games have been played here, but none more memorable than the one that began on the night of April 18,1981, and continued until 4 a.m.—at which time the game, tied at 2-2, was suspended after Rochester and the hometown "PawSox" had played 32 innings. The game was resumed on June 23, and it ended in the 33rd inning when Pawtucket's Dave Koza delivered a bases-loaded single. Among the participants in the longest game in professional baseball history were Rochester third baseman Cal Ripken Jr., Pawtucket third baseman Wade Boggs and Sox pitcher Bob Ojeda. Ripken went 2 for 13 at the plate and Boggs was 4 for 12. Ojeda pitched one inning and got the victory in the 8-hour, 25-minute game.

Historic Cardines Field

20 America's Cup Avenue
Newport
Rhode Island
401-862-4494

It might be America's oldest ballpark. No one is sure when this stadium was built, but a substantial portion of its existing grandstand might date back as far as 1889. If so, that would make Cardines the only surviving example of 1800s-era baseball stadium architecture in the world. (LaBatt Field in London, Ontario, is an older ball field, but its structure has been rebuilt over the years.) Cardines was home for the Newport Colts of the New England League from 1897-99. In 1919, the George S. Donnelly Sunset League began

Future Indians teammates Satchel Paige (left) and Larry Doby played at Cardines.

playing at Cardines and various Negro League teams made frequent barnstorming stops in the 1930s and '40s. Cardines Field almost was torn down in the 1980s, but a local group raised funds and made overdue repairs on the aging facility. Today, the Friends of Cardines Foundation works hard to improve the historic landmark, which now is home to the Newport Gulls of the New England Collegiate Baseball League. Over the years, many baseball legends have played at Cardines, including Jimmie Foxx, Larry Doby and Satchel Paige, who would sit in his rocking chair between the dugouts thinking up colorful names for his many pitches.

Vermont

Centennial Field

City: Burlington
Location: University of Vermont

The University of Vermont's baseball team has played at Centennial Field since 1906. Though many renovations were made to the park in the 1990s—the Vermont Expos of the short-season Class A New York-Penn League began play here in 1994 and remain a tenant—the existing grandstand was put in place in 1922. Tris

Centennial Field, which dates back to 1906, is used today by the Vermont Expos of the Class A New York-Penn League.

Speaker is one of many great stars of yesteryear who visited Centennial Field for exhibition games. And Barry Larkin, Ken Griffey Jr. and Omar Vizquel are among those who called the park home when they played for the Vermont team in the Class AA Eastern League in the 1980s.

Birthplace of Larry Gardner

City: Enosburg Falls
Location: 14 School St.

A marker reveals that third baseman Larry Gardner, a member of four World Series championship teams, was born here on May 13, 1886. A local high school star and a standout at the University of Vermont, Gardner joined the Boston Red Sox in 1908 and was a regular on Sox teams that won the Fall Classic in 1912, 1915 and 1916. In 1920, he was a key player on Cleveland's Series champions. It was Gardner's fly ball that drove home the Series-winning run against the New York Giants in 1912. In 1916, Gardner managed only three hits in the Series (against the Dodgers)—but two of them were home runs. He later served two decades as University of Vermont baseball coach.

Virginia

Ron Necciai's 27 strikeout game

City: Bristol
Location: DeVault Memorial Stadium
1501 Euclid Avenue

Ron Necciai, a hard-throwing righthander for Pittsburgh's Bristol farm team in the Appalachian League, gained national prominence when he struck out 27 batters in a nine-inning 1952 no-hitter.

On May 13, 1952, 19-year-old Bristol righthander Ron Necciai struck out 27 Welch hitters in a nine-inning no-hitter that put the Appalachian League on the baseball map. Necciai, a Pirates farmhand, faced 31 batters—walking one, hitting another and losing two outs when his catcher dropped a third strike and a fielder committed an error. One out was recorded on a ground ball. Necciai's remarkable feat gained national attention and prompted Branch Rickey to say, "There have been only two young pitchers I was certain were destined for greatness. ... One of those boys was Dizzy Dean. The other is Ron Necciai." Rickey was only half right. Necciai was 4-0 at Bristol with 109 strikeouts and allowed only 10 hits in 43 innings. He was 7-9 with 172 strikeouts in 126 innings when he moved up to Burlington of the Carolina League before finishing his 1952 season at Pittsburgh, where he struggled to a 1-6 record and 7.08 ERA in 54 innings. After that 1952 season, physical problems took a toll on Necciai and his stock tumbled quickly. But a baseball that Necciai threw in his memorable 1952 game remains on display at the Baseball Hall of Fame in Cooperstown, and a commemorative marker at DeVault Memorial Stadium honors his monumental pitching performance. DeVault is the current home of the Bristol

White Sox, a Chicago affiliate in the Appalachian League, but the original park where Necciai tossed his no-hitter is gone. The original ballpark, located about a mile from the current park at Gate City Highway and Catherine Streets, was torn down in the 1960s and is now the current location of a dairy.

Bing Crosby Stadium

City: Front Royal
Location: 8th Street behind the Youth Center
In 1948, while serving as Grand Marshall of the Apple Blossom Festival in Winchester, Bing Crosby came to the small town of Front Royal at the invitation of Sen. Raymond R. Guest to help with a fund-raising campaign for a new ballpark. The actor/crooner contributed $1,000 to the effort. In 1950, Crosby returned for the premiere of his movie, "Riding High," and he made another contribution of $3,572.92, which completed the fund-raising campaign. Now, after more than five decades of athletic activity at the park and numerous renovations, Bing Crosby Stadium stands as a tribute to the man and the citizens who worked hard to create recreational facilities in Front Royal and Warren County. Today, the field is used by the local high school and the Front Royal Cardinals, who play in the Valley League. The Valley League is one of only eight summer collegiate baseball leagues certified by the National Collegiate Athletic Association and endorsed by Major League Baseball. The eight leagues are members of the National Alliance of College Summer Baseball. A plaque within the stadium pays tribute to Bing Crosby.

The Virginia Sports Hall of Fame and Museum has a quaint feel and an impressive collection of artifacts and memorabilia.

Virginia Sports Hall of Fame and Museum

City: Portsmouth
Location: 420 High St.
757-393-8031
Established in 1972, the Virginia Sports Hall of Fame and Museum is the Commonwealth's official sports Hall of Fame, honoring champions from every region of Virginia. The Museum houses one of the country's largest collections of sports artifacts and memorabilia, including a tennis racquet used by Arthur Ashe, the signature straw hat of leg-

endary golfer Sam Snead and the game ball from a 1903 football battle between Virginia Tech and Navy. But baseball is well-represented, too. More than 20 local players from the major leagues and Negro leagues are honored, including such performers as Al Bumbry, Ray Dandridge, Leon Day, George Lacy and Jim Lemon.

West Virginia

Bowen Field

City: Bluefield
Location: Route 460 at Westgate
Located on the state line that divides Virginia and West Virginia, historic Bowen Field has a charming, tree-shaded "country" feel. The park was built in 1939 and has undergone numerous renovations. But fans still flock through the turnstiles to experience its throwback environment. Bowen Field today is home of the Bluefield Orioles in the Appalachian League.

George Brett earned Hall of Fame distinction in Kansas City, but his roots can be traced to Glen Dale in north-central West Virginia.

Watt Powell Park

City: Charlestown
Location: 3403 MacCorkle Ave. SE

Another of the great old minor league parks in the Appalachian League, Watt Powell is home today for the Class A Charleston Alley Cats of the South Atlantic League. Anybody who wants to experience its throwback aura should be advised that Watt Powell will be torn down after the 2004 season and replaced by a new park. It is named for Watt Powell, the man who financed part of its construction, which started in August of 1948. Powell's efforts were aided by a $350,000 government bond issue. The park was needed because Kanawha Park, the former home of professional baseball in Charleston, had burned to the ground in 1944. Sadly, Powell died just two months before the park opened, so he never got to experience a game at the place that was fittingly named for his efforts.

Hometown of George Brett

City: Glen Dale

Signs north and south of town proclaim it to be the "Birthplace of George Brett—Baseball Hall of Fame"

The tough-as-nails Kansas City third baseman was born in Glen Dale, which is located in north-central West Virginia. Brett's major league career started in 1973 and lasted 21 years, all with the Kansas City Royals. Brett was the American League MVP in 1980, when he hit .390, the highest batting average since Boston's Ted Williams hit .406 in 1941. He played in two World Series, contributing to the Royals' first championship in 1985. A participant in 10 All-Star Games, the lefthanded-swinging Brett was named to the Hall of Fame in 1999.

Hall of Famers buried in West Virginia

Lewis "Hack" Wilson
Rosedale Cemetery
2060 Rosedale Road
Martinsburg

Hack Wilson's 190 RBIs in 1930 is still a major league record.

The South

Site of **Durham Athletic Park**
Durham, North Carolina

Grave of
Bill Dickey
Little Rock, Arkansas

Hank Aaron Stadium
Mobile, Alabama

The **Astrodome**
Houston, Texas

Dodgertown
Vero Beach, Florida

Alabama

Alabama Sports Hall of Fame

City: Birmingham
Location: 2150 Civic Center Boulevard
205-323-6665

Founded in 1967, this world-class sports museum boasts three floors of memorabilia focusing on state athletes, interactive kiosks, a film room, a gift shop and other displays and exhibits. Baseball fans will get a great feel for the history of the game in Alabama. Willie Mays, Satchel Paige, Cleon Jones, Hank Aaron, Don Sutton—many enthusiasts do not realize what a major league breeding ground the state has been over the years.

Rickwood Field—An old, old story

City: Birmingham
Location: 2100 Morris Avenue
205-458-8161

Built in 1910, Rickwood Field was the vision of a young Birmingham industrialist named Rick Woodward. While still in his 20s, Woodward bought controlling interest in the city's professional baseball team, the Coal Barons, and sought help from legendary baseball star and Philadelphia Athletics manager

The impressive Alabama Sports Hall of Fame chronicles the considerable baseball history of the state that produced home run king Hank Aaron.

Rickwood Field, modeled after Pittsburgh's Forbes Field when it was built in 1910, has been the playground of such Hall of Famers as Ty Cobb, Christy Mathewson, Babe Ruth, Honus Wagner and Rogers Hornsby.

Connie Mack in designing "the finest minor league ballpark ever." Woodward's passion was contagious and, fueled by fervent publicity, the entire city of Birmingham turned baseball-crazy and many businesses closed to celebrate the facility's grand opening. Modeled primarily after Pittsburgh's Forbes Field, Rickwood lived up to its owner's wildest dreams. Over the years, local fans were dazzled by some of baseball's greatest stars. Standing-room-only crowds watched such future Hall of Famers as Ty Cobb, Christy Mathewson, Honus Wagner and hometeam sensation Burleigh Grimes—the last legal spitball pitcher in the major leagues.

By the 1920s, the newly formed Black Barons of the Negro League also were drawing overflow crowds, most of whom were mesmerized by the considerable talents of such black immortals as Mule Suttles, Satchel Paige, Jimmie Crutchfield, Piper Davis and Willie Mays, who would go on to greater glory in the major leagues. The New York Yankees and Babe Ruth also were frequent visitors to Rickwood; occasional stops were made by such stars as Rogers Hornsby, Shoeless Joe Jackson and Dizzy Dean. Old Diz, the St. Louis Cardinals' ace righthander, lost 1-0 to the Barons after guaranteeing a victory—one of the most famous games in Rickwood history.

Today's Rickwood Field, technically "The oldest stadium in America" is on the National Register of Historic Places and the Class AA Birmingham Barons

Attending a game at Rickwood Field, one of baseball's oldest fields, is like stepping back into another era.

come back once a year to play in the Rickwood Classic. In addition, this park is used frequently by Birmingham city schools, men's amateur leagues, junior colleges and other groups.

Optimist Park

City: Huntsville

Location: Corner of Oakwood Avenue and Andrew Jackson Way

Built in 1928 and originally called "Dallas Park," this was home to Dallas Mill baseball teams coached by H.E. "Hub" Myhand, who came to Huntsville in 1927 as physical director for Dallas Manufacturing Co. Until the 1940s, Myhand was a local Huntsville legend who spearheaded the rise of semi-pro baseball featuring local mill teams that drew loyal crowds of 6,000-plus fans. In 1935, the Lincoln and Dallas Mill teams merged to form the Redcaps. The Huntsville Dr. Peppers (1937-43), a women's semi-pro softball team coached by Cecil Fain, also played here. This also was one of the few early ballparks open to all races and was used during the 1950s and '60s for exhibition games by the Birmingham Black Barons and other Negro League teams. Jackie Robinson, Willie Mays and other African American baseball legends were routine visitors in Huntsville. The park was renovated and reopened for baseball in 1994 by the city. Known today as "Optimist Park," there is an historical marker that celebrates its colorful past.

Mobile native Hank Aaron lends his name to a stadium that has become a hub of baseball activity in southern Alabama.

Hank Aaron Stadium

City: Mobile
Location: 755 Bolling Bros. Blvd.
334-479-2327

Officially opened on April 17, 1997, beautiful Hank Aaron Stadium is the home of the Mobile Bay Bears in the Southern League. It also is the annual site for the Hank Aaron High School Baseball Classic featuring Mobile County and Baldwin County high school baseball teams; the Satchel Paige Invitational, an event featuring area independent schools, and the Willie McCovey Challenge and Billy Williams Showdown, classics featuring local college teams. The ballpark is named after baseball's all-time home run king and Alabama native Hank Aaron, who was born in Mobile on February 5, 1934. Aaron grew up in an area called "Toulminville," which also was home to Paige, McCovey, Williams, Cleon Jones, Tommie Agee, Amos Otis and Hank's brother, Tommie Aaron. A nearby street is called Hank Aaron Loop.

Walt Cruise Field

City: Sylacauga
In May, 1973, the local Babe Ruth Field was renamed for Walton "Walt" Cruise, who grew up in Sylacauga. The 82-year old Cruise was presented with a plaque (he played for the Cardinals and Braves, 1914-24).

Keep your eyes peeled for...

- A highway sign and Community Center touting Titus as "Home of Joe Sewell."

- A water tank with the words, "Home of Don Sutton" on its side in Clio—where there's also a Don Sutton Street.

- A sign reading "Hometown of Don Kessinger" in Forrest City.
- Early Wynn Field in Hartford.

Hall of Famers Joe Sewell (top left), Don Sutton (above) and Early Wynn are Alabama natives who are honored in their hometowns.

Arkansas

Lamar Porter Field

City: Little Rock
Location: 7th and Johnson Streets
Completed in 1936 as part of the Works Progress Administration, this charming, classic piece of baseball history has played host to thousands of Arkansas-born athletes, including Hall of Fame third baseman Brooks Robinson. Still used by Boys Club and other youth leagues, Lamar Porter Field also has been the location for several films shot in Arkansas, including 1983's *A Soldier's Story.*

Ray Winder Field is a cozy experience for fans who want a throwback aura while watching the Arkansas Travelers.

Ray Winder Field War Memorial Park

City: Little Rock
Location: Jonesboro Drive at I-630
501-664-1555

This historic stadium is home to the state's only professional baseball team, the Arkansas Travelers of the Class AA Texas League (affiliated with the Anaheim Angels). Built for the Travelers in 1932, the stadium originally was called Travelers Field and also served as home for a team in the Negro Southern League that debut season. The Travelers previously had played their games at Kavanaugh Field, which now is the site of Little Rock's Central High School football stadium. Travelers Field was renamed in honor of the late Ray Winder, a man who dedicated himself for more than a half century to the promotion of professional baseball for the Little Rock and Arkansas Travelers. Now one of the five oldest stadiums still in use in professional baseball, Ray Winder Field can seat 6,000-plus fans, although twice that many crammed through its gates on June 1, 1991, to see pitcher Fernando Valenzuela make a rehabilitation start. Ray Winder, a cozy, old-fashioned park with open seating, features box seats that jut out past the dugouts, allowing fans a clear view of the player benches. Several historic plaques and markers are located throughout the ballpark.

George Kell Park

City: Newport
Location: Off Highway 367 about five miles from downtown Newport

During World War II, when many players had gone off to serve their country, third baseman George Kell emerged as one of the best players in the major leagues. Long after the war was over, Kell remained as a mainstay hot corner specialist for five American League teams. His best seasons were with the Detroit Tigers, where he earned All-Star stature and national prominence by dramatically edging Ted Williams for the 1949 A.L. batting crown (.343). The hard-working, hard-throwing Kell topped the .300 plateau nine times and topped A.L. third basemen in fielding percentage seven times. Kell was elected to the Hall of Fame by the Committee on Veterans in 1983. The park dedicated to Kell is not far from Swifton, where

The memory of third baseman George Kell's Hall of Fame exploits live on at the Newport-area ballpark named in his honor.

he was born in 1922. The American Legion and Newport High School baseball teams play at the park, which also plays host to several state tournaments. The complex has baseball and softball fields as well as the Newport city pool, tennis courts and a volleyball playing area.

Hall of Famers buried in Arkansas

Bill Dickey
Roselawn Memorial Park
2801 Asher Avenue
Little Rock, Arkansas

Travis Jackson
Waldo Cemetery
Columbia County Road 27 and U. S. Hwy. 82
Waldo

Bill Dickey (top), an eight-time All-Star, had a career batting average of .313. Travis Jackson, an excellent defensive shortstop, batted over .300 six times.

Florida

Jackie Robinson Ballpark (formerly called City Island Ballpark)

A statue honoring Jackie Robinson stands at the entrance to the Daytona Beach ballpark named in his honor.

City: Daytona Beach
Location: 105 E. Orange Avenue
386-258-3106

This historic ballpark can claim a milestone moment in American history. City Island Ballpark was the place where Jackie Robinson, on March 17, 1946, began his professional career as a member of the Montreal Royals, a Brooklyn Dodgers Class AAA farm team that trained in Daytona Beach. The spring training game between the Royals and the Dodgers was the first integrated major league game of the 20th century and a preview of Robinson's major league debut in 1947. The ballpark was renamed in Robinson's honor in 1990 and a statue bearing his likeness is located at the entrance. Jackie Robinson Park was built in 1930 and has served as temporary home to many Hall of Famers. In November 1998, the ballpark was listed on the National Register of Historic Places for its status and contributions to the civil rights movement. Today, the ballpark is home of the Daytona Cubs, a Chicago Cubs Class A farm team that plays in the Florida State League.

Tate High School

City: Gonzalez
Location: 1771 Tate Road
850-937-2300

Since 1954, 45 players from Tate High School have been drafted by major league teams, including Hall of Famer Don Sutton, who pitched in the major leagues for 23 years, earned four All-Star Game selections and pitched in four World Series. Other Tate High School products include Jay Bell and Travis Fryman. A nearby billboard touts the major leaguers the school has produced and there's an exhibit within the school.

Ted Williams Retrospective Museum & Library, Inc.

City: Hernando
Location: 2455 North Citrus Hills Blvd.
352-527-6566

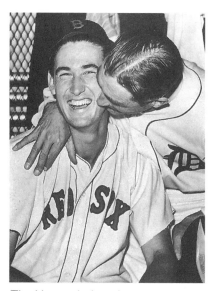

The Hernando-based museum honors great Ted Williams moments, such as his 1941 All-Star home run.

On February 9, 1994, a few blocks from where Ted Williams lived, the Ted Williams Museum was dedicated. The museum is laid out like a baseball diamond—each base representing a different chapter in the Splendid Splinter's legendary career. First base begins with Williams playing for the Minneapolis Millers and the San Diego Padres before arriving in the major leagues with the Boston Red Sox. Second base documents Williams' military exploits during World War II and the Korean War. The theme continues, chronicling Williams' spectacular career, 1960 retirement, managerial career and beyond. Williams memorabilia takes up most of the outer rim of the diamond, with inside space devoted to such other players as Cal Ripken and Don Mattingly. On a platform in the middle of the diamond (where the pitcher's mound would be) is a statue of Williams, immortalized in his classic batting stance. In the "Hitter's Wing," there are displays honoring Williams' choices as the 20 greatest hitters of all time, a list that includes Hank Aaron, Willie Mays, Mickey Mantle, Stan Musial, Frank Robinson and Babe Ruth. In addition to the numerous displays, visitors can see thousands of pieces of memorabilia, much of it from private collectors, and video clips showing classic moments involving Williams and other legends. The museum holds induction ceremonies every year to honor Williams and other worthy players from the past and present. In Williams' own words,

"Through the Ted Williams Museum and Hitters Hall of Fame, we hope to build a lasting monument, an architectural tribute to what I think is the single most difficult thing in all of sports; hitting a baseball. We hope the Museum will become a place millions of baseball fans will visit and enjoy for generations to come. I hope you'll join us as we transform our dreams into reality." More than 50,000 fans visit the museum annually and it already has become one of the true shrines of baseball. Enhancing the displays are the ideas submitted by the man many consider the greatest pure hitter who ever lived.

Tinker Field is dwarfed by the Citrus Bowl football stadium that was built perilously close to its right field fence.

Tinker Field

City: Orlando
Location: 287 South Tampa Avenue
407-849-2001

Though the current ballpark was built in 1963, pro baseball has been played on this field since 1914. It served as the spring training facility for several major league teams as well as the home for Florida State League and Southern League teams until being abandoned in 2000. The stadium is named for Hall of Famer Joe Tinker (of "Tinker-to-Evers-to-Chance" fame), who lived in Orlando after retiring and managed Orlando's first semi-professional team. Interestingly, several hundred grandstand seats from Washington's Griffith Stadium are used at Tinker Field and a monument to Senator's owner Clark Griffith stands out front. (The Senators used to train here.) The Citrus Bowl football stadium is built ridiculously close to Tinker, almost touching the right field exterior wall. In the late 1980s, Boston's Sam Horn hit a monster shot that cleared the exterior of Tinker Field and landed in the football stadium.

The hometown of Chipper Jones

City: Pierson

"Fern Capital of the World and Hometown of Chipper Jones."

(There is also a street and ballpark named after Jones in Pierson.)

Pierson, Fla., has honored favorite son Chipper Jones with a sign, a street and a ballpark.

The Swain Apartments

City: St. Petersburg

Location: 1511 22nd Street South

In the 1950s and '60s, Dr. Robert James Swain, Jr., a prominent African-American dentist in St. Petersburg, helped lead the struggle against segregation in the city. This area was the heart of the African-American community during the civil rights era and the apartments on 22nd Street housed many of the black major league players of the St. Louis Cardinals and New York Yankees when they arrived in St. Petersburg for spring training. Blacks in that period were often denied housing in areas where their white teammates would stay. Built in 1956, the apartments offered a sanctuary while Swain and other leaders fought through the system to expose the racial injustice. Attitudes started to change after 1961 and the Cardinals eventually made an effort to integrate their housing. The Yankees already had relocated their spring facilities to Fort Lauderdale. The former Swain Apartment building is still used for commercial purposes and was recently granted landmark status for its significant role in the American civil rights era.

St. Petersburg's Al Lang Field has served as a spring training base since 1916, thanks to the inspired thinking of the city's former mayor.

Progress Energy Park at Al Lang Field

City: St. Petersburg
Location: 230 First St. S.
727-825-3284

Al Lang Field is named after St. Petersburg's former mayer, the local "father of baseball" who provided the impetus for bringing spring training to this Gulf Coast community. For more than 80 years, Al Lang has been a spring training home. The Philadelphia Phillies played here from 1916-21; the Boston Braves from 1922-24; the New York Yankees (Babe Ruth, Lou Gehrig, Joe DiMaggio) from 1925-37; the St. Louis Cardinals (Stan Musial, Bob Gibson, Lou Brock) from 1938-97, and currently, the Tampa Bay Devil Rays. During the summer, the field serves as home to the St. Petersburg Devil Rays, a Class A farm team for Tampa Bay. A marker in the shape of home plate stands just north of the stadium, detailing some of the field's rich history.

One of Babe Ruth's longest home runs

City: Tampa
Location: Pepin-Rood Stadium (former site of Plant Field)
University of Tampa
401 West Kennedy Boulevard
813-253-3333

In 1919, during an April 4 spring training game between the defending World Series-champion Red Sox and the New York Giants, young Babe Ruth hit one of his most memorable home runs out of Plant Field. George Smith, pitching for the Giants, fired a fastball that the Red Sox pitcher-turned-slugger crushed an estimated 587 feet—purported by some to be the longest ball ever hit in baseball history. Ruth's home run was not the only significant moment or event that occurred here. One of the most memorable was a barnstorming football game between Red Grange's Chicago Bears and a pickup team led by Jim Thorpe called the Tampa Cardinals. More recently, hurdler Roger Kingdom won a national championship at reconfigured Pepin-Rood Stadium on his way to winning a second Olympic gold medal. The stadium also has been used by the Tampa Smokers of the International League and the Cincinnati Reds as a spring training site. Pepin-Rood Stadium, now considered the finest collegiate soccer venue in NCAA Division II, has been the site of two national championship finals. A nearby plaque commemorates the blast.

Dodgertown

City: Vero Beach
Location: 3901 26th Street
772-569-4900

This is easily the most historic spring training site in major league baseball. The Dodgers were lured to the area in 1948 by Bud Holman, director of Eastern Airlines, who persuaded Brooklyn farm director Buzzy Bavasi to econ-

Dodgers players (from left) Steve Garvey, Bill Russell, Ted Sizemore, Don Sutton and Ron Cey look up to manager Walt Alston in this 1976 photo.

omize and bring together all 30-plus Dodgers farm teams to one central facility. In 1952, the current Dodgertown, featuring Holman Stadium, was constructed in the city of Vero Beach. Dodgertown was a former Naval air base and Brooklyn players originally were housed in former Navy barracks. When Holman Stadium opened in 1953, 1,500 of its steel chairs were former seats used at Brooklyn's Ebbets Field. The original barracks eventually were replaced by more comfortable villas (90 of them), many of which are still in use. Dodgertown also has added 27 holes of golf, 70 acres of citrus groves and Safari Pines Estates, a residential development. Although most of the compound has changed significantly since 1948, this spring training "Dodger Blueprint" remains one of the true archetypes of a successful training facility and also one of the best places for fans to visit and get a sense of what the preseason is really like. During the regular season, Holman Stadium is home to the Vero Beach Dodgers of the Class A Florida State League and the Gulf Coast Dodgers of the Rookie Gulf Coast League.

Nap Lajoie (top) batted .338 lifetime, while Bill Terry's career batting average was .341.

Hall of Famers buried in Florida

Nap Lajoie
Bellevue Cedar Hill Memory
1425 Bellevue Avenue
Daytona Beach
904-253-7603

Dazzy Vance
Stage Stand Cemetery (East Side of U. S. Hwy. 19, a quarter mile south of Yulee Road)
Homosassa Springs

Bill Terry
Evergreen Cemetery
4535 N. Main Street
Jacksonville
904-353-3649

Bill Klem
Graceland Memorial Park
4580 SW 8th Street
Coral Gables
305-446-2922

Jimmie Foxx
Flagler Memorial Park
5301 W. Flagler Street
Miami
305-446-7625

Max Carey
Woodlawn Park North Cemetery and
Mausoleum
3216 SW 8th Street,
Miami
305-445-5425

Ed Walsh
Forest Lawn North
200 West Copans Road
Pompano Beach
954-523-6700

Joe Tinker
Greenwood Cemetery
1603 Greenwood Street
Orlando
407-246-2616

Ray Dandridge
Fountainhead Memorial
7303 Babcock Street SE
Palm Bay
407-727-3977

Bill McKechnie and Paul Waner
Manasota Memorial Cemetery
1221 53rd Avenue East
Bradenton
941-755-2688

Hoyt Wilhelm
Palms Memorial Park
170 Honore Avenue
Sarasota
941-371-4962

(From top) Max Carey,
Joe Tinker, Bill McKechnie
and Paul Waner.

Heinie Manush had a .330 career batting average.

Heinie Manush
Sarasota Memorial Park
5833 S. Tamiami Trail
Sarasota
941-924-1993

Billy Herman
Riverside Memorial Park
4534 County Line Road
Tequesta
561-747-1100

Georgia

Hank Aaron statue at Turner Field

City: Atlanta
Location: Turner Field
755 Hank Aaron Dr. SE
404-577-9100

On the north side of the Braves' current home ballpark, facing downtown Atlanta, is a 10-foot bronze statue of Hank Aaron. Hammerin' Hank hit a major league-record 755 home runs, drove in a record 2,297 runs and collected a record 6,856 total bases in his storied 23-year career with the Braves and Milwaukee Brewers. Aaron became a first-ballot Hall of Famer in 1982.

Ty Cobb, executing his distinctive fadeaway slide, is a fixture outside the entrance of Atlanta's Turner Field.

Ty Cobb statue at Turner Field

City: Atlanta
Location: Turner Field
Located outside the northern entrance to Turner Field is a bronze statue of Ty Cobb sliding into a base. The plaque under the statue reads:
Tyrus Raymond Cobb
1886 -1961
Known as the Georgia Peach
Charter member of Baseball
Hall of Fame

Leading Batsman of all Major League History
.367 Average, 4,191 Hits

Phil Niekro statue at Turner Field

City: Atlanta
Location: Turner Field
The famed knuckleballer also has been immortalized with a bronze statue outside the northern entrance of Turner Field. The plaque under it reads:

Five times an All-Star, Phil was always an All-Star to Atlanta and baseball fans everywhere. He won 318 games in a 24-year Major League career, including a 9-0 no-hit victory in Atlanta-Fulton County Stadium on August 5, 1973. He struck out 3,342 batters in 864 games. Led N.L. in games started 4 times, in complete games 4 times and in victories twice. Phil and brother Joe, the winningest brothers in Major League history, won a combined record total 539 M.L. games.

Knuckleballer Phil Niekro, a longtime fan favorite in Atlanta, has been immortalized by a bronze statue outside Turner Field.

"There's no better Braves fan anywhere than I." —Phil Niekro

Ivan Allen Jr. Braves Museum and Hall of Fame

City: Atlanta
Location: Turner Field
755 Hank Aaron Dr. SE
404-614-2311

This great in-stadium museum and Hall of Fame contains more than 500 franchise artifacts from its history in Boston, Milwaukee and Atlanta—including the bat and ball from Hank Aaron's record-breaking 715th home run. Through the museum, you also can arrange a guided tour of Turner Field and behind-the-scenes looks at the press box, broadcast booth, clubhouse, dugout and other areas not generally open to the public. A tour of the Hall of Fame triggers memories of special moments and provides inside looks at such Braves legends as Aaron, Eddie Mathews, Dale Murphy, Phil Niekro, Warren Spahn,

The Braves Museum is filled with memorabilia celebrating the long history of a franchise that has been located in Boston, Milwaukee and Atlanta.

Greg Maddux and owner Ted Turner. Walk-up tickets can be purchased and free parking is available in the north lot.

Spot where No. 715 landed

City: Atlanta
Location: Former site of Fulton County Stadium
Parking lot at Turner Field
When Fulton County Stadium was demolished to make way for Turner Field, Braves officials were careful to preserve the landing spot for one of baseball's most historic home runs. In the large reserved parking lot (the green lot) at Turner Field, a portion of the original Atlanta Stadium fence still stands—the section where the ball left the park—with a big sign proclaiming "715." The original outer wall from Fulton County also remains, serving as a barrier between the green and the blue lots. Aaron's record-breaking homer was hit on April 8, 1974, in a dramatic season home opener against the Los Angeles Dodgers. The image of Aaron triumphantly circling the bases remains imbedded in the city's baseball history.

Birthplace of Jackie Robinson

City: Cairo
Location: Hadley Perry Road

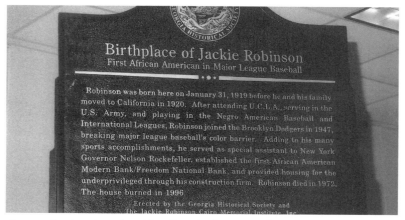

Birthplace of Jackie Robinson
First African American in Major League Baseball

Robinson was born here on January 31, 1919 before he and his family moved to California in 1920. After attending U.C.L.A., serving in the U.S. Army, and playing in the Negro American Baseball and International Leagues, Robinson joined the Brooklyn Dodgers in 1947, breaking major league baseball's color barrier. Adding to his many sports accomplishments, he served as special assistant to New York Governor Nelson Rockefeller, established the first African American Modern Bank/Freedom National Bank, and provided housing for the underprivileged through his construction firm. Robinson died in 1972. The house burned in 1996.

Erected by the Georgia Historical Society and The Jackie Robinson Cairo Memorial Institute, Inc.

A recently placed marker identifies the location of the wooden house where Cairo native Jackie Robinson was born in 1919.

The tin-roofed wooden house in this small southwest Georgia town burned down in 1996, leaving only the brick chimney and double fireplace as a physical reminder of Jackie Robinson's birthplace. Born on January 31, 1919, to sharecropper parents on what was once a slave-worked plantation, Robinson was 2 years old when his mother packed up their belongings and headed to California with Jackie and his four siblings. A recently unveiled marker, placed by the Georgia Historical Society, identifies the exact spot where the house was located.

Other Jackie Robinson tributes in Cairo

A 10-mile stretch of State Highway 93 between Cairo and Beachtom is now called the "Jackie Robinson Memorial Highway." And Cairo High School recently renamed its baseball grounds, "Jackie Robinson Field."

Golden Park

City: Columbus
Location: 100 4th Street
706-571-8866

Golden Park, built in 1926, was named for T.E. Golden, the man who led the drive to land the town's first South Atlantic League team. In the 1940s, a minor league club called the Cardinals played here; through the 1960s, it was home to a Yankees farm club. In 1994, the remodeled stadium was chosen to play host to the softball competition in the 1996 Summer Olympic Games. Golden Park today is an historic landmark, featuring a wall of fame honoring Babe Ruth, Hank Aaron, Willie Mays, Ernie Banks and other legends who played there over the years.

Former site of Ponce de Leon Park

City: Atlanta
Location: 650 Ponce de Leon Road

Baseball was played on this site as far back as 1907. Home of the legendary Atlanta Crackers, the wooden park burned to the ground in 1923 and was rebuilt with concrete and steel. Originally called Spiller Park in honor of Rell J. Spiller, the club's president, Ponce de Leon served as primary home for Atlanta baseball through 1964, at which point the Crackers (a Braves' farm team) moved over to new Atlanta-Fulton County Stadium. The Crackers played their last season there in 1965. Ponce de Leon was especially busy during the 1930s when Georgia Tech used the park and the Atlanta Black Crackers called it home for a period. Ponce de Leon provided proving grounds for such future Hall of Famers as Eddie Mathews and Luke Appling while entertaining numerous legendary stars in both exhibitions and minor league games. In April of 1949, Jackie Robinson and the Brooklyn Dodgers played a three-game exhibition against the Crackers, marking the first time in Atlanta history that blacks and whites competed against each other in a professional sports event. The only reminder of Ponce de Leon Park today is a magnolia tree, once part of the outfield, that stands in the parking lot of a Home Depot store.

Home of Johnny Mize

City: Demorest
Location: Corner of Georgia and Oak Streets, 1 block east of US 441 Bus.

A historical marker (left) is placed here to commemorate the "Home of Johnny Mize, the Big Cat."

Johnny Mize monument

City: Demorest
Location: Demorest Springs Park
Between Georgia Street and Massachusetts Boulevard

Johnny Mize, "The Big Cat," was born in Demorest on January 7, 1913. The big, burly first baseman played for the St. Louis Cardinals, New York Giants and New York Yankees during a storied career that lasted from 1936-53. He led or tied for the National League lead in home runs four times while winning three RBI crowns and one batting championship. The Yankees were unstoppable during Mize's five-year stay, winning five straight World Series championships (1949-53). In the 1952 classic against Brooklyn, he hit three homers and drove in six runs. Mize finished his career with 359 home runs and a .312 average, earning induction into the Hall of Fame in 1981. He died in his hometown of Demorest in 1993. The park where the monument stands is just down the street from city hall.

Johnny Mize Center & Museum

City: Demorest
Location: Piedmont College
165 Central Avenue
1-800-277-7020

While attending high school at the former Piedmont Academy, Johnny Mize played for the varsity baseball team. When Piedmont College opened a 51,000-square-foot facility with gymnasium, fitness center, classrooms and training rooms in November of 2000, officials decided to name it the Johnny Mize Athletic Center. The Center also houses the Johnny Mize Baseball Museum, a collection of Mize memorabilia from his major league playing days (1936-53) with the Cardinals, Giants and Yankees.

Mize is buried at Yonah View Memorial Gardens, 441 Historic Highway S. in Demorest.
706-778-8599

Piedmont College named its 51,000-square-foot athletic center after Johnny Mize, who was born and raised in Demorest.

Historic Luther Williams Field

City: Macon
Location: Central City Park, Riverside Drive
Luther Williams Field, which dates back to 1929, has served as home to several South Atlantic League minor league teams as well as a team in the Negro American League in the 1940s. As current home of the Macon Braves, Luther Williams Field has provided proving grounds for such future Atlanta players as Chipper Jones, Andruw Jones, Kevin Millwood and Rafael Furcal. The field also achieved status in 1976 when it was used to film the movie *The Bingo Long*

Traveling All-Stars and Motor Kings starring Billy Dee Williams, Richard Pryor and James Earl Jones.

Georgia Sports Hall of Fame

City: Macon
Location: 301 Cherry Street
478-752-1585
Among the many historic baseball items on display at this excellent museum are a book autographed by Hank Aaron while in the minor leagues, a Thomasville Orioles uniform from the Georgia-Florida league, 1915-17 Crackerjack cards of selected Georgia baseball players, the Boston Red Sox uniform of Willard Nixon, images and reproductions from the Atlanta Black Crackers and a 1962 opening day ticket to an Atlanta Crackers game at Ponce de Leon Park. There are even some items on display in actual lockers from Fulton County Stadium, former home of the Atlanta Braves. More than 30 players have been inducted into the Georgia Sports Hall of Fame, including Hank Aaron, Luke Appling, Ty Cobb, Josh Gibson and Jackie Robinson.

Sherry Smith Historical Marker

City: Mansfield
Location: Ga. 11 just south of the railroad tracks
"Mansfield's Famous Southpaw" was honored with an historical marker bearing that inscription in 1994. Sherrod Malone "Sherry" Smith (1891-1949) was

The Georgia Sports Hall of Fame is a worthwhile stopover for baseball fans traveling through Macon.

The memory of Sherry Smith, a former big-league pitcher and Georgia baseball legend, is honored by a prominent marker in Mansfield.

born in Monticello and played town ball in Mansfield, Madison, Elberton and Newborn before turning pro in 1910. Babe Ruth called Smith "the greatest pickoff artist who ever lived." Smith played 14 major league seasons with Pittsburgh, Brooklyn and Cleveland, posting a 114-118 record. But his remarkable legacy is the pickoff move that baffled runners and resulted in only two stolen bases against him in 2,052 2/3 innings. Smith appeared in two World Series and worked 30 1/3 innings in three games, compiling an 0.89 ERA. In a 1916 thriller against Boston, the Dodgers lefty pitched 14 innings before losing, 2-1, to Red Sox lefty Babe Ruth. Ruth failed to get a hit and struck out twice against Smith, who doubled once in his five trips against the Babe. Smith managed the Macon Peaches in his last professional season (1932) and served in the Army during World War I. He later served as Chief of Police in Porterdale and Madison. Smith, who is buried in Mansfield, was inducted into the Georgia Sports Hall of Fame in 1980.

Ty Cobb Museum

City: Royston
Location: 461 Cook Street, in the Joe A. Adams Professional Building of the Ty Cobb Healthcare System
706-245-1825

Ty Cobb, who moved to Royston as a young boy, remains a celebrated figure in this small Georgia city. The museum is an outgrowth of a major donation Cobb made in 1949. Royston, in need of a hospital, received $100,000 from the Georgia Peach and began building what would become the Cobb Memorial Hospital—a facility dedicated to the memory of Cobb's parents, Herschel and

Amanda Cobb. The hospital has grown into the Ty Cobb Healthcare System, which now includes two hospitals, two long-term care facilities, a personal care unit and an elderly housing complex. The museum, dedicated in 1998, features an impressive collection of Cobb artifacts and memorabilia, including a Detroit Tigers uniform, one of Cobb's gloves, his childhood Bible, a Shriner's cap, his shotgun and much more. An audio-visual presentation spans the life of the man considered by many the greatest player in baseball history. Cobb became a charter member of the Hall of Fame in 1936 and he built an off-field reputation as an astute businessman, an investment-savvy operator who was dubbed "baseball's first millionaire athlete." Cobb died at Atlanta's Emory hospital on July 17, 1961.

Other Ty Cobb-related sites in Royston:

- The Ty Cobb Memorial Statue
  Royston City Hall
  634 Franklin Springs Street
  706-245-7232

- The "Royston Welcome Sign" coming into town features Cobb.

- Ty Cobb's ornate family mausoleum is visited by many who come to Royston. It is located at Rosehill Cemetery, Route 17, Royston.

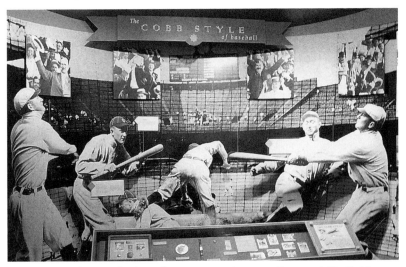

This is one of many displays that attract visitors to Royston's Ty Cobb Museum, a fitting memorial to one of baseball's greatest players.

Historic Grayson Stadium, home to the Savannah Sand Gnats, is a beautiful Southern baseball gem that has been playing host to minor league baseball teams since 1941.

William L. Grayson Stadium

City: Savannah
Location: Daffin Park on Victory Drive between Bee Road and Waters Avenue
912-351-9150

The Class A Savannah Sand Gnats play their games at Grayson Stadium, a beautiful, old-fashioned brick ballpark that dates back to 1941. Located in picturesque Daffin Park, Grayson has been the stomping grounds for numerous future major leaguers on teams affiliated with the Los Angeles Dodgers, Atlanta Braves, St. Louis Cardinals, Texas Rangers and currently the Montreal Expos. The stadium is named for Savannah native and Spanish American War hero William Grayson, who spearheaded the drive to build the stadium which has long existed as one of the true baseball gems of the south.

Luke Appling was a 16-time .300 hitter.

Other Hall of Famers buried in Georgia

Luke Appling
Sawnee View Gardens
1390 Dahlonega Highway (Hwy. 306)
Cumming
770-887-2387

Kentucky

Louisville Slugger Museum

City: Louisville
Location: 800 West Main Street
502-588-7228

The 120-foot bat that stands at the front of the museum suggests something special. And few visitors are disappointed. The legacy of Hillerich & Bradsby dates back to 1884, when the company started making Louisville Slugger bats in its family woodworking shop. The legend goes like this: The owner's son, Bud Hillerich, attended a local baseball game and, noticing that local star Pete Browning was in a hitting slump, brought him to the shop to have a new bat made. With his new weapon, Browning clubbed three hits the next day, and soon word spread of the effective new bat manufactured by Hillerich & Bradsby. Today, visitors to the factory and museum in downtown Louisville watch bats being made and experience a baseball history museum that is rivaled only by Cooperstown. Everyone, from Honus Wagner and Ty Cobb to Babe Ruth, have sworn by the famous bats made from Pennsylvania white ash.

The Hillerich name is still prominent in the business; the Bradsbys have been gone since the late 1930s. The company has always been located in Louisville, except for a few years when it moved across the Ohio River to Indiana. The company produces 2,000 wooden bats per workday, using high-speed lathes. Some go to young players, but 60-70 percent of all major league players have contracts with Hillerich & Bradsby. The bats crafted for professionals match precise computer specifications for each player. The company also makes golf clubs, hockey sticks and aluminum bats at other facilities, but wooden baseball bats are made exclusively at the Louisville plant.

Tours end at the gift shop, appropriately named "A League of Your Own." Every person who takes a tour also receives a miniature Louisville Slugger as a souvenir. The Louisville Slugger Museum, which entertains 300,000 visitors a year, is open Monday through Saturday.

Parkway Field

City: Louisville

Location: Brook Street just south of Eastern Parkway

Edge of the Belknap Campus, University of Louisville

Historic Parkway Field opened in 1923 and was quickly recognized as one the finest minor league ballparks in the nation. Over the years, Parkway also served as home to several Negro League teams, including the Colonels, the Black Caps and the Buckeyes. Many area baseball fans

The 120-foot Louisville Slugger bat guards a baseball museum that hosts 300,000 visitors a year.

remember Parkway best for memorable barnstorming games and exhibitions that featured such stars as Babe Ruth, Lou Gehrig, Honus Wagner, Grover Cleveland Alexander, Satchel Paige, Pee Wee Reese and Jackie Robinson. In 1961, the permanent stands were torn down, but the diamond remained intact, as did part of its original brick outfield wall. Until recently, Parkway Field served as home field for the the Louisville Cardinals. Today, the facility is no longer used on a regular basis.

Birthplace of Pee Wee Reese

City: Ekron

Location: Corner of Third Street & Broadway

County of Meade

Born July 23, 1918, in Ekron, Reese was one of six children. He made his major league debut in 1940 and spent 16 years with the Brooklyn and Los Angeles Dodgers. One of the premier shortstops of his era, "Pee Wee" (his nickname comes from his marble-shooting prowess as a youngster) captained the dominating Dodgers teams of the 1950s. An outstanding defensive player and

Former Brooklyn shortstop Pee Wee Reese still holds a special place in the hearts of Ekron residents.

inspirational leader, he led the Dodgers to seven National League pennants and one World Series championship in his 16 seasons and is credited with providing an emotional lift to teammate Jackie Robinson during his efforts to integrate major league base-ball. Reese and Robinson formed one of the game's top double-play combinations for a decade. Reese, who lost three prime years to military service during World War II, played in 44 World Series games and collected 46 hits, which ranks fifth all time. He retired after the 1958 season (the Dodgers' first in Los Angeles) with a .269 career average and was elected to the Hall of Fame by the Committee on Veterans in 1984. A plaque marks the site.

"Pee Wee" Reese died August 14, 1999, and is buried at:

Resthaven Memorial Park

4400 Bardstown Road

Louisville

Birthplace of Earle Combs

City: Pebworth

Location: Highway 11, County of Owsley

An historic marker identifies Pebworth as the birthplace of the former Yankees center fielder (1899-1976). Combs played for the Bronx Bombers from 1924-35 and served as a Yankees coach from 1936-43. As a player, Combs contributed to four American League pennants and three World Series championships, retiring with a lifetime average of .325. Combs, the outstanding leadoff hitter for teams that featured Babe Ruth, Lou Gehrig, Tony Lazzeri and Lefty Gomez, was elected to the Kentucky Athletic Hall of Fame in 1963 and to the Baseball Hall of Fame by the Committee on Veterans in 1970. When he

died in 1976, he was buried at:
Richmond Cemetery
606 E. Main Street
Richmond

Jackie Robinson marker

City: County of Union
Location: $2^1/4$ miles from Morganfield at entrance to Earle C. Clements Job Corps Center, U.S. 60

There is a marker here stating that Jackie Robinson began his professional career in 1944 while he was a lieutenant at Camp Breckinridge. The next year, Brooklyn general manager Branch Rickey signed the four-sport letterman from UCLA to a minor league contract with the Montreal Royals, a Class AAA team in the Dodgers' chain. In 1947, Robinson was promoted to the major league roster and went on to lasting fame as the man who broke baseball's color barrier.

Earle Combs was a key member of the 1927 Yankees, considered by many the greatest team of all time.

Marker for Gov. Albert B. Chandler

City: County of Woodford
Location: Junction of Pisgah Pike & US 60

Better known as Happy Chandler, this Henderson County native was a state Senator and Lieutenant Governor before winning election as Governor in 1935 and '55. (He also served as a U.S. Senator from 1939-45.) As baseball commissioner, it was Chandler who approved Jackie Robinson's contract, giving him the go-ahead to become the first black player in modern major league history. Chandler, who was elected to the Hall of Fame in 1982, is buried at:

Pisgah Presbyterian Church
710 Pisgah Road
Versailles

Kentuckian Happy Chandler took time away from his political career to serve as commissioner of baseball.

There is another historic marker for Happy Chandler at
Park Field
Adkinson Park, off Elm St., Henderson
County of Henderson

Louisiana

Delhi Municipal Baseball Park

City: Delhi
Location: Chicago and Louisiana Streets
(Also known as Billy Bryan Memorial Park)

This quaint little field with the old wooden grandstand is the first sporting facility in Louisiana to be placed on the National Register. Built in 1948, it was the community's first permanent baseball facility and the first to provide lighting for night games. In its early years, amateur baseball competition was fierce among town teams and the acquisition of a permanent baseball facility with bleachers and lighting in 1948 was an event of considerable magnitude in the life of a town. It was built especially for the Delhi Oilers, who were in a six-team amateur league and played two games per week—40 per season. The park was paid for by a local stock drive and its first game was played in May of 1948. The first night game at Delhi was later than planned because of a delay in getting all the lighting equipment in place. But its "first night game in history" (as it was described in the local paper) occurred on July 15, 1948, and was accompanied by a local celebration. Baseball parks with covered wooden grandstands,

The wooden grandstand at Delhi Municipal Baseball Park gives it an ambience long forgotten in most American cities.

once typical in towns throughout rural America, are now scarce, which is why this charming slice of a history has earned its place on the National Register. Today, the field is used by various local groups.

Mel Ott Park

City: Gretna
Location: Belle Chase Highway (Highway 23)
Dedicated to "Master Melvin" Ott, this park (and the monument within) shows the undying pride of a city for a player who ended his major league career in 1947. Born in Gretna, Ott was only 16 when New York Giants manager John McGraw spotted him in a tryout. McGraw, intrigued by the Louisiana kid with the odd batting stance and impressive lefthanded power stroke, signed him straight out of high school and kept him on the big-league roster in 1926 and '27, watching and learning at the side of the master. By the end of Ott's 22-year career, he had compiled Hall of Fame numbers. He was a .304 hitter whose stroke was tailor-made for the Polo Grounds' short right field fence. His 511 home runs ranked third on the all-time list and he had driven in 1,860 runs. He topped .300 10 times, played in three World Series and was the National League home run leader six times. Ott is best remembered for his "foot in the bucket" batting stance—he would step high and shift his weight into the pitch with his bat swooping low and nearly upright. Ott played his

The monument to Gretna native Mel Ott has its own quiet section in Mel Ott Park, which is dedicated to the former New York Giants slugger.

entire career with the Giants and managed the team from 1942-48, all but one of those years as a player/manager. He was the toast of the town, the "favorite ballplayer" of actress Tallulah Bankhead and restaurateur Toots Shor, and a New York personality dwarfed only during his playing days by Babe Ruth, Lou Gehrig and Joe DiMaggio. After retiring as a player, Ott managed the Oakland Oaks of the Pacific Coast League in 1951 and '52, and then opted for a second career as a Detroit broadcaster. On November 21, 1958, Ott was tragically killed in an automobile accident while returning home from dinner with his wife. The car driven by Ott was slammed head-on by a drunk driver. In addition to Mel Ott Park and the accompanying monument, Gretna also honors its favorite son with a photo exhibit at city hall on Huey P. Long Avenue and 2nd Street.

Ted Lyons won 260 games.

Hall of Famers buried in Louisiana

Mel Ott
Metairie Cemetery
5100 Pontchartrain Boulevard
New Orleans

Ted Lyons
Big Woods Cemetery
Hwy. 388 and Big Woods Cemetery Road
Edgerly

Mississippi

Mississippi Sports Hall of Fame and Museum

City: Jackson
Location: 1152 Lakeland Drive

This 22,000-square-foot museum, which was opened in the early 1990s, has become one of the state's exceptional sports facilities and a vital part of its sports heritage. What makes it particularly special to a baseball history fan are the artifacts it inherited from the former Dizzy Dean Museum. On the second floor, visitors will discover the best collection of Dizzy Dean memorabilia in America—items that make the legendary St. Louis Cardinals pitcher come alive. There are personal items donated by Dean's family, including his 1934 World Series and Hall of Fame rings, many photos, vintage newsreel clips, an original uniform and much more. Among the other Mississippi-born former baseball stars honored at the museum are James "Cool Papa" Bell and Guy Bush, a pitcher best best remembered for giving up Babe Ruth's last two major league home runs.

Cool Papa Bell marker

City: Starkville
Location: McKee Park
Cool Papa Bell Drive

The historic marker is across from the concession stand between the two largest baseball fields.

"Cool Papa" Bell's Hall of Fame career is saluted by a marker in McKee Park, a sports facility in his home-town of Starkville.

Directions: As you enter Starkville from the south on Highway 25, turn left at the traffic light marking the intersection of Lynn Lane and Highway 25. Go approximately 1 mile on Lynn Lane and turn right on Cool Papa Bell Road, which is the entrance to McKee Park. McKee Park is to the right of Lynn Lane and not to be confused with the Starkville Sportsplex, which is on the left just before the entrance to McKee Park.

James "Cool Papa" Bell, born in Starkville, enjoyed his reputation as the fastest man in baseball. Rumor had it that Bell, who starred as a Negro League outfielder, could hit the light switch in his bedroom and hop into bed before the light went out. Bell was an offensive and defensive force for almost three decades with such teams as the St. Louis Stars, Detroit Wolves, Kansas City Monarchs, Homestead Grays, Memphis Red Sox, Chicago American Giants and the legendary Pittsburgh Crawfords—a team that boasted a lineup with Josh Gibson, Judy Johnson and Buck Leonard, three future Hall of Famers. While Bell never got a chance to play in the majors, there's little doubt he would have succeeded. He was a consistent .300-plus hitter, a speedy Tris Speaker-caliber center fielder and one of the best basestealers at any professional level. The tales of Bell's speed have been greatly exaggerated over the years, but there was little doubt he deserved a place in the Hall of Fame when a special committee announced his selection in 1974.

Dizzy Dean led the league in strikeouts four times and posted a 30-7 record in 1934.

Hall of Famers buried in Mississippi

Dizzy Dean
Bond Cemetery
Bond (in town to the east side of U. S. Hwy. 49)

Bill Foster (unmarked)
Carbondale Cemetery
S. R. 552, 3 miles northwest of Alcorn and 2 miles southeast of the Windsor Ruins, Claiborne County

North Carolina

Historic McCormick Field

City: Asheville

Location: 30 Buchanan Pl.

Babe Ruth called it "the prettiest ballpark in America." Over the years, that opinion has been seconded many times. Built into a scenic hillside, McCormick Field opened in 1924 and remained largely intact until it was rebuilt in 1992. Throughout its existence, the park has served as home for the minor league Asheville Tourists. Willie Stargell played for the Tourists in 1961 and his monumental home runs here are still the stuff of legend. For a while, the Ebbets Field clock sat over the scoreboard in center field, reportedly because Dodgers boss Branch Rickey loved the smell of the honeysuckle in the outfield and felt it would provide a fitting home for the former Brooklyn relic. McCormick played a small part in the so-called "Bellyache Heard 'Round the World" in 1925 when Ruth, who was scheduled to play an exhibition there with the Yankees, collapsed at an Asheville train station and was rushed to a hospital. Rumors quickly circulated that the Bambino had died in Asheville. Ruth returned to the city for an exhibition game in 1926, but it was rained out. He finally played at McCormick on April 8, 1931, in a game that also featured Yankees teammate Lou Gehrig.

Today's McCormick Field is still the home of the Asheville Tourists Professional Baseball Club, a Class A team in the South Atlantic League now affiliated with the Colorado Rockies.

McCormick Field, once called 'the prettiest ballpark in America' by Babe Ruth, is still the home of the Class A Asheville Tourists.

Durham Athletic Park is best remembered by baseball fans as the setting for the popular 1988 movie *Bull Durham*.

Historic Durham Athletic Park

City: Durham
Location: 409 Blackwell Street
Though many notable major leaguers, including Chipper Jones, David Justice, Mickey Lolich, Rusty Staub and Joe Morgan, have played at this little gem of a ballpark in Durham, the stadium is probably best known as the setting for the 1988 movie *Bull Durham*. Built in 1940 on the same site as El Toro Park, which had burned to the ground, Durham served as home for minor league teams in both the Piedmont League and Carolina League. But its professional association ended in 1995, when nearby Durham Bulls Athletic Park played host to its first game. Today, Durham Athletic Park is used primarily by college summer and high school leagues.

Babe Ruth's first professional home run

City: Fayetteville (Cumberland County)
Location: Gillespie Street (near the North Carolina Department of Transportation building)
The historic marker here commemorates Babe Ruth's first home run in professional baseball. In March of 1914, the Baltimore Orioles, offered free lodging by the Baltimore-born owner of the Lafayette Hotel, traveled to

Fayetteville for spring training. That season's Orioles team featured an 18-year-old phenom pitcher named George Herman Ruth. During an Orioles intrasquad game at the old Cape Fear Fairgrounds, Ruth clobbered a ball out of the park and into a lake, marking his "unofficial" first home run as a professional player. The ballpark has long been gone and replaced by a local Department of Transportation building. But the marker was erected in 1951, thanks to the persistence of Maurice Fleishman, a 1914 bat boy who witnessed the historic blow. The ceremony at the marker's dedication was attended by former Philadelphia A's manager Connie Mack and Babe Ruth's wife, among other notables.

A bed and breakfast at Fuquay Varina keeps alive the memory of pitcher Tommy Byrne, a former teammate of Joe DiMaggio with the Yankees.

The Fuquay Mineral Spring Inn and Garden

City: Fuquay Varina
Location: 333 South Main Street

The owner of this cozy bed and breakfast is John Byrne, whose father, Tommy Byrne, pitched for the New York Yankees in the 1940s and '50s—for teams that included Joe DiMaggio and Mickey Mantle. Byrne led the American League in winning percentage in 1955, when he went 16-5. One of the game's better hitting pitchers, he belted 15 career homers and was used as a pinch-hitter 80 times. John, who has entertained many of his father's former teammates, honors his legacy by displaying some of his

Yankees memorabilia. If you visit Byrne, be sure to check out his finger—he still wears his father's 1950 World Series ring.

Historic World War Memorial Stadium

City: Greensboro
Location: Yanceyville and Lindsay Streets
Built in 1926 as a memorial to Greensboro casualties of World War I, War Memorial currently ranks as the fourth-oldest minor league ballpark still in use. Originally built for football and track, it became a baseball facility in 1930. Amazingly, night games were played here four years before the first major league game was played under the lights. War Memorial played its first night game on July 28, 1930, and an overflow crowd watched as the local Patriots lost to the Raleigh Caps, 22-6. In that game, playing for the Caps, was future Hall of Famer Hank Greenberg. Later that season, another Hall of Famer joined the Patriots—Johnny Mize. Ted Williams, making a stopover during World War II, blasted a famous ninth-inning bomb into the trees in right field while playing for the Carolina Pre-Flight team of Chapel Hill. In 1950, throngs turned out to see Jackie Robinson's Dodgers play an exhibition game at War Memorial. Carl Yastrzemski played here when he was in the Carolina League, Bob Hope once staged a benefit here and, more recently, Don Mattingly, Derek Jeter, Otis Nixon, Mariano Rivera and Curt Schilling all spent time at War Memorial. Today, the Greensboro Bats, the city's entry in the Class A South Atlantic League for the past 17 years, call War Memorial home, as do Greensboro College and North Carolina A&T.

After his banishment from baseball, Shoeless Joe Jackson lived a quiet life in Greenville.

"Shoeless Joe" Jackson Memorial Park

City: Greenville
Location: West Avenue
This park, which contains a memorial to Jackson, is on the original field where, in 1903, at the age of 13, Shoeless Joe began his baseball career. He started here in the old textile league for the Brandon Mill team in Greenville and went on to become one of the outstanding—and controversial—players in baseball history. Initially brought to the majors by Connie Mack in 1908, Jackson was sent to

Cleveland where his career took off. Jackson starred for the Indians from 1910-1915, batting .408 in 1911 with a near-perfect swing that was copied by a young Babe Ruth. An outstanding outfielder as well as one of the game's most dangerous hitters, Jackson was traded to Chicago in 1916 and helped the White Sox win a 1917 World Series championship. But in 1919, after playing in a World Series loss to Cincinnati, he was caught up in one of the most infamous gambling scandals in sports history—the "Black Sox" incident that resulted in his lifetime banishment from baseball. Jackson returned to Greenville's West End and quietly resumed his life. Until his death in 1951, he operated a liquor store on Pendleton Street. Near the park today is a life-size bronze statue at Shoeless Joe Jackson Plaza, located at the intersection of Augusta, South Main and Pendleton streets. This area is in the middle of the West End District, where Shoeless Joe spent much of his life.

Joe Jackson is buried beside his wife in Woodlawn Memorial Park on Wade Hampton Boulevard in Greenville.

Jim "Catfish" Hunter statue

City: Hertford
Location: Perquimans County Courthouse lawn
Church Street

Jim "Catfish" Hunter was a beloved figure in Hertford, the rural town where he was born on April 8, 1946. Hunter, one of the top righthanders in the game from 1965-79, earned five World Series championships—three with the Oakland Athletics in the early 1970s and two more with the New York Yankees. The unassuming Hunter won 224 games over his 15-year career, topping the 20-win plateau five times, earning a 1974 Cy Young and pitching a perfect game in 1968. Arm trouble finally ended his career at age 33, setting the stage for his Hall of Fame induction in 1987. Hunter died tragically in his hometown at age 53 of Amyotrophic Lateral Sclerosis (ALS), the same disease that claimed the life of former Yankee great Lou Gehrig in 1941.

"Catfish" Hunter is buried at:
Cedarwood Cemetery
Hyde Park Road
Hertford

Catfish Hunter, a 'country boy' from Hertford, was a championship-winning machine for the Oakland A's and New York Yankees.

Jim Thorpe's professional baseball debut

City: Rocky Mount (Nash County)
Location: US 301 Business (Church Street)

A state historic marker commemorates the area where legendary multiple-sport athlete Jim Thorpe made his professional baseball debut with the Rocky Mount Railroaders in 1909. It was because of his role as a pitcher on this Eastern Carolina League team in 1909 and '10, as well as the time he spent playing for the Fayetteville Highlanders, that Thorpe was stripped of his 1912 Olympic gold medals—a pounishment for violating the amateur status rules of that era. In his Class D career, Thorpe batted only .250 in 89 games.

Enos Slaughter museum exhibit

City: Roxboro
Location: Person County Museum
309 North Main

Enos Slaughter is remembered as a Cardinal and a Yankee, but his baseball roots were in North Carolina.

Located in historic Uptown Roxboro, the Person County Museum opened in 1992. Operated over its first few years out of the old post office building on Main Street, it is located today in the lovely and historic "Kitchin House," the one-time residence of the former North Carolina Gov. W.W. Kitchin. One of the museum's permanent exhibits is a tribute to local legend Enos "Country" Slaughter, who was born at Roxboro in 1916. The hard-nosed Hall of Fame outfielder, best remembered for his 1946 "Mad Dash" that gave the St. Louis Cardinals a seven-game

World Series win over the Boston Red Sox, was a career .300 hitter who never stopped hustling over a 19-year career that also included stints with the New York Yankees, Kansas City Athletics and Milwaukee Braves. The lefthanded-hitting Slaughter, who was devastated by his shocking 1954 trade from the Cardinals to the Yankees, helped the New Yorkers win three American League pennants and two World Series before ending his career in 1959 at Milwaukee. The museum's Slaughter exhibit offers an impressive collection of trophies, news articles, baseballs, pictures and other interesting items. Slaughter, who was named to the Hall of Fame in 1985 by the Committee on Veterans, died in 2002 at age 86 and is buried at:

Allensville United Methodist Church Cemetery
80 Dirgie Mine Road, Roxboro.

Other Hall of Famers buried in North Carolina

Rick Ferrell
New Garden Friends Cemetery
801 New Garden Road
Greensboro

Walter "Buck" Leonard
Gardens of Gethsemane
3020 N. Raleigh Street
Rocky Mount

Willie Stargell
Oleander Memorial Gardens
306 Bradley Drive
Wilmington

Rick Ferrell hit over .300 four times and caught all nine innings of baseball's first All-Star Game in 1933.

Buck Leonard was a home run leader in the Negro Leagues.

Riley Park is home to the Charleston RiverDogs and plenty of fan-friendly promotions, thanks to team president Mike Veeck.

South Carolina

Riley Park—the Veeck legend lives on

City: Charleston
Location: Fishburne Street near Lockwood Drive

Riley Park, affectionately called "The Joe", is named for Joseph P. Riley, Jr., the Mayor of Charleston. While The Citadel plays its home games here (the park is located near campus), the fun really starts when the Charleston RiverDogs square off against an opponent in a South Atlantic League game. Anything goes because the RiverDogs' president is none other than Mike Veeck, son of immortal baseball innovator Bill Veeck. In his father's unpredictable and sometimes-zany tradition, Mike works overtime to dream up the most fan-friendly, off-the-wall promotions in sports, making a RiverDogs game a once-in-a-lifetime experience. Actor Bill Murray is part owner of the RiverDogs, who also are a Class A affiliate of the Tampa Bay Devil Rays.

Historic Duncan Park

City: Spartanburg
Location: On Duncan Street off Union Street

It is billed as "the oldest minor league stadium in the nation." Opened in 1925, Duncan Park served for decades as home to the Spartanburg Phillies, the South Atlantic League's affiliate of the Philadelphia Phillies. Duncan is one of those cozy, small-town parks that feels blissfully trapped in another, simpler era. Given its longtime association with the Phillies, Duncan Park was fortunate to

Duncan Park, a ballpark from a simpler era, is now the stomping grounds for college, high school and American Legion teams.

have inherited some of the box seats from Philadelphia's Connie Mack Stadium when that park was torn down. Today, though no longer associated with minor league baseball, Duncan Park is home to Wofford College, the University of South Carolina at Spartanburg and the American Legion in addition to high school and summer league games.

Tennessee

Historic Joe Engel Stadium

City: Chattanooga

Location: Fifth and O'Neal Streets

Built in 1930, this venerable old park was the longtime home of the Lookouts, initially a Washington-affiliated franchise that played in the Southern Association. Senators owner Clark Griffith built the franchise from scratch with the help of scout and former pitcher Joe Engel, who was dispatched to Chattanooga to get things organized. It didn't take long for Engel to become the southern version of Bill Veeck, a brainstorming promoter whose crazy promotions made every visit to the park an event to remember. Engel gave away a house at one game and swapped a player for a turkey at another. But it was his Jackie Mitchell stunt that gained the most publicity and shocked the baseball world.

In 1931, Mitchell was a 17-year old southpaw, honing her skill as a pitcher in Atlanta, when Engel offered her a minor league contract. His plan was to have the young lady pitch in an exhibition game against the New York Yankees. One New York newspaper reporter snidely remarked: "The Yankees will meet a club here that has a girl pitcher named Jackie Mitchell, who has a swell change of pace and swings a mean lipstick. I suppose that in the next town they will find a squad that has a female impersonator in left field, a sword swallower at short and a trained seal behind the plate." The game went off as planned on April 2, 1931, and 4,000 fans turned out, including dozens of reporters and other media—just the kind of response Engel had anticipated.

The first batter Mitchell faced was Babe Ruth, who gamely swung at and missed her first pitch—a sinker. At 2-1, Ruth missed on another swing. At 2-2, the Babe was called out looking, a borderline pitch that prompted a futile protest before Ruth sulked back to the dugout. Next up was Lou Gehrig. Like Ruth, Gehrig missed the first pitch. But he also missed the second and third, giving the teenager strikeouts against the two most feared hitters in baseball. Mitchell walked the next hitter, Tony Lazzeri, before being pulled from the game. The story was huge, splashed across the top of major newspapers throughout the country; film of the event played in theaters everywhere. Whether or not the players were merely going along with the stunt has been debated for years, but many in attendance believe Mitchell's nasty sinker was, indeed, effective and that the strikeouts were legitimate.

Within days, baseball commissioner Kenesaw Mountain Landis came down hard on the stunt, voiding Mitchell's contract on the grounds that professional baseball was too strenuous to be played by a woman. By 1937, tired of the publicity that followed her everywhere, Mitchell retired and went to work in her father's optometry office. In 1982, she returned to Joe Engel Stadium to throw out the first pitch for the Lookouts on opening day. Mitchell died in 1987. The Lookouts have since moved to a new park, but Joe Engel Stadium proudly remains, a host for high school and college games.

Former site of Sulphur Dell

City: North Nashville

Location: Marker located on Fourth Avenue between Jackson St. and the railroad tracks (Farmer's Market area of downtown)

Today, it's a parking lot used by state workers. But one of the minor leagues' most historic stadiums once sat here. Baseball reportedly was played on this site as far back as 1876—the reputed first-ever game in Nashville. When the Southern League was organized in 1885, Nashville was a charter city and the state capital fielded several different teams that played in the league over the

SULPHUR DELL

Nashville's first (1885) professional baseball was played in the Athletic Park which
formerly occupied this block. Traditionally
baseball was introduced in Nashville in 1862
by soldiers of the Union army of occupation
who played the game here. This low-lying area,
originally called Sulphur Spring Bottom,
was first called "Sulphur Dell" by local
sports writer, Grantland Rice. In 1963 this
was the oldest playing grounds still in use
in professional baseball.

A parking lot and marker stand at the site of Sulphur Dell, a former minor league landmark.

next 10 years—including the Americans, the Blues, the Tigers and the Seraphs. When the Southern Association was formed in 1901, Sulphur Dell, then known as Sulphur Spring Bottom (it was the site of an historic sulphur spring), became the permanent home to the Nashville Volunteers. In time, legendary writer Grantland Rice, while working as a newspaper reporter in Nashville, nicknamed the park "Sulphur Dell" and the name stuck. One of the park's more interesting quirks was its right field area, which was defined by irregular-shaped hills. One incline rose to 25 feet, forming a "shelf" that forced fielders to position themselves at its top. Right fielders at Sulphur Dell became known as "mountain goats," a reference to the unusual hill climbing they had to do during a typical game. The Vols called Sulphur Dell home for 61 years, until the Southern Association disbanded. In addition to the Vols, the Negro American League Elite Giants called the park home in 1933 and '34. Sulphur Dell was torn down in 1963 and the only reminder of its colorful past is a historic marker at its former site.

Tennessee Sports Hall of Fame Museum

City: Nashville
Location: 501 Broadway
615- 242-4750

Located inside the Gaylord Entertainment Center, this relatively new museum, while dedicated primarily to college football, does contain some memorabilia related to local baseball history (including some Negro League uniforms worn by teams that played at Sulphur Dell).

Texas

Nolan Ryan Center

City: Alvin
Location: On the campus of Alvin Community College
2925 South Bypass 35

This is Nolan Ryan country, pure and simple, and you can get a full appreciation of the "Ryan Express" at Alvin Community College's Nolan Ryan Center for Continuing Education. The Center was built by the Ryan Foundation and donated to the college in the summer of 1996. About one-third of the building functions as a museum dedicated to Ryan. This area chronicles the life and baseball career of Alvin's favorite son in many state-of-the-art displays, including an interactive pitch-catch

It's difficult to visit Alvin without encountering Nolan Ryan, either physically or in spirit.

exhibit where the visitor "feels" a Nolan Ryan fastball in a catcher's mitt. There are video clips of Ryan's career with the Mets, Angels, Astros and Rangers, the full chronology of his 27 major league seasons and much more. The Rawlings Hall of Records sells replica strikeout balls depicting each of Ryan's 5,714 strikeouts with "owners" listed in a computer database.

Also in Alvin, outside of their city hall at 216 West Sealy, is a statue of Ryan.

Alvin High School

City: Alvin
Location: 802 South Johnson

Ryan graduated from Alvin High School in 1965. His wife, Ruth, followed in 1967 and their two sons and daughter attended school there. The baseball diamond has been named Nolan Ryan Field and a trophy case there includes Ryan's high school jersey. Ryan fans should also look for signs proclaiming Alvin as the "Hometown of Nolan Ryan" and the Nolan Ryan statue that stands beyond the center field seats at The Ballpark in Arlington.

Meadowbrook Park

City: Arlington
Location: East Abram St.

Built in 1921 by the "Optimist Club," Meadowbrook was Arlington's first ballpark. Donkey baseball was once played on a diamond in the area where the recreation center is now located, and a Texas sandstone building on the knoll inside the loop road once housed a small monkey zoo.

The Legends of the Game Museum at The Ballpark in Arlington

City: Arlington
Location: 1000 Ballpark Way
817-273-5600

This museum and learning center, opened with the new Texas Rangers' ballpark in 1994, features the largest collection of baseball-related artifacts outside Cooperstown. With more than 140 items from the Hall of Fame (and more than 1,000 objects from private donors and the Rangers), the story of baseball's greatest legends is told through jerseys, bats, gloves, words and much more. The

The center field complex at The Ballpark in Arlington is home to Rangers offices as well as the Legends of the Game Museum.

Legends of the Game features outstanding exhibits about Arlington's own "boys of summer," the Texas Rangers. You can trace the roots of the Rangers back to their previous life as the Washington Senators and learn about the top players throughout the club's history.

The Legends of the Game Museum features baseball memorabilia second in scope only to that found at Cooperstown.

You'll also find exhibits on:

- Texas League—Fort Worth Cats, Dallas Spurs and more

- Heroes of the Negro Leagues

- Women in professional baseball

- A replica of the KLIF radio broadcast booth

- Famous ballparks

Along with the permanent exhibits, the museum offers outstanding temporary exhibits as well as a display dedicated to "Baseball's 25 Greatest Moments," selected by *The Sporting News* and including historic photographs and interpretive text. The three-story, 24,000-square-foot museum also features an interactive Learning Center, designed for all those fans curious about the history and science of baseball. Visitors can examine the insides of a 4-foot baseball, predict the trajectory of a pitch on a windy day and stand in for former Rangers catcher Ivan Rodriguez while catching a curveball from Nolan Ryan.

Former site of Arlington Stadium

City: Arlington
Location: Next to The Ballpark in Arlington
1000 Ballpark Way

Now a parking lot, the area immediately adjacent to The Ballpark in Arlington was where Arlington Stadium once stood. "Turnpike Stadium" opened in 1965 as home for the local Texas League club and eventually was expanded to accommodate major league baseball. The Washington Senators relocated to renamed Arlington Stadium in 1972. Arguably, the park's most memorable moment occurred on May 1, 1991, when 44-year-old Rangers righthander Nolan Ryan fired his record seventh no-hitter while beating the Toronto Blue Jays on Arlington Appreciation Night. The final score was 3-0 and Ryan struck out 16 batters with a fastball that averaged 93 mph. The final game at Arlington Stadium was played October 3, 1993, and the ballpark was demolished a year later. There is nothing to mark the former site of the historic ballpark.

Former site of Stuart Stadium

City: Beaumont
Location: 3330 Avenue A
The Stadium shopping center

The site today is covered by a parking lot and small shopping center, but a plaque in front of the post office reminds visitors that this once was the home of the Texas League's Beaumont Exporters. The plaque reads, "Home plate—On this spot the Beaumont Exporters took their final swing. Rube Stuart's contribution is fondly remembered and appreciated." Stuart Stadium, which opened in 1923, was a baseball hotbed for more than 30 years. The former Detroit Tigers farm team featured such stars as Hank Greenberg, Dizzy Trout and Rip Sewell. By the mid-1940s, the team was known as the Roughnecks and it was here that Rogers Hornsby ended his career in 1950 as a manager. The ballpark was torn down in 1955.

Reagan County High School Baseball—home of The Rookie

City: Big Lake
Location: 1111 12th Street

This is where Jim Morris, a high school science teacher and baseball coach of the Owls, made a bargain with his players: If they made the playoffs, he would try out for the majors. His team delivered and Morris, a lefthanded pitcher, began an amazing journey that ended in the major leagues. Morris pitched as a 35-year-old rookie for the Tampa Bay Devil Rays in 1999. A movie starring Dennis Quaid told Morris' improbable story in 2002.

Jack Lummus marker

City: Ennis
Location: Ennis Public Library
501 West Ennis Avenue

In 1999, a Texas historical marker was placed near this library to honor athlete and war hero Jack Lummus. A standout athlete as a youth in Ennis, Lummus attended Baylor University on scholarship and played minor league baseball in Texas and one season of pro football for the NFL's New York Giants. He joined the Marines in 1942 and landed in 1945 with the Fifth Marine Division in the first wave of assault troops on Iwo Jima. After fighting without rest for two days and nights, Lummus singlehandedly destroyed three enemy placements before stepping on a land mine and getting killed. There also is a small exhibit to Lummus inside the library.

Former athlete and war hero Jack Lummus is honored with an historical marker in Ennis.

LaGrave Field

City: Fort Worth
Location: 301 NE 6th Street

This is a story of two ballparks. The first, built in 1926, was used by the Fort Worth Cats until 1964. The second was built on the exact same site in 2001 and ramains in use today. Suffice to say LaGrave Field has enjoyed a "Texas-size" history.

Spring exhibitions over the years brought Ty Cobb, Babe Ruth, Lou Gehrig, Rogers Hornsby and many other great players to the Fort Worth ballpark. Because Branch Rickey chose Fort Worth as a pillar of the Brooklyn Dodgers farm system, the Dodgers made frequent spring stops there with such players as Jackie Robinson, Gil Hodges, Duke Snider, Don Newcombe and Pee Wee Reese. But the Cats also made a little of their own history. Five future Hall of Famers called Fort Worth home—Carl Hubbell, Hornsby, Snider, Sparky Anderson and Billy Williams. (Anderson earned his nickname at LaGrave in 1955 when Cats broadcaster Bill Hightower remarked on his fiery demeanor following a loud argument with an umpire.) In 1949, the first Texas League game was televised from LaGrave and, later that year, the park's grandstands caught fire and were destroyed. (The Cats played San Antonio the next day with the stands still smoldering.) The Dodgers rebuilt in 1950 and, at the urg-

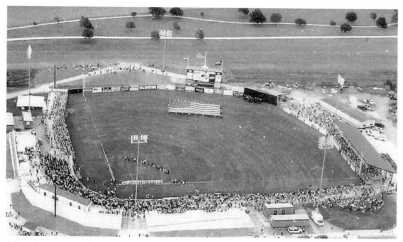

New LaGrave Field is built on the exact site of the old ballpark, where the legendary Fort Worth Cats once played.

ing of Rickey, dedicated the ballpark to Paul LaGrave, who spearheaded the modern baseball era in Fort Worth. But expansion eventually pushed baseball out of LaGrave and the park hosted its final game on September 4, 1964; the historic home of the Cats was torn down in 1967. With the Cats gone, the site sat vacant for years with bits and pieces of the old stadium buried beneath the weeds.

Then came the rebirth. The Central League's Fort Worth Cats, an independent professional team, came to town and, fittingly, set up operations at new LaGrave Field. The old dugouts have been restored as suites, the view of downtown is perfect and the Cats have succeeded in breathing new life into one of the great baseball fields of all time.

Former site of Majors Stadium

City: Greenville
Location: 1807 Church Street

A walking tour of this historic northeast Texas town puts visitors in touch with former actor and war hero Audie Murphy, a native of Greenville, and a former ballpark that claimed some significant history of its own. At 2714 Washington Street, a plaque describes a baseball game that took place about six blocks away at Majors Stadium—an event described enthusiastically by Judy Woods of the Hunt County Historical Commission: "Greenville's baseball team belonged to the East Texas Baseball League in the 1930s and '40s. In 1949, the Greenville Majors became a Class B team in the Big Texas League. They also became famous that year. Our minor league team beat the celebrated New York

The old brick arch entryway is a physical reminder of Majors Stadium, where the Greenville minor league team once defeated the Yankees.

Yankees, with Joe DiMaggio in center field, in a preseason exhibition game!"

It happened on April 10, 1949, as documented by historian John Mark Dempsey. It was common in those days for major league teams to barnstorm through the south near the end of spring training. Because no major league teams were stationed farther south than St. Louis at the time, Majors owner George Schepps, the owner of several minor league teams, had to pull strings to bring the Yankees to Greenville. DiMaggio started in center that day and wound up with a single and a run scored in two at-bats. Righthander Allie Reynolds started for the Yankees, who also posted a lineup with second baseman Snuffy Stirnweiss, shortstop Jerry Coleman, third baseman Bobby Brown and right fielder Gene Woodling. The Yankees committed four errors and the winning run was scored by aging former St. Louis "Gas House Gang" shortstop Pepper Martin, who ended his career in the minors. The game was costly for the Yankees, who lost DiMaggio with a heel injury that would plague him the rest of the season.

Majors Stadium is gone, its former location now occupied by the Greenville Transformer Co. But there are some reminders. A building that stands on the corner of Houston and Church streets is part of the old stadium locker rooms. The old brick arch through which fans entered the stadium still stands, with the words "Majors Stadium" in welded metal letters across the top. Also in Greenville is a Little League park named after former major league pitcher Monty Stratton, who grew up in the city. Stratton, who played for the Chicago White Sox, lost his leg in a tragic 1938 hunting accident and returned to play minor league baseball with an artificial leg. Hollywood made a movie (*The*

Stratton Story) about his life, starring James Stewart and June Allyson, both of whom came to Greenville for the film's 1949 premiere.

Former site of Buff Stadium

City: Houston
Location: Finger Furniture Center
4001 Gulf Freeway

A furniture store occupies the former site of Buff Stadium, the only reminder a marker that sits on the floor in the exact spot where home plate used to sit. Buff Stadium, built in 1928, opened as home of the Texas League's Houston Buffaloes. The Spanish-style park was renamed Busch Stadium for a period when the Buffs were part of the St. Louis Cardinals farm system. Red Schoendienst, Joe Garagiola and Solly Hemus all played at Buff Stadium, as did numerous other

Buff Stadium's home plate lies in state—on the floor of a Houston furniture store.

major league stars in exhibition games. The ballpark, damaged in 1961 by Hurricane Carla, was sold at auction for $19,750 and demolished in 1963. When the Finger Furniture Center was built, a plaque was imbedded to mark home plate and from that seed grew the Houston Sports Museum, which also is located in the store. In addition to chronicling Houston baseball from its Texas League beginnings, the museum celebrates the major league Astros as well as professional teams from other sports.

Houston Astrodome

City: Houston
Location: 8400 Kirby Drive

Dubbed the "Eighth Wonder of the World" by Astros owner Judge Roy Hofheinz, the Harris County Domed Stadium became the world's first air-conditioned, domed, all-purpose stadium when it opened in 1965. The Astrodome, as it came to be known, was home of the Houston Astros through 1999. In addition to introducing the world to indoor baseball and cookie-cutter ballparks, the stadium spawned the use of synthetic playing surfaces. After experimenting with a natural grass field, Houston officials turned to an artificial surface that became known as AstroTurf. As new multi-purpose ballparks

The Astrodome, baseball's renowned former Eighth Wonder of the World, remains intact, though mostly unused.

sprang up in other cities, artificial carpets were installed to safeguard against wear and tear—a trend that proved offensive to baseball purists. Today's Astrodome is used sporadically, no longer associated with major league baseball.

Some memorable moments in Astrodome history:

- April 28, 1965: New York Mets announcer Lindsey Nelson broadcasted a game from a hanging gondola, 208 feet above the infield.

- June 10, 1974: Phillies slugger Mike Schmidt crushed a ball that bounced off the public address speaker hanging from the Astrodome roof, 117 feet up and 300 feet from the plate. It was ruled a single.

- September 25, 1986: Mike Scott's no-hitter beat the Giants and clinched a West Division title for the Astros.

Former site of Colt Stadium

City: Houston
Location: Parking lot of Astrodome
Colt Stadium was located a few yards northwest of the Astrodome, in the area now occupied by its north parking lot. Used by the Houston Colt .45s from 1962-64, the 32,000-seat ballpark was home to the expansion Houston franchise until the Astrodome opened in 1965. Colt Stadium, famous for its heat and huge mosquitoes, played host to its final game on September 27, 1964. It remained standing for five more years, used primarily as a storage facility. But it became such an eyesore that Astros owner Roy Hofheinz painted its exterior gray so that it wouldn't be visible in aerial photos of his sparkling new

Astrodome. Colt Stadium, after being sold to a minor league team in the late 1960s, was taken apart, moved to Torreon, Mexico, and moved again to Tampico, Mexico. It exists today as part of a public playground.

Tris Speaker exhibit

City: Hubbard
Location: Hubbard Museum
304 NW 6th

Tris Speaker remains popular in his hometown of Hubbard.

This small museum, which is housed in a restored high school, contains an exhibit dedicated to Tris Speaker, who was born and buried in Hubbard. Speaker's incredible numbers sometimes get overshadowed because he played in the same era as Ty Cobb. The Grey Eagle, who spent 20 of his 22 big-league seasons with the Indians and Red Sox, hit .380 or better five times, but won only one American League batting title (1916). He compiled a .345 lifetime average, struck out only 220 times and was considered one of the great defensive center fielders of all time. The first Texan inducted into the Hall of Fame, Speaker always returned to Hubbard in the offseason and was a lifelong Hubbard volunteer firefighter.

Tris Speaker is buried at:
Fairview Cemetery, 201 West 3rd, Hubbard.

Tris Speaker historic plaque

City: Hubbard
Location: Hubbard City Hall
118 Magnolia Street (Route 171)

In addition to the museum exhibit, Hubbard also placed an historic marker that chronicles Speaker's major league career.

Driller Park

City: Kilgore
Location: Hunter Street, one block east of Commerce

One of the few landmarks still standing from the town's oil boom days is Driller Park, former home of the Kilgore Drillers of the Texas Lone Star League.

Driller Park is a vivid reminder of Kilgore's oil boom days.

Built in 1946 from oil field pipe, tank steel and concrete, Driller Park may be one of the sturdiest little parks ever constructed. The stadium bears a Texas Historical Marker and today is home for the Kilgore High School baseball team. Driller Park also is the site of numerous postseason high school playoff games.

Zychlinski Park

City: Pearland
Location: 2319 Grand Blvd.

Captain Wilhelm Zychlinski, a Polish nobleman, arrived in the Pearland area in the late 1880s and fell in love with its flowering pear trees. He bought 5,991 acres of land, including the Zychlinski Park site, completed his town plat and then sold most of his holdings before disappearing. In 1911, two land developers, in an attempt to promote the Pearland area, created a baseball team called the Suburban Gardens. For nearly two generations, the team (as well as the people of Pearland) played baseball in Zychlinski Park, a particularly popular activity during the depression era. Until the late 1990s, Zychlinski Park was the playground for the C.J. Harris Elementary School. Today an historic marker documents the town baseball that was played there for so many years.

Texas Sports Museum and Hall of Fame

City: Waco

Location: 1108 South University Parks Dr.

Tris Speaker was the first Texas Sports Hall of Fame inductee in 1951. Over the years, he has been joined by Ernie Banks, Norm Cash and Roger Clemens, among others. The museum was established to celebrate and preserve Texas' sports history. It boasts an impressive array of classic baseball memorabilia, including Speaker's Cleveland Indians jersey, a complete Rogers Hornsby Cardinals uniform, Silver Slugger Awards from Norm Cash and Pete Reynolds, a Nolan Ryan jersey and, amazingly, the last-out ball from the 1920 World Series when Cleveland beat the Brooklyn Dodgers.

The Texas Sports Hall of Fame honors such Texas-born stars as Tris Speaker, Ernie Banks, Norm Cash and Roger Clemens.

Rogers Hornsby Field

City: Winters

Location: In Ted Meyers Park off Main Street, on Novice Road (310 South Main).

Rogers Hornsby had roots in this small Texas town. His ancestors settled there in 1830, in an area now known as "Hornsby Bend." Hornsby was born in 1896 on his father's Hereford ranch and played minor league baseball with Texas teams based in Hugo, Dallas and Denison before moving up to the St. Louis Cardinals in 1915. He went on to make legitimate claim as the greatest righthanded hitter in baseball history. Hornsby led the National League in batting seven times, topped the magical .400 plateau three times and posted one of the most incredible five-year stretches in major league history. From 1921-25, Hornsby batted .397, .401, .384, .424 and .403 while compiling 1,078 hits. His six consecutive

One of baseball's greatest players, Rogers Hornsby is also one of Texas' favorite sons.

batting titles were unprecedented and he won two League MVP citations. Hornsby also managed the St. Louis Cardinals to their first World Series championship in 1926. Rajah, who was elected to the Hall of Fame in 1942, finished his long baseball association as a manager in the Mexican League. Hornsby died in 1963 from a heart attack following an operation for cataracts. The field named in his honor also features a plaque and monument.

Rogers Hornsby is buried at:
Hornsby Bend Cemetery
Highway 969
Hornsby Bend

Rube Waddell led the A.L. in strikeouts six times and had a lifetime ERA of 2.16

Other Hall of Famers buried in Texas

Willie Wells
Evergreen Cemetery
3304 East 12th Street
Austin

Mickey Mantle
Hillcrest Memorial Park
7403 W. Northwest Highway
Dallas

Ross Youngs and Rube Waddell
Mission Park Cemetery
1700 SE Military Drive
San Antonio

The Midwest

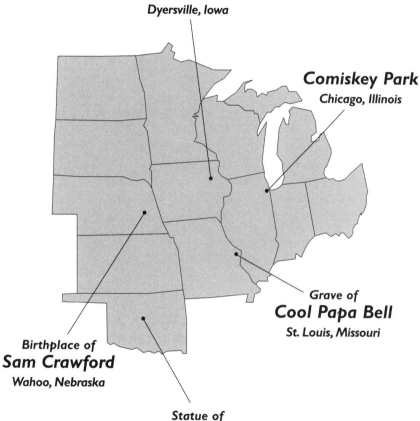

Field of Dreams
Dyersville, Iowa

Comiskey Park
Chicago, Illinois

Grave of
Cool Papa Bell
St. Louis, Missouri

Birthplace of
Sam Crawford
Wahoo, Nebraska

Statue of
Mickey Mantle
*Oklahoma City,
Oklahoma*

The memory of Albert Spalding, a 19th-century baseball pioneer, is preserved throughout his hometown of Byron.

Illinois

Albert Spalding birthplace

City: Byron
Location: 133 E. 2nd St.

One of the premier pitchers of the 1870s, Albert Spalding is described on his Hall of Fame plaque as an "organizational genius of baseball's pioneer days." His 47 wins in 1876 led the Chicago White Stockings to the first-ever National League championship. Spalding, who helped draft the N.L.'s first constitution, retired as a player to join the White Stockings' front office in 1882, a move that also allowed him to tend to the thriving sporting goods business he had founded with his brother. A plaque marking the house where Spalding was born on September 2, 1850, is located about 80 miles west-northwest of Chicago.

Albert Spalding exhibit

City: Byron
Location: The Byron Public Library
109 N. Franklin Street
815-234-5107

The Byron Public Library houses two large display cases of Albert Spalding memorabilia, including signed baseballs, photos, awards and more.

Wrigley Field remains true to its early century heritage, a ballpark that charms even the most hard-core baseball fan.

Historic Wrigley Field

City: Chicago
Location: 1060 West Addison
773-404-CUBS

Being a Cubs fan is a challenge. But being a fan of Wrigley Field is easy. The brick, the ivy, the neighborhood—all combine to make this one of baseball's most beloved environments. Originally known as Weeghman Park, Wrigley originally was home to Chicago's entry in the short-lived Federal League. The first major league game at the ballpark took place in 1914 with the hometown Federals defeating Kansas City, 9-1. When the Federal League folded in 1916, team owner Weeghman headed a group that bought the Cubs, who defeated Cincinnati in the first National League game at renamed Cubs Park. William

Wrigley Jr. bought the team in 1918 and the stadium became Wrigley Field in 1926. The bleachers, the scoreboard on its center field perch and many of the other nuances that contribute to Wrigley's lore came during a 1937 renovation. Baseball at Clark and Addison streets remains refreshingly simple, from the hand-updated scoreboard to the quaint, earthy atmosphere. One longstanding tradition is the flying of a flag bearing either a "W" or "L" atop the scoreboard after each game—a signal to fans whether the Cubs won or lost. The original ivy vines that cover the outfield walls were planted by a young Bill Veeck in 1937. He strung bittersweet from the top of the wall to the bottom, then planted ivy at the base of the wall. And if you look up at the flags atop the foul poles, Ernie Banks' uniform number (14) is on the left field foul pole and Billy Williams' No. 26 adorns the right field pole. For many years, the Cubs resisted the temptation to install lights, preferring to keep Wrigley as the lone bastion of daytime baseball. But they finally gave in, installing the standards in 1988 and agreeing to a limited number of night games. Wrigley Field exists today as the second oldest ballpark in the major leagues, second only to Boston's Fenway Park.

Some memorable moments at Wrigley Field:

- During Game 3 of the 1932 World Series, Babe Ruth executed his famous "called shot." Allegedly, Ruth pointed to the bleachers in center field, then hit Charlie Root's next pitch for a homer. (Root always denied Ruth was calling his shot.)

- September 28, 1938: Gabby Hartnett hit his famous "Homer in the Gloamin' " against the Pittsburgh Pirates.

- May 12, 1970: Ernie Banks hit his 500th career home run off Atlanta's Pat Jarvis.

- September 8, 1985: Pete Rose collected career hit 4,191 off Chicago's Reggie Patterson, tying him with Ty Cobb for the all-time hits record.

Murphy's Bleachers

City: Chicago
Location: 3655 N. Sheffield Avenue
This legendary open-air bar/restaurant, located just across the street from Wrigley Field, features the famous Murphy's roof where you can sit and watch Cubs games while knocking back one of their many available brews. Bill Veeck used to greet fans here, and it's not uncommon for a player or two to stop in

after a game. The walls are covered with Chicago-related sports memorabilia in what might be the most perfectly located sports bar in the country.

Black Sox Courthouse

City: Chicago
Location: 54 West Hubbard Street
"Say it ain't so, Joe" were the words allegedly uttered by a devastated kid as the disgraced Joe Jackson entered this former courthouse. Whether that really happened is anybody's guess. But what did happen here was a trial involving the eight members of the Chicago White Sox who conspired to fix the 1919 World Series against the Cincinnati Reds. Despite their acquittal in the so-called "Black Sox" scandal, the players received a lifetime baseball ban from commissioner Kenesaw Mountain Landis, a ruling that still stands today despite repeated efforts to get Jackson reinstated for election to the Hall of Fame. Shoeless Joe compiled a Series average of .375 and played error-free defense, but he was implicated in the scandal. The trial attracted huge headlines and made a nation of fans feel betrayed. This building, which housed the Cook County Criminal Courts for 35 years, also was the site of other legendary trials, including the Leopold and Loeb murder case.

National Italian American Sports Hall of Fame

City: Chicago
Location: 1431 West Taylor Street
312-226-5566
When businessman George Randazzo decided to raise money for a struggling local Catholic youth program in 1977, he organized a dinner featuring 21 former Italian boxing champions. The event was so successful that another local businessman, Don Ponte, encouraged Randazzo to start an entire hall of fame to honor all Italian-American athletes. Just one year later, the first National Italian American Sports Hall of Fame banquet was held honoring Lou Ambers, Eddie Arcaro, Charlie Trippi, Gino Marchetti, Joe and Dom DiMaggio and (posthumously) Vince Lombrdi. In 1978, the National Italian American Sports Hall of Fame officially opened in Elmwood Park, Illinois, and over the years it grew into one of the most impressive sports memorabilia collections in the world. Among the baseball inductees are Roy Campanella, Dolph Camilli, Tony Conigliaro, Joe and Dom DiMaggio, Tony Lazzeri, Tommy Lasorda and Tony LaRussa. The National Italian American Sports Hall of Fame is slated to relocate from Elmwood to its new address in the fall of 2003. Located in Chicago's historic Little Italy neighborhood, the expansive 40,000-square-foot

limestone building will feature two spacious exhibition halls with special exhibit galleries on each of the four floors. An elegant staircase will lead visitors from a 150-seat theater in the lower level to a third-floor banquet hall that will seat as many as 400 dinner guests.

Piazza DiMaggio

City: Chicago
Location: On Taylor Street, just across from the new location of the National Italian American Sports Hall of Fame.

Piazza DiMaggio, a small Romanesque park in Chicago's Little Italy, is dedicated to New York Yankee legend Joe DiMaggio. The centerpiece is a 9-foot statue of DiMaggio that was dedicated in 1991 to commemorate the 50th anniversary of the Yankee Clipper's 56-game hitting streak and rededicated in 1998. DiMaggio was present at both ceremonies.

A 9-foot Joe DiMaggio still swings freely in Chicago's 'Little Italy.'

Former site of Comiskey Park

City: Chicago
Location: Parking lot of new Comiskey Park

When it was closed after the 1990 season, old Comiskey Park had survived 81 seasons and was baseball's oldest major league ballpark. It opened on July 1, 1910, replacing the 39th Street Grounds where the White Sox had played from 1901-10. After the 1926 season, a $1 million renovation replaced the original wooden bleachers with seats and totally enclosed the stadium grandstand. The seating capacity was increased from 32,000 to 52,000. In addition to the White Sox, Comiskey was home to the National Football League's Chicago Cardinals for 35 seasons and it played host to the Negro leagues' yearly east-west all-star game from 1933-50. The inventive Bill Veeck bought the White Sox in 1959 and had the red brick façade painted white. He also created a picnic area in left field and installed the first electric scoreboard behind the center field bleachers. In 1960, Veeck took his scoreboard fascination a step further, installing baseball's first exploding board complete with fireworks, aerial bombs and sound effects. In 1969, AstroTurf was installed to save money, but it was

Old Comiskey Park, site of baseball's first All-Star Game in 1933, is now a parking lot adjacent to new Comiskey Park.

removed in 1976. By the 1980s, with Comiskey showing signs of wear and tear, the White Sox threatened to leave town if a new park wasn't built. Comiskey Park's days were numbered. New Comiskey was built next door to its predecessor and the final old Comiskey game was played on September 30, 1990—the team's 3,024th regular-season victory at the ancient park. A parking lot now covers the former site with a home plate area marked by a plaque.

Some memorable moments at Comiskey Park

- September 5, 1918: Babe Ruth pitched the Red Sox to a 1-0 Game 1 victory over the Cubs in the World Series. The Cubs played the classic at Comiskey because of its larger capacity.

- October 9, 1919: The Cincinnati Reds ended the World Series by beating the White Sox, 10-5. It later was learned the Series was thrown by the infamous "Black Sox."

- July 6, 1933: The first All Star Game was played at Comiskey with Babe Ruth's home run leading the American League to a 4-2 victory.

- July 5, 1947: Cleveland Indians pinch-hitter Larry Doby became the first black player in the American League.

- July 12, 1979: Disco Demolition Night, a Bill Veeck promotion, went awry when a fan riot broke out between games of a doubleheader, forcing the White Sox to forfeit the nightcap to Detroit.

The exact spot of old Comiskey Park's batter's box is preserved outside of new Comiskey Park.

The Chicago White Sox Hall of Fame

City: Chicago
Location: Comiskey Park (Now U.S. Cellular field)
333 W. 35th Street
312- 674-1000
A good selection of White Sox history is on display in this Hall of Fame, located in the stadium gift shop on the main concourse behind home plate. You can see Shoeless Joe Jackson's original White Sox contract.

Andrew "Rube" Foster home

City: Chicago
Location: 39th Street and Wentworth Avenue
Rube Foster is considered by many historians the "Father of Negro League Baseball." Although the former player founded the Negro National League in Kansas City in 1920 (at the Paseo YMCA), he lived near this corner where an historical marker has been placed.

A small Nokomis museum is primarily dedicated to three Hall of Famers—Jim Bottomley, Red Ruffing and Ray Schalk.

Bottomley-Ruffing-Schalk Baseball Museum

City: Nokomis
Location: 121 West State Street
217- 563-2516

This small museum honors three players from the Nokomis area. Jim Bottomley, a standout first baseman and two-time RBI champion for the St. Louis Cardinals, Cincinnati Reds and St. Louis Browns, was voted League MVP in 1928. Righthander Red Ruffing posted 273 victories, four 20-win seasons and seven World Series wins with the New York Yankees from 1930-46. Ray Schalk was a top defensive catcher for the White Sox from 1912-28 and the first catcher to routinely back up plays at first and third base. The museum has many more honorees, including umpire Al Barlick, Hall of Fame righthander Robin Roberts and former slugging first baseman Mark McGwire. The museum's displays include baseballs, bats, hats, books, articles, personal letters, scrapbooks and uniforms.

Abe Lincoln played baseball here

City: Postville
Location: Postville Park
5th & Washington

In 1965, a marker was erected to acknowledge a Baltimore adventurer named Russell Post, who laid out the town of Postville in 1835. The marker also notes that Abraham Lincoln and his friends played Town Ball, a predecessor to baseball, in the park in addition to throwing the maul, a heavy wooden hammer, and pitching horseshoes. While in his 30s, the future U.S. president visited Postville as part of his circuit law practice. His athletic endeavors took place during his free time.

Billy and Ma Sunday historical marker

City: Sleepy Hollow
Location: Route 72 at Sleepy Hollow Road
Erected in the early 1970s, the marker indicates the area where former Chicago Cubs outfielder William Ashley "Billy" Sunday held a month-long religious revival from May to June, 1900, in West Dundee Park. Billy Sunday owned the farm with his wife, Helen "Ma" Sunday, from the end of the 19th century to the mid-1910s.

Robin Roberts Stadium at Lanphier Park

Robin Roberts is still remembered in his hometown of Springfield.

City: Springfield
Location: North Grand near 11th Street
Opened in 1928, Lanphier has at different times been home to minor league teams serving the Browns, Tigers, Giants and Cardinals organizations. It also played host briefly to games in the All-American Girls Professional Baseball League. Situated several blocks from old Route 66, the stadium is named for local hero Robin Roberts, the former Phillies Hall of Fame pitcher. Lanphier today is used primarily for college baseball.

Hall of Famers buried in Illinois

Charles "Old Hoss" Radbourne
Evergreen Memorial Cemetery

William Hulbert, Cap Anson, Kenesaw Mountain Landis and Gabby Hartnett (top to bottom)

302 East Miller Street
Bloomington
309-827-6950

Chicago Metropolitan Area
Andrew "Rube" Foster
Lincoln Cemetery
12300 Kedzie Ave.
Blue Island
773-445-5400

Urban "Red" Faber
Acacia Park Cemetery
7800 W. Irving Park Road
Chicago
773-625-7800

William Hulbert
Graceland Cemetery
4001 N. Clark Street
Chicago
773-525-1105

Cap Anson and Kenesaw Mountain Landis
Oak Woods Cemetery
1035 E. 67th Street
Chicago
773-288-3800

Gabby Hartnett and Fred Lindstrom
All Saints Cemetery
700 N. River Road
Des Plaines
847-298-0450

Charles Comiskey
Calvary Catholic Cemetery
301 Chicago Avenue
Chicago
847-864-3050

Ray Schalk
Evergreen Cemetery
8700 S. Kedzie Ave.
Evergreen Park
773-776-8434

Lou Boudreau
Pleasant Hill Cemetery
East side of Elsner Road, 1.5 miles south of
U. S. Hwy. 30
Frankfort

William Harridge
Memorial Park Cemetery
9900 Gross Point Road
Skokie

Warren Giles
Riverside Cemetery
6th Avenue and 29th Street
Moline

Lou Boudreau (top) and
Will Harridge

Indiana

Historic grandstand

City: Brookville
Location: 8th and Mill Streets
Baseball has been played in Brookville since at least 1867, when local amateur teams competed against out-of-town teams. A local team joined the semi-pro Southern Indiana Baseball Association in 1922 and other regional leagues in later years. This grandstand was built in 1922 to seat 1,000 and serve fans of the new Brookville semi-pro team. The structure, renovated in 1992 for use by the community, is recognized today with an historic marker.

An historic marker salutes the grandstand that seated 1,000 fans when it was built in 1922.

Big Sam Thompson gave new meaning to the term power hitter in the 19th century.

Sam Thompson Plaque at Sam Thompson Field

City: Danville
Location: In Ellis Park, right off Highway 36

Born in Danville on March 5, 1860, Sam Thompson went on to fame as one of the game's first true power hitters. Playing for National League teams in Detroit and Philadelphia, Thompson hit 126 home runs and collected 200-plus hits three times while compiling a .335 career average. Big Sam was elected to the Hall of Fame in 1974. This Danville plaque and field were dedicated to Thompson in 1998.

Huntingburg League Stadium—A League of Their Own

City: Huntingburg
Location: 1st and Cherry Streets

This stadium, originally built in 1894, was used for the filming of the 1992 hit movie, *A League of Their Own*, starring Tom Hanks, Geena Davis, Madonna and Rosie O'Donnell, among others. When Columbia Pictures decided to film here in 1991, they expanded and renovated the old park to give it a more nostalgic feel and make it more true to the 1940s time period the film took place. That look and atmosphere has been maintained ever since and, thanks to the movie, this has the feel of a true throwback park. (Except for the orange and red plastic box seats salvaged from Atlanta-Fulton County Stadium.) During the spring months, the field is home to the Southridge Raiders and it also hosts the high school sectional and regional playoffs. The Dubois County Dragons, a Class A professional team of the Independent Frontier League, play their home games here as well.

Oscar Charleston Park

City: Indianapolis
Location: 2800 East 30th Street

Oscar Charleston was the first Indianapolis-born player to get a plaque at Cooperstown. The former Negro League star, who was elected to the Hall in

1976, was considered by many of his peers the greatest player ever—black or white. As a youth he served as batboy for the local ABCs. After a short stint in the Army, he came home and played with that team, helping lead the ABCs to a 1916 victory in the Black World Series. After playing 30 seasons for the ABCs, Chicago American Giants, Hilldale Daisies and other Negro League teams, the outstanding defensive center fielder returned to Indianapolis as manager of the Clowns. In 1998 this park, less than a mile from where he was born and raised, was dedicated. Oscar Charleston, "The Hoosier Comet," died in 1954 and is buried at:

Floral Park Cemetery
3659 Cossell Road
Indianapolis

Few players, black or white, could match Oscar Charleston's incredible skills.

Indiana Baseball Hall of Fame

City: Jasper
Location: Hwy. 162 S. & College Ave.
Campus of Vincennes University–Jasper
Ruxer Student Center

The first inductions to this Hall were made in 1979 with Mickey Mantle serving as guest speaker. Over the years, other speakers have included Ernie Banks, Johnny Bench and Lefty Gomez. There are 114 inductees in the Hall of Fame covering four categories: Pro-Player, Coach-Manager (high school, college, pro), Contributor and Veteran. In addition to plaques honoring the inductees, memorabilia includes an impressive selection of bats and jerseys dating from the early 1900s as well as photos, autographed baseballs and more.

Mordecai Three-finger Brown farm site

City: Nyesville
Location: Nyesville Road
Travel east of Rockville on U.S. 36 to Billy Creek Village, then head north about two miles on Nyesville Road until you reach the plaque.

Mordecai Brown was born October 19, 1876, in Nyesville, a tiny farming community just north of Terre Haute. At age 5, Brown's right hand was mangled when he stuck it into a running feed-cutter machine. Missing an index finger, he learned to throw a baseball with a peculiar spin, a "handicap" that gave him what Ty Cobb called "the best curveball in the game." Over Brown's 14-year career, 11 with the Chicago Cubs, he compiled a 239-130 record, a 2.06 ERA and a 5-4 mark in World Series play. He is best remembered for his stirring pitching duels against Giants ace Christy Mathewson. The historical marker placed here by family and friends in 1994 is on the land where the Brown family farm existed, approximately 50 yards from where the family house stood. Brown died in 1948 at Terre Haute and was inducted into the Hall of Fame in 1949. He is buried at:

Roselawn Memorial Park
7500 N. Clinton Street
Terre Haute

Edd Roush was a member of the Reds team that won the 1919 World Series.

Edd Roush hometown marker

City: Oakland City
Location: Main Street
Born at Oakland City in 1893, Edd Roush played for the Chicago White Sox, New York Giants and Cincinnati Reds over a major league career that spanned 18 seasons. The center fielder, a career .323 hitter, won batting crowns in 1917 and '19, the latter while leading the Reds to a World Series victory over the infamous Chicago Black Sox. Roush, who was known for his breathtaking outfield catches, was

elected to the Hall of Fame in 1962, the same year his plaque was mounted on the wall of a bank on Main Street in his hometown. Roush died in 1988 and is buried at:

Montgomery Cemetery

200 S., one-fifth mile east of 1200 E.

Oakland City

Gil Hodges statue

City: Petersburg

Location: Pike County Courthouse

801 Main Street

In the rotunda of the county courthouse is a large bronze bust of Gil Hodges, who was born in Princeton, Indiana, and grew up and attended school in Petersburg. There also is the Gil Hodges Memorial Bridge, located just north of Petersburg on SR 57 at White River.

Gil Hodges Memorial Field/Rueth-Fitzgibbon Baseball Facility

City: Rensselaer

Location: Saint Joseph's College

U.S. Highway 23

In 1994, Saint Joseph's College named its baseball field in honor of former Brooklyn Dodgers first baseman Gil Hodges, who attended school there. The college also presents each year a "Gil Hodges Award" to its outstanding senior player.

Billy Sunday Home and Visitor Center

City: Winona Lake

Location: 1101 Park Avenue

Billy Sunday, one of the 20th century's best-known evangelists, was a major league outfielder for Chicago, Pittsburgh and Philadelphia before pursuing a more spiritual career. Born in Ames, Iowa, in 1862, the aptly-named Sunday went straight from semi-pro baseball in Marshalltown, Iowa, to the majors in Chicago. He was converted to Christ in 1886 through the street preaching of Harry Monroe of the Pacific Garden Mission in Chicago and gave up his baseball career in 1891, after eight seasons. Sunday, ordained to the ministry in 1903 by the Presbytery of Chicago, eventually began preaching at his own services. He preached in the Army camps during World War I and later held city-

Billy Sunday made his name as an evangelist, but his roots were in baseball.

wide meetings across the United States. In one celebrated meeting in Philadelphia, more than 2.3 million people attended his eight-week crusade. Sunday held campaigns for more than 20 years—a practice called "hitting the sawdust trail" because the tabernacle floors were covered with sawdust—and at the close of each service, throngs of people came forward to grasp the evangelist's hand, signifying their conversion. Sunday also was known for wild acrobatic feats on the platform while he preached. Sunday and wife Helen settled in Winona Lake, Indiana, home of the Winona Lake Bible Conference and famed Chautauqua meetings, in 1911. He died in Chicago in 1935. Today at this museum, near the home where the Sunday family lived until 1957, the Billy Sunday legacy is alive and well.

Hall of Famers buried in Indiana

Chuck Klein

Chuck Klein
Holy Cross/St. Joseph Cemeteries
Meridian Street and Pleasant Run Parkway
Indianapolis

Stan Coveleski
St. Joseph Polish Roman Catholic Cemetery
24980 State Rd. 2
South Bend

Ban Johnson
Riverside Cemetery
W. Wayne Street and S. West Street
Spencer

Iowa

Community Field

City: Burlington

Location: Mount Pleasant Avenue east of Route 61

Community Field was built in 1947 as home for Burlington's professional team in the Central Association of Professional Baseball. Burlington joined the Class A Midwest League in 1962 and the franchise has been competing in that circuit ever since. Over the years, Community Field has been home for many outstanding teams and future major leaguers. Chicago Cubs legend Billy Williams started his Hall of Fame journey at Burlington in 1958. Sal Bando, who would gain World Series fame with the Oakland Athletics and later serve as Milwaukee's general manager, led the team to its first Midwest League championship in 1965. In 1968, young Oakland farmhand Vida Blue struck out a Midwest League-high 231 batters—a mark that still stands as the Burlington single-season record. On June 8, 1971, Community Field's original grandstand burned to the ground. Although the rebuilding process wasn't completed until 1973, play continued with temporary bleachers, and community volunteers, demonstrating their dedication to professional baseball, spent countless hours returning the stadium to working order. Today, the Burlington Bees, a Kansas City Royals affiliate, call this historic field home.

Alliant Energy Field

City: Clinton

Location: Riverview Park

6th Ave. N. & 1st St.

The former Riverview Stadium, built in 1937, has played host to Clinton professional baseball since the original Owls were affiliated with the Brooklyn Dodgers. The historic ballpark sits in Clinton's Riverview Park, a 65-acre city recreational area on the Mississippi River. Over the years, Clinton teams have been affiliated with the Chicago Cubs and White Sox, Seattle Pilots, Milwaukee Brewers, Pittsburgh Pirates, Detroit Tigers, San Francisco Giants, Los Angeles Dodgers, San Diego Padres, Cincinnati Reds and, today, the Texas Rangers—as the Clinton Lumber Kings. The Mount St. Clare College baseball team also uses the field for games and the historic stadium hosts activities in conjunction with Clinton Riverboat Days, an annual Fourth of July festival.

Davenport's John O'Donnell Stadium, located on the banks of the Mississippi River, has survived three major floods.

John O'Donnell Stadium

City: Davenport
Location: 209 South Gaines Street

The current home of the Midwest League's Quad City River Bandits (Twins) was built in 1931, just yards from the Mississippi River. The stadium has experienced three major floods—1965, 1993, 2001—and has been rebuilt several times, but it retains a nostalgic charm. Originally called Municipal Stadium, the historic ballpark was renamed for John O'Donnell, the sports editor of the *Quad City Times* during the 1940s and '50s. The stadium is nothing if not picturesque. The Centennial Bridge creates a scenic view beyond first base foul territory; a railroad line runs along the third-base side. Fans get a spectacular view of downtown Davenport beyond the outfield walls.

Field of Dreams

City: Dyersville
Location: 28963 Lansing Road
888-875-8404

Located on two farms, 3.3 miles northeast of Dyersville.

"If you build it, they will come," the voice in the movie promises. And they still do, in droves, to see, experience, dream and play on the very field where the 1989 movie starring Kevin Costner, Amy Madigan and James Earl Jones was filmed. One of the ultimate baseball landmarks in the country exists on two Iowa farms near a small east-central Iowa community. Tourists are allowed to run bases, play catch and bat on the *Field of Dreams*, or they can simply sit in the bleachers and enjoy its considerable aura. The house, part of the Lansing family farm, also is open to visitors. And so, of course, is the cornfield. Great efforts have been taken to not over-commercialize the field and surrounding area. It is pristine and simple. Since the movie, more than 60,000 people have flocked to Dyersville. Though privately owned, the attraction is open daily, 10 a.m. -6 p.m., April through November.

Bill Zuber's Dugout Restaurant

City: Homestead
Location: 2206 44th Avenue
The restaurant is located in the historic Amana Colonies, a religion-inspired commune that was founded by German immigrant members of the Community of True Inspiration in 1854. Even though sports were frowned on by the church, colony native Bill "Goober" Zuber crafted an 11-year major league pitching career (1936-47) with the Indians, Senators, Yankees and Red Sox. Zuber, a righthander, retired with a 43-42 record. After baseball, he returned to Homestead and bought the commune-run eatery and operated it until his death in 1982. The restaurant still serves up the same rich, authentic German meals that made it popular in 1862.

Bob Feller Museum

City: Van Meter
Location: 310 Mill Street
This small town museum was opened in 1995 as a tribute to Van Meter's native son, Hall of Famer Bob Feller. "Rapid Robert" compiled a 266-162

A large sign urges travelers to stop in Van Meter, where a worthwhile Bob Feller Museum pays tribute to one of the game's great pitchers.

record over 18 major league seasons (1936-56) with the Indians while pitching three no-hitters and setting numerous strikeout records. Although Feller lives in retirement near Cleveland, he has retained an active interest in the museum and donated many of its displays. He also shows up occasionally to meet visitors and autograph balls and photos. Among the artifacts are Feller uniforms, trophies he earned, newspapers trumpeting his victories and photos of him on the field and in the presence of U.S. presidents. One display case features the bat Babe Ruth carried on June 13, 1948, when he made his final Yankee Stadium appearance. The Indians were playing the Yankees that day and the bat belonged to Feller. The museum also has an outstanding gift shop with many autographed and collectible items.

Kansas

Kansas Sports Hall of Fame

City: Old Town Wichita
Location: 238 North Mead
Slated to open in the fall of 2003, this museum dedicated to Kansas sports will include substantial baseball displays honoring such noteworthy Kansans as Walter Johnson, Fred Clarke, Ralph Houk, Joe Tinker, Elden Auker, Darren Daulton, Mike Torrez, Ralph Terry, Joe Rogan and Dummy Taylor. A display for the National Baseball Congress also will be included, as will a tribute to the Wichita State University national championship team.

Mickey Mantle is discovered

City: Baxter Springs
Location: Kiwanis Park
Located on Highway 166, one block from the Spring River Bridge
It was one of those mythical stories that color baseball history. Just 10 miles up the road from Commerce, Oklahoma, Mantle's hometown, is Baxter Springs—a small town tucked into the southeastern corner of Kansas. A teenage Mantle played for the Baxter Springs Whiz Kids in 1948, the same year Yankees scout Tom Greenwade traveled to Baxter Springs to scout a third baseman named Billy Johnson. The young Mantle blasted two homers into the nearby river that day, one from the right side and another from the left, and Greenwade immediately targeted the speedy youngster. Since Mantle was only 16, Greenwade promised to return with a Yankees contract on his high school graduation day in 1949, which he did. Mantle signed a minor league contract

with the Yankees' Class D team in Independence, Kansas. The ballpark where Mantle performed his impromptu audition no longer exists. The grandstand is gone and kids now play mostly soccer where baseball was once king. But the river is a physical reminder of where a 16-year old future star hit two gigantic home runs so many years ago, the day he was discovered by the New York Yankees.

Baxter Springs Little League Museum

City: Baxter Springs
Location: 14th and Grant Avenue

Mickey Mantle is an Oklahoma kid, but Kansas baseball fans remember him well.

Baxter Springs has one of the most successful Little League programs in the country. The small Kansas community has long been the state's Little League power, the winner of 15 state titles from 1976-2000. The city also has an impressive ballpark with a Little League Museum that features awards and memorabilia from such local sports heroes as Mickey Mantle, Hale Irwin and Bill Russell in addition to collectibles from such other stars as Yogi Berra and Whitey Ford.

Mickey Mantle Exhibit

City: Baxter Springs
Location: Baxter Springs Heritage Center and Museum
740 East Avenue
620-856-2385

This impressive local museum, which celebrates the rich history of Baxter Springs, "The First Cowtown in Kansas," is a small display featuring artifacts from Mickey Mantle's brief time spent in Baxter Springs and other Baxter Springs Whiz Kids memorabilia and photographs.

Site of historic baseball game

City: Blue Rapids
Location: Baseball diamond located at West 5th at Riverside Park

(Blue Rapids is located in southwest Marshall County at the junction of the Little Blue River and the Big Blue River, about 46 miles north of Manhattan, Kansas.)

On October 24, 1913, Blue Rapids was the proud host of an exhibition game between the Chicago White Sox and New York Giants. The stopover was a prelude to a 1913 worldwide barnstorming tour. More than 3,000 fans watched the game at the Riverside Park field that is still in use today. (Advance tickets sold for $1.00; tickets were $1.50 at the gate.) Sam Crawford, John McGraw, Bill Klem, Christy Mathewson and Jim Thorpe all were part of the contest, which the White Sox won, 8-5. After leaving Blue Rapids, the teams traveled through the Southwest and up the Pacific Coast to Vancouver where they caught a ship for Japan. They played games along the Pacific rim, passing through Ceylon, India and the Suez Canal all the way to Egypt. They also played several games in Europe, the last of which was witnessed by King George V in England. The teams arrived back in New York on March 6, 1914.

Walter Johnson Park

City: Coffeyville
Location: 8th and Park

The Coffeyville Red Ravens play their home games at Walter Johnson Field, located in Walter Johnson Park. Construction of the field began in the summer of 1998 and was completed almost a year later with the installation of tournament lighting and grandstand seating. The field is named for Johnson because he lived in Coffeyville for several years during his heyday as a star pitcher for the Washington Senators. (His house, a private residence, is located at 1701 E. 8th Street.) Guarding the field is an exact replica of the monument that was posthumously dedicated to Johnson and originally stood at Griffith Stadium in Washington. The original now stands outside Walter Johnson High School in Bethesda, Maryland.

Walter Johnson exhibit

City: Coffeyville
Location: The Dalton Museum
113 East 8th Street
620-251-5944

This museum, dedicated to local history, contains an exhibit of memorable Walter Johnson moments. There's also a mural of Johnson in Coffeyville, one of many murals featuring various subjects painted by Don Sprague. They are visible throughout the city.

A simple marker alerts visitors to the location of Walter Johnson's birth site in Humboldt.

Walter Johnson birth site

City: Humboldt

Location: Two miles N. on old Hwy. 169 to sign (west) and two miles west to the intersection of 900 Road and Iowa Street.

Allen County

Walter Johnson was born November 6, 1887, to Swedish emigrants on a rural farm four miles west of Humboldt in Allen County—about an hour drive from Coffeyville. His family left the Humboldt area for the oil fields of California in 1901, six years before the 19-year-old fireballing righthander began his phenomenal major league career with the Washington Senators. Over 21 seasons, the "Big Train" carved out 417 wins, second all time only to Cy Young, and recorded two 30-win seasons and 12 more of 20 or more victories while pitching for generally weak Senators teams. His fastball was legendary and the 3,509 strikeouts he recorded stood as a record for many years. The Johnson birth site marker resulted from the dedicated efforts of local baseball historian Richard Davis, who has worked for more than 30 years to preserve the Johnson legacy throughout Humboldt. In 2001, Davis staged a banquet for the third annual Walter Johnson-George Sweatt World Series Classic that was attended by Negro League legend Buck O'Neil, Johnson's daughter Carolyn and grandson Hank Thomas. Davis and wife Gloria even hand-painted the sign that directs people to the Johnson birthplace and the sign at the marker. He also runs the Walter Johnson Fan Club and is a driving force for all of the annual baseball events that take place in Humboldt.

Walter Johnson pitched the first ball in the inaugural game at this athletic field named in his honor in Humboldt.

Walter Johnson Athletic Field

City: Humboldt
Location: 6th and Pine
Here are excerpts from the October 27, 1921, edition of the *Humboldt Union* newspaper that described the dedication of Walter Johnson Athletic Field:

> *"Well, it was a great and glorious day. Humboldt closed up shop at 1:30 on this Wednesday, October 26th, 1921, and drilled out to Walter Johnson Athletic Field to see the great Walter Johnson pitch and the Monarch Cement Plant ball team win a ten inning game 5 to 4.*

> *"The crowd was the best ever, packing the grandstand and bleachers while an immense fringe of occupied automobiles and pedestrians hugged the foul lines on either side.*

> *"The Field was formally and officially dedicated as Walter Johnson Athletic Field. Mr. Charles L. McKnight, acting for Mayor J. W. Braucher and in well chosen words, explained the motive that actuated the planning and naming of the ground, on behalf of the citizen of Humboldt. Mr. McKnight also had a half dozen league base balls upon which Walter Johnson had written his name and were for sale at $2 each.*

"Walter Johnson pitched the first ball and Mr. Gilliland caught it. The ball was then given to C. M. Hilleary, who explained that it had on it the name of Walter Johnson, October 26, 1921, and was to be placed in the corner-stone of the new high school building in honor of the man who is an exponent of clean sport, true manhood and right living. There are Sporting men and Sportsmen. Walter Johnson never confounded them. A Sportsman every inch. A more Sporting man he does not know. He is one of the cleanest and

Walter Johnson's autographed ball is imbedded in the cornerstone at the field bearing his name.

most respected men in his calling of the day and age. We speak not by the book but have lived where we could see and judge for ourselves."

This was the last of eight times Walter Johnson traveled to Humboldt for exhibition games that raised money to buy the land for the field that is still in use today. And that first ball he signed? It is still in the cornerstone at:

Humboldt High School
1011 Bridge Street
Humboldt

George A. Sweatt Park

City: Humboldt
Location: 12th Street and Wulf Drive

Walter Johnson is not the only professional player from Humboldt. George Sweatt, a former Negro League star, also was born there in 1893. Sweatt, an outstanding athlete, attended Pittsburg (Kansas) Normal College on scholarship and excelled in baseball, football, basketball and track. After college, he taught in Coffeyville while playing semi-pro baseball. When World War I erupted, Sweatt enlisted in the 816th Pioneer Infantry Division, which arrived in France only two weeks before the Armistice, and he returned to teaching and semi-pro ball after his discharge. Sweatt got his big break when the owner of the Negro National League's Kansas City Monarchs saw him play in a Pittsburg game. Sweatt signed his first professional contract and played for Kansas City in 1921, a second baseman, third baseman and outfielder who helped the Monarchs win the 1924 Negro World Series—the same year Johnson and the Washington Senators won the major league World Series. Sweatt retired from professional baseball in 1928 but remained involved with youth leagues and semi-pro teams for the rest of his life. He died in 1983 in Los Angeles. In honor of Sweatt and with the heartfelt persistence and leadership of Richard Davis, Humboldt dedicated this baseball field, Sweatt Park, to him. It plays host every summer to the Johnson-Sweatt Classic baseball tournament.

The George A. Sweatt Memorial can be found one block away from the park at 11th and Wulf Drive.

Exhibit featuring Walter Johnson and George Sweatt

City: Humboldt
Location: Humboldt Historical Society Museum
Corner of Second and Neosho Streets
The Humboldt Museum is divided into five buildings. The first opened to the public as a museum in October of 1967. In building No. 5, several very special displays, featuring many rare artifacts, are dedicated to both major league great Walter Johnson and Negro League star George Sweatt. The museum is open from Memorial Day through the second weekend of October. Interestingly, these two Humboldt-born ballplayers lived near each other in the tiny town at the turn of the century. Sweatt's home was just across from the site where the Walter Johnson Field was built, in the block between 6th and 7th streets. The Johnson home was located at 3rd and Cherokee.

Walter Johnson Information Center

City: Humboldt
Location: The Humboldt Union Newspaper
8th and Bridge Street
Baseball historian Dick Davis has created a display with some of his Walter Johnson and George Sweatt memorabilia, photos and information. A visit here also provides visitors with all of the location information they might need to catch the interesting baseball-related sites in Humboldt. Davis' displays also include information about and photographs of other legendary stars who have played in the area—Hall of Famers like Lou Gehrig and Christy Mathewson who made offseason exhibition visits to Blue Rapids, Kansas. This is a good starting point before touring the town.

Walter Johnson carved out his Hall of Fame career in Washington, D.C., but it is obvious his roots were in rural Kansas.

The first night game in organized baseball

City: Independence
Location: Shulthis Stadium
Riverside Park

An historic marker at the former Producer Park identifies the stadium as the location of the first lighted night game ever played in organized baseball. The game took place on April 28, 1930, and 1000 fans saw the Class C Western Association Muskogee Chiefs defeat the Independence Producers, 13-3. By the end of the 1930 season, 38 minor league teams had lights—five years before major league baseball took its first night-game plunge at Cincinnati.

Independence also was the city where Mickey Mantle played his first minor league season in 1949—for the Independence Yankees in New York's minor league system. Other notables who played at Independence are Bill Virdon and Lou Skizas. The current stadium hosts high school football, track and other local events.

National Baseball Congress (NBC) Hall of Fame

City: Wichita
Location: Lawrence-Dumont Stadium
Corners of Sycamore and Maple
316-267-3372

The National Baseball Congress and its NBC World Series were the brainchild of a Wichita sporting goods salesman named Hap Dumont. During the

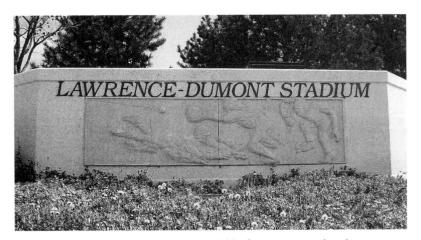

Lawrence-Dumont Stadium, the brainchild of sporting goods salesman Hap Dumont, is home to the National Baseball Congress World Series. Satchel Paige headlined the first tournament.

depression, Dumont hatched the idea after watching a Sunday baseball game between circus clowns, who were in Wichita for the week, and local firemen. The circus wasn't allowed to perform on Sunday because of the blue laws still in effect, but the baseball-playing clowns drew a large crowd, triggering Dumont's brainchild. He created the National Semi-Pro Baseball Congress Kansas State Tournament, which premiered in 1931 on Island Park in the middle of the Arkansas River. Over the years, as the event grew more popular, Dumont approached Wichita about building him a new stadium so he could expand his tournament and include teams from all over the country. The city built his stadium on the west bank of the river, just south of the old park, and named it after Wichita pioneer Robert Lawrence. In a brilliant public relations move in 1935, Dumont paid Satchel Paige $1,000 to bring his touring team to town for the first NBC tournament. The idea paid off. Paige struck out 60 batters and won four games, thrilling the local crowds. The national tournament was a hit. Since then, thousands of young prospects and former major leaguers have played here. Today's tournament features mostly college players with a few former professionals and some outstanding former college or high school players who were never drafted by a professional team. The museum outside the center field wall is dedicated to the NBC and memories of its long-running tournament. More than 600 future major leaguers have played in the event. The stadium also displays historical information about the Congress—a fitting tribute to Hap Dumont, the sporting goods salesman with big baseball dreams.

The history of Lawrence-Dumont Stadium, where the NBC Hall of Fame is located:

Lawrence-Dumont Stadium, built in 1934 as a Work Projects Administration assignment, is one of the 15 oldest baseball stadiums still in use in professional baseball. The stadium has undergone renovations in 1972, '89 and 2001, resulting in the current facility. Lawrence-Dumont is the second oldest stadium in the Texas League. Only Ray Winder Field in Little Rock, Arkansas, is older (built in 1932). From 1935, the NBC tournament has drawn huge crowds and hundreds of future major league players to Wichita. Since Dumont's death, the NBC has had five different ownerships, including the current owner, Rich Products Corporation. The Wichita Wranglers, a Class AA team of the Kansas City Royals, have captured three Texas League championships since moving to Lawrence-Dumont Stadium in 1987.

Lawrence-Dumont Stadium is one of the 15 oldest facilities still in use in professional baseball.

Hall of Famers buried in Kansas

Fred Clarke

St. Mary's Cemetery

E. 12th Street, between Wheat Road and Alexander Avenue

Winfield

Fred Clarke

Michigan

Former site of Recreation Park

City: Detroit

Location: Brush Street Mall behind Harper Hospital

Recreation Park, home of the National League's Detroit Wolverines from 1881-88, was built on this site in 1879. The park extended from Brady Street to Willis Avenue. It was here on May 2, 1881, that the first major league baseball game in Detroit was played—the first of more than 800 over its eight-season big-league association. Hall of Famers Dan Brouthers and Sam Thompson played for the Wolverines at Recreation Park, but the team went out of existence after the 1888 season. That's when the Wolverines moved to Cleveland and the park was used sporadically by other teams until being closed in 1894, at which point it was torn down. The historical marker that stands here now is located where left field used to be.

Lou Gehrig bows out

City: Detroit

Location: The Book-Cadillac Hotel

220 Michigan Avenue (corner of Washington)

When this grand hotel opened in 1924, it was the largest in the world, with 1,200 rooms and 33 stories. On May 2, 1939, it became the scene of a dramatic baseball moment—a simple meeting that took place in its lobby. New York Yankees first baseman Lou Gehrig, hitting an anemic .143 after eight games in the new season, met with manager Joe McCarthy. Gehrig said to his boss, "I'm taking myself out, Joe." McCarthy asked why. "For the good of the team," Gehrig said. "Nobody has to tell me how bad I've been and how much of a drawback I've been to the club." This was the the beginning of the end to Gehrig's incredible 2,130 consecutive-games streak. That afternoon at Detroit's Briggs Stadium, Gehrig was not in the starting lineup. The crowd, sensing the weight of the event, applauded for two minutes. Without the Iron Horse, the Yankees posted an inspired 22-2 victory over the Tigers with Gehrig replacement Babe Dahlgren collecting a home run and a double. The hotel closed in 1986 and has remained vacant ever since. The Baseball Hall of Fame in Cooperstown has a letter written by Gehrig on Book-Cadillac Hotel stationery to his wife Eleanor, recounting his conversation with McCarthy and his decision to take himself out of the lineup. Though it isn't dated, researchers believe it was most likely written on May 3, the day after the meeting.

The Ernie Harwell Sports Collection

City: Detroit
Location: Detroit Public Library
5201 Woodward Avenue
313-833-1480

Part of the Burton Historical Collection at the Detroit Library is the Harwell Collection, donated by legendary sportscaster Ernie Harwell in 1967. It consists primarily of baseball books, team annuals, scorecards, clippings and photographs that were amassed by Harwell throughout his broadcasting career. The immensely popular broadcaster was working for the Atlanta Crackers when Dodgers owner Branch Rickey took notice of him. So impressed was Rickey that he brought Harwell to Brooklyn to broadcast Dodgers games in 1948. Harwell later had stints with the Giants and Orioles before arriving at Detroit in 1960. Harwell retired following the 2002 season, after 55 years in broadcasting.

Detroit Tiger Statues and Walk of Fame

City: Detroit
Location: Comerica Park
2100 Woodward Ave.
313-962-4000

The main concourse at Comerica Park is like a tour through baseball history. Divided into 20th century eras, the concourse lets fans progress through dif-

Six former Tigers greats are honored with life-size statues, just beyond the center field fence at Comerica Park.

ferent time frames of baseball lore. "Decade Monuments" covering two 10-year periods each are placed through the concourse, towering from floor to ceiling and featuring artifacts and memorabilia. In center field (just beyond the General Motors Fountain), the Tigers have honored some of the franchise's greatest players with larger-than-life statues. Al Kaline, Hank Greenberg, Willie Horton, Ty Cobb, Charlie Gehringer and Hal Newhouser are the players immortalized.

Tiger Stadium

City: Detroit
Location: Corner of Michigan and Trumbull

This is one of the few former major league ballparks to be honored by a state historical marker—and with good reason. From 1912-99, Tiger Stadium was a baseball Mecca for fans throughout Michigan. Three generations witnessed the magical play of such stars as Ty Cobb, Hal Newhouser, Mickey Cochrane, Hank Greenberg, George Kell, Al Kaline, Denny McLain, Mickey Lolich, Alan Trammel, Jack Morris, Lou Whitaker, Kirk Gibson and Willie Horton. Baseball actually was played at the Michigan and Trumbull site as early as 1896, when 10,000-seat Bennett Park was built. From 1901-12, Bennett was home for the American League Tigers. The stadium opened as Navin Field in 1912 and also existed through its 87-year run as Briggs Stadium and Tiger Stadium—the home of four World Series championship teams. The final game was played at Tiger Stadium on September 27, 1999, and many former players returned to pay tribute. They shared in the "transfer of power" to new Comerica Park, a cer-

Tiger Stadium has not hosted a major league game since 1999, but the venerable old ballpark is still standing today.

emony in which home plate was dug up (for use at Comerica) and the Tiger Stadium flag was passed from player to player. Detroit won its last game at the old park, 8-2 over Kansas City—a win accentuated by an eighth-inning grand slam from Rob Fick. Tiger Stadium remains in place today, a crumbling, seldom-used relic awaiting its final fate.

Some memorable moments at Tiger Stadium

- July 8, 1941: Ted Williams hit a three-run, ninth-inning home run to give the American League a 7-5 All-Star Game victory.

- October 7, 1935: In Game 6 of the World Series, Tigers catcher/manager Mickey Cochrane scored the winning run in the bottom of the ninth inning, beating the Cubs and giving the Tigers their first World Series championship.

- September 14, 1968: Denny McLain, thanks to a ninth-inning Tigers rally, posted a victory over Oakland and became baseball's first 30-game winner since 1934.

- July 13, 1971: Reggie Jackson's All-Star Game blast off Pittsburgh pitcher Doc Ellis hit the light standard positioned atop the right field bleachers—one of the stadium's most memorable home runs.

- October 14, 1984: In Game 5 of the 1984 World Series, Kirk Gibson's dramatic eighth-inning, three-run homer off Padres pitcher Goose Gossage sealed the team's fourth championship.

Michigan Sports Hall of Fame

City: Detroit
Location: 1 North Washington Blvd
Cobo Conference Center
248-540-6248
Started in 1955, this is one of the oldest "state" sports Hall of Fames. Located within a hallway at the Cobo Conference Center, hundreds of plaques are displayed along the walls honoring athletes and other notable figures from Detroit professional teams. Among the baseball players included in this "Hall of Heroes" are Charlie Gehringer, Sam Crawford, Hank Greenberg, Ty Cobb, Al Kaline, Lance Parrish, Jack Morris, Alan Trammel and Norm Cash. Honorees are voted in each year by living Hall of Fame members and local sports media. Admission is free (whenever Cobo Conference Center is open).

National Polish-American Sports Hall of Fame and Museum

City: Orchard Lake
Location: 3535 Indian Trail (Intersection of Commerce Road and Orchard Lake Road)
248-683-0401
(Open by appointment, call for information)

The National Polish-American Sports Hall of Fame and Museum was founded in 1973 to honor and recognize outstanding American athletes, both amateur and professional, of Polish descent. A Hall of Fame Room and Museum was established in the Dombrowski Fieldhouse on the campus of St. Mary's College, Orchard Lake, 25 miles northwest of Detroit. The organization has inducted many baseball players, including Stan Musial, Ted Kluszewski, Carl Yastrzemski, Tony Kubek and Bill Mazeroski. When inducted, each member is asked to provide a piece or two of related memorabilia, an idea that has resulted in a sizable and impressive collection. A special display honors charter inductee Musial, the former St. Louis great who has been extremely generous in his involvement with the museum.

The tomb of Frank Navin

City: Southfield
Location: Holy Sepulchre Cemetery
25800 W. 10 Mile Road
248-350-1900

The former Detroit owner loved his team so much that his gravesite is "guarded" by two very realistic looking, life-size bronze tigers. Navin died suddenly while horseback riding in November of 1935. Ironically, it was just five weeks after his beloved Tigers won their first World Series championship, beating the Cubs in six games.

Hall of Famers buried in Michigan

Larry MacPhail
Elkland Township Cemetery
6897 Cass City Road
Cass City
517-872-1112

Detroit Metropolitan area
Norman "Turkey" Stearnes
Lincoln Memorial Park Cemetery

21661 E. 14 Mile Road
Clinton Township
810-791-3486

Sam Thompson
Elmwood Cemetery
1200 Elmwood Street
Detroit
313-567-3453

Hal Newhouser
Oakland Hills Memorial Gardens
43300 W. 12 Mile Road
Novi
248-349-2784

Charlie Gehringer and Harry Heilmann
Holy Sepulchre Cemetery
25800 W. 10 Mile Road
Southfield
248-350-1900

Charlie Gehringer (top) and
Harry Heilmann

Minnesota
Former site of Metropolitan Stadium

City: Bloomington
Location: Mall of America
Crossroads of Interstate 494 and Highway 77 (Look for Camp Snoopy in the Mall)

Metropolitan Stadium was built on a farm in 1956 for the American Association's Minneapolis Millers, who had just abandoned Nicollet Park. The Class AAA Millers played there five years, giving way in 1961 to the relocated Washington Senators, who gave the city its first taste of major league baseball. The Senators began their first Metropolitan Stadium season as the "Twins" and were joined by a National Football League expansion team, the Minnesota Vikings, who helped finance the building of a double-deck grandstand in left

Metropolitan Stadium, former home of the Twins, was located on property now occupied by the Mall of America.

field. The renovation brought capacity to 45,919, where it stayed until the park closed after the 1981 season when the Twins and Vikings moved to the new Metrodome. Three years after shutting down operations, Metropolitan Stadium was demolished to make way for the Mall of America. The former site of home plate is marked by a plaque in the Camp Snoopy area of the mall. There also is a Metropolitan Stadium seat bolted to a wall, marking the landing spot for Harmon Killebrew's mammoth 520-foot home run in 1967.

Some memorable moments at Metropolitan Stadium:

- October 7, 1965: Twins pitcher Jim Kaat gave Minnesota a two-games-to-none World Series lead over the Dodgers, driving in two runs and outpitching Sandy Koufax, 5-1.

- July 13, 1965: Twins star Harmon Killebrew homered, but the A.L. lost 6-5 in the stadium's only All-Star Game.

- Rod Carew won seven A.L. batting titles here.

- August 10, 1971: Killebrew hit his 500th home run in a game against the Orioles.

Keep your eyes peeled for...

- Harmon Killebrew Drive (83rd Street, Bloomington) near the site of old Metropolitan Stadium

Original Baseball Hall of Fame Museum of Minnesota

City: Minneapolis
Location: 910 South Third Street

The Baseball Hall of Fame Museum of Minnesota may be small, but it has an impressive collection of memorabilia and artifacts.

The Original Baseball Hall of Fame and Museum, discreetly hidden behind a Third Street sportswear store, is a treasure-trove of autographed baseball memorabilia, including jerseys, bats, balls, cards and much more. This small but packed baseball museum is the brainchild of Ray Crump, a man dedicated to Minnesota baseball history.

Former site of Nicollet Park

City: Minneapolis
Location: Nicollet Avenue South and 31st Street
Fabled Nicollet Park, home to minor league baseball from 1896-1955, was the stomping grounds of the Class AAA American Association's Minneapolis Millers for 54 years. The Millers compiled the Association's best won-lost record over that span and also won nine pennants, tying the total of their cross-river neighbors, the St. Paul Saints. The Millers provided a proving ground for 15 players who eventually ended up in the Hall of Fame, including Philadelphia lefty Rube Waddell, Boston's Ted Williams, Giants center fielder Willie Mays and Red Sox star Carl Yastrzemski. Nicollet Park also was 1944 home to the Minneapolis Millerettes of the All-American Girls Professional Baseball League, the wartime circuit that inspired the 1992 movie, *A League of Their Own*. Babe Ruth played several memorable exhibition games at Nicollet, one during the 1924 Ruth/Walter Johnson barnstorming tour.

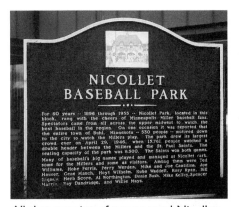

All that remains of once-proud Nicollet Park is this historic marker.

In 1955, the year before it was torn down, Nicollet Park played host to the Junior World Series in which the Millers beat the Rochester Red Wings to win their first and only Series title. The games in that Series were the final ones played at Nicollet. In 1983, an historic marker was erected on the former site of the ballpark, paid for in large part by donations from former players and fans whose fondness for the cozy, slightly decrepit but always loved ballpark stretched on for years after it was gone.

Some memorable moments at Nicollet Park:

- On a 1933 billboard posted on an outfield wall, Wheaties first used its slogan, "Breakfast of Champions." According to the The Wheaties Franchise, an American Sports icon since 1933: "General Mills' broadcast deal with the minor league Minneapolis Millers on radio station WCCO included the large signboard that Wheaties would use to introduce its new advertising slogan. The late Knox Reeves (of the Minneapolis-based advertising agency) was asked what should be printed on the signboard for his client. He took out a pad and pencil, it is said, sketched a Wheaties package, thought for a minute, and then printed 'Wheaties—The Breakfast of Champions.' "

- July 4, 1940: Millers outfielder Ab Wright hit four home runs and a triple in five at-bats for 19 total bases.

- In 1938, a brash-but-brilliant Millers outfielder named Ted Williams took the league batting title with a .366 average.

- In 1951, the New York Giants assigned Willie Mays to Minneapolis. In 35 games, Mays collected 71 hits, 8 home runs and 30 RBIs. This prompted a recall from Giants manager Leo Durocher.

Missouri

Jake Beckley monument

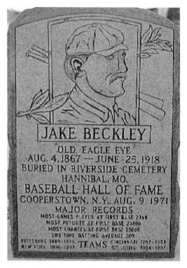

City: Hannibal

Location: 300 block of North Main Street

This recently-restored memorial to Jake Beckley was originally unveiled on August 11, 1971. Beckley was born in Hannibal on August 4, 1867, and played first base in the major leagues for 20 years. Over that tenure, he played more games (2,386), made more putouts (23,696) and handled more chances (25,000) than any other player at his position. Beckley retired with a .308 average, 87 home runs and 1,575 RBIs. Beckley had the bizarre habit of screaming the nonsensical word "Chickazoola" at pitchers while approaching the plate,

Jake Beckley is long gone, but not forgotten in Hannibal.

presumably to rattle them. Beckley, who was inducted into the Hall of Fame in 1971, just a few days before the dedication of his memorial, died in 1918 and is buried at:

Riverside Cemetery
State Route 79
Hannibal

Historic Joe Becker Stadium

City: Joplin

Location: 1301 E. Third Street

Joplin's historic Joe Becker Stadium, built in 1918, is where Mickey Mantle played in 1950, his second professional season. Mantle batted .383 with 26 home runs, 30 doubles, 12 triples and 136 RBIs for the Western Association Class C team. That performance earned him an invitation to 1951 spring training with the Yankees. The venerable little park has survived two fires, countless storms and thousands of games from Little League to semi-pro. In addition to Mantle, such other stars as Stan Musial, Joe Garagiola and Ken Boyer played here. Today's Joe Becker Stadium is home to Missouri Southern State College,

Joplin High School, American Legion Post 13 and several regional tournaments. The stadium is named for Joe Becker, a professional baseball umpire and scout who also served as business manager for the Joplin Miners minor league team from 1936-42.

Gabby Street Park

City: Joplin

Location: Gabby Street Boulevard (26th Street) between Main Street and Maiden Lane

Gabby Street, a one-time batterymate of Washington Senators great Walter Johnson and the manager who led the St. Louis Cardinals to National League pennants in 1930 and '31, first visited Joplin in 1923 as a minor league player/manager. He met and married a local girl, then became a full-time Joplin resident until he died in 1951. The city held a day in Street's honor on January 19, 1950, dedicating the park and a street to his name. On hand to celebrate the affair were longtime friends Stan Musial, Joe Garagiola, Red Schoendienst and Enos Slaughter. Also present was Harry Caray, whose career Street influenced as a Cardinals radio broadcaster in the 1940s. The park today is mostly used for youth baseball.

Satchel Paige Memorial Stadium

City: Kansas City

Location: 51st Street and Swope Parkway

This stadium, used by amateur baseball organizations and for special events, is named for pitching legend Satchel Paige, who played for the Kansas City Monarchs in the old Negro National League. Originally called the Catholic Youth Council Athletic Field, the 5,000-seat stadium was renamed in Paige's honor in 1982. Three days after the ceremony, Paige died, a tragedy that galvanized the community to renovate the then-deteriorating stadium.

Satchel Paige Comprehensive Community School

City: Kansas City

Location: 3301 E 75th St.

Satchel Paige Elementary School was opened originally as a kindergarten through fifth grade magnet school with the unlikely name "Satchel Paige Classical Greek Academy." The name referred to the school's focus on sports from the original Olympic Games. In 1998, the school was renamed Satchel Paige Comprehensive Community School. A statue of Paige stands inside the

Satchel Paige Memorial Stadium serves amateur baseball leagues in the Swope Park district of Kansas City.

building, as well as a display case featuring an autographed baseball, a uniform, a pair of cleats and some other personal items.

Lou Gehrig's last game

City: Kansas City
Location: Municipal Stadium (former site)
A mile and a half southeast of downtown Kansas City at the intersection of 22nd street and Brooklyn Avenue.

Home to four different teams from 1923-72, Kansas City's Municipal Stadium, once called Muehlebach Field, was originally built as a home base for the Negro League's Kansas City Monarchs and the Kansas City Blues minor league team of the American Association. The stadium was the early stomping grounds for such black baseball greats as Satchel Paige and John Henry Lloyd as well as many of the great players it developed as a longtime farm team for the New York Yankees. In 1938, the stadium was re-christened Ruppert Stadium, in honor of Yankees owner Jacob Ruppert, and a few years later it was renamed Blues Stadium. From 1955-66, now called Municipal Stadium, the Brooklyn Avenue ballpark was strictly big league—home of the Kansas City Athletics, relocated from Philadelphia. The ballpark was rebuilt with a double deck to accommodate more fans.

Many Kansas Citians will remember the 1960s primarily as the era of flamboyant Charles O. Finley, the innovative, always-controversial owner who kept things stirred up with his contrary personality and futuristic ideas. Finley made ballpark changes that incurred the wrath of commissioner Bowie Kuhn, parad-

Municipal Stadium, formerly called Blues Stadium, was home for two major league teams, the Athletics and Royals.

ed his mascot, Charlie O. the Mule, around the city and stadium, installed a small zoo and picnic area down the right field line and installed a mechanical rabbit (Harvey) that would rise from the ground behind home plate to supply balls to the umpire. He also pulled off Bill Veeck-like stunts that kept everyone shaking their head. Finley's final "stunt" was to make the A's disappear. He moved his club to Oakland in 1968, at which point the expansion Kansas City Royals were formed and Municipal Stadium took on yet another tenant—a relationship that lasted until Royals Stadium (now Kauffman Stadium) was opened in 1973.

Few fans know that Municipal Stadium played an emotional role in the tragic career-ending story of Lou Gehrig. It was in Detroit that the Iron Horse pulled himself out of the Yankees' lineup, ending his 2,130-game streak on May 2, 1939. But it is widely believed he never played again. He did, more than a month later on June 12, when the New Yorkers played an exhibition game at Blues Stadium against their top farm club. A frail, weakened Gehrig, whose illness had yet to be diagnosed, played three innings, batted once (eighth in the order) and grounded out to second base in his final professional at-bat. He cleanly handled four putouts while playing first base. Gehrig was still traveling with the team at that point and had not yet been diagnosed as terminal. Teammate Tommy Heinrich was quoted as saying, "He actually didn't want to do that in Kansas City. But Gehrig, for the sake of those fans, went up to home plate." The 23,864 fans who watched that game were part of the largest crowd ever to attend an exhibition game in the history of the American Association.

The day after the game, the Yankees returned to New York while Gehrig took a train to the Mayo Clinic in Minnesota, where he would learn the details of his fatal disease. The next month, in a stirring Fourth of July ceremony at Yankee Stadium, Gehrig made his famous "Luckiest Man Alive" speech. Two years later, he was dead.

Municipal Stadium was demolished in 1976 and the site is now a community garden.

Some memorable moments at Municipal Stadium

- August 9, 1930: Smoky Joe Williams of the Negro league Homestead Grays struck out 27 Kansas City Monarchs and allowed just one hit in 12 innings. The losing pitcher, Chet Brewer, struck out 19 and allowed four hits.

- September 8, 1965: Kansas City A's shortstop Bert Campaneris became the first man in modern baseball to play all nine positions in one game. (The A's lost 5-3 to the California Angels.)

- September 25, 1965: Satchel Paige, at age 59, pitched three scoreless innings against the Boston Red Sox in another of Finley's many Kansas City promotions.

Negro Leagues Baseball Museum

City: Kansas City
Location: 1616 E. 18th Street

Negro League legend and baseball goodwill ambassador Buck O'Neil serves as board chairman at the Negro Leagues Baseball Museum, which was opened in January of 1991. The museum, originally located in the historic Lincoln Building, recounts in great detail the formation and history of the Negro Baseball League. Displays include rare Negro League pennants, autographed baseballs, photographs and an 8-minute video tape about the league's history—narrated by newsman Bernard Shaw. From old photos, contracts, scorecards and equipment, to a room honoring the nine best (one at each position) Negro League ballplayers, this museum does an excellent job of documenting a special group of athletes who excelled in the face of great adver-

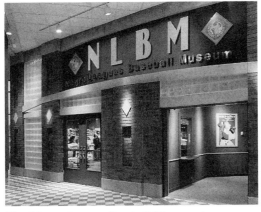

The Negro League Baseball Museum is a must-see for baseball fans visiting Kansas City.

The Negro League Museum features a display honoring the greatest players at each position.

sity. When you visit, you might even bump into O'Neil, one of the more charismatic heroes baseball has produced.

Birthplace of the Negro League

City: Kansas City
Location: Paseo YMCA
1800 Paseo Boulevard between 18th and 19th Streets
In 1920, team owner (and former Negro League pitcher) Andrew "Rube" Foster met here with other independent team owners to brainstorm a plan to create a stable league for black baseball. This summit resulted in the formation of the Negro National League (NNL). In addition to Foster's American Giants, charter members included the Chicago Giants, the Dayton Marcos, the Detroit Stars, the Indianapolis ABCs, the St. Louis Giants and the Kansas City Monarchs. Before this historic session, Negro League teams were primarily rudderless barnstormers. After the NNL was formed, however, black baseball grew into a popular, nationally recognized association. Over the next 40 years, Negro League Baseball expanded to include more than 2,600 athletes and dozens of teams.

Missouri Sports Hall of Fame

City: Springfield
Location: 3861 E. Stan Musial Drive
417-889-3100

This museum/hall of fame features a great second-floor display devoted to baseball, complete with a Mark McGwire area and Heavy Hitters area that includes memorabilia from many Missouri teams and players, including autographed jerseys, helmets, gloves and more. Some of baseball's most historic names—Babe Ruth, Willie Mays, Mike Schmidt, Reggie Jackson—are represented. Interactive displays include a broadcast booth and a pitching cage where visitors can stand behind home plate and witness, up close and personal, a major league pitch traveling 100 mph.

St. Louis Cardinals Hall of Fame Museum

City: St. Louis

Location: 111 Stadium Plaza

The St. Louis Cardinals Hall of Fame is the official repository for more than 100 years of St. Louis baseball history. Through photographs and memorabilia, visitors experience the evolution of the game as witnessed by St. Louisans from the 1880s to the present. The museum, located inside the International Bowling Museum, includes artifacts from the Cardinals' 15 World Series and nine championships, complete with the 1967 and '82 trophies, championship rings, scorebooks, programs, autographed balls and bats. An impressive Stan "The Man" Musial exhibit covers his amazing major league career. Ozzie Smith, Bob Gibson, Lou Brock, Dizzy Dean, Rogers Hornsby, Joe Medwick and many other Cardinals greats are showcased as well. Mark McGwire's 1962 Corvette, which was presented to him by the Cardinals in 1998 when he broke Roger Maris' single-season home run record, is on display. There also is a Mark McGwire "Bat Bench"—a sitting area made from bats, balls and bases. The St. Louis Browns are well-represented, too, as are the St. Louis Stars, the Negro National League team of St. Louis and James "Cool Papa" Bell. The museum, strategically located across from Busch Stadium, is a great stopover for fans heading to a game. With admission you get the Cardinals Hall of Fame, the International Bowling Museum and four free frames of bowling.

Plaza of Champions

City: St. Louis

Location: Busch Stadium

250 Stadium Plaza

Don't miss the statues of "Cool Papa" Bell, Ozzie Smith, Bob Gibson, Lou Brock, Rogers Hornsby, George Sisler, Dizzy Dean, Enos Slaughter, Red

Inspiration at Busch Stadium can be found at the Plaza of Champions, which is manned by statues of former baseball greats.

Schoendienst and Jack Buck, located on the Plaza of Champions outside Busch Stadium, near the oversized Stan Musial statue.

Cool Papa Bell Avenue

City: St. Louis

Location: James "Cool Papa" Bell Avenue runs between Dr. Martin Luther King, Jr. Drive and Jefferson Avenue on what used to be called Dixon Street. It's named for the lightning-fast Bell, the legendary Negro league center fielder who played from 1922-50.

Cool Papa Bell Memorial

City: St. Louis

Location: St. Peters Cemetery

2101 Lucas & Hunt Road

Northwest of downtown St. Louis

The 10-foot-high memorial is located at the gravesite of Cool Papa Bell. Made of African granite, it honors "A Universal Legend" and commemorates Bell's 1974 induction into the Hall of Fame. The monument was designed by Connie Bell Brooks, Cool Papa's only child, and was dedicated on July 20, 1996—a day the state of Missouri proclaimed "James 'Cool Papa' Bell Day."

Former site of Sportsman's Park

City: St. Louis

Location: The Herbert Hoover Boys and Girls Club

2901 North Grand Avenue

The former site of Sportsman's Park, the once-proud home of the St. Louis Browns and Cardinals, now belongs to a youth club.

Baseball at the intersection of Grand and Dodier dates all the way back to 1875, but the 20th century brand that St. Louis fans can still remember began in 1902, when the American League's Browns moved into the modern-era Sportsman's Park. The Browns were the lone inhabitants of Sportsman's for 18 years while the Cardinals played their games at Robison Field. Neither team enjoyed a lot of success over that period and in 1920 the Browns accepted their cross-league rivals as tenants, a Sportsman's Park relationship that would last for 34 years.

While the Browns continued to flounder for most of their St. Louis existence, the Cardinals suddenly jumped into the spotlight with their first National League pennant and World Series championship in 1926. It was the first of 10 pennants and seven fall classic wins they would bring to the ballpark. The Browns, who would move to Baltimore in 1953 and become the Orioles, managed only one A.L. pennant—and lost to their co-tenant Cardinals in an all-St. Louis World Series in 1944. When the Browns moved in 1953, Anheuser-Busch, the new owner of the Cardinals, renamed the park Busch Stadium. It remained home to the Cardinals until May 8, 1966, when they moved into new Busch Memorial Stadium in downtown St. Louis. After the move, August A. Busch, Jr., donated the property for use as a private recreational facility that eventually became the Herbert Hoover's Boy's Club. Several signs and a plaque still commemorate the decades of baseball that was played there, and there's even a youth baseball field with home plate located in what was the right field area of Sportsman's Park. It's still possible for diehard fans to play on the exact spot where almost 100 years of St. Louis baseball history took place.

Some memorable moments from Sportsman's Park:

- May 5, 1925: Detroit player-manager Ty Cobb hit three homers, a double and two singles, driving in five runs in a game against the Browns.

- October 9, 1944: The Cardinals won Game 6 of the all-St. Louis World Series, 3-1, over the Browns.

- October 15, 1946: Enos Slaughter's "Mad Dash" around the bases gave the Cardinals a stirring Game 7 victory over Boston in a dramatic World Series.

- August 19, 1951: Midget Eddie Gaedel drew a walk in a pinch-hitting appearance for the Browns, another wild promotion by owner Bill Veeck.

- May 2, 1954: Stan Musial homered five times in a double-header split with the New York Giants.

Keep your eyes peeled for...

- McGwire Highway (Interstate 70). When Cardinals first base-man Mark McGwire hit his 70th homer of the 1998 season, his adopted state of Missouri named a section of I-70 in his honor. The six-mile stretch runs just past Busch Stadium and is marked in both directions.

- St. Louis Walk of Fame on the sidewalk of Delmar Boulevard in the Loop District of University City. Brass stars are laid into the sidewalk honoring actors, writers, musicians, teachers and, of course, baseball players. Look for Cool Papa Bell, Yogi Berra, Lou Brock, Dizzy Dean, Bob Gibson, Rogers Hornsby, Stan Musial, Branch Rickey, Red Schoendienst, Jack Buck, Harry Caray, Bob Costas and Joe Garagiola.

Hall of Famers buried in Missouri

Bullet Joe Rogan

Blue Ridge Lawn Memorial Gardens
2640 South Blue Ridge Boulevard
Kansas City

Zack Wheat and Satchel Paige
Forest Hill & Calvary Cemetery
6901 Troost Avenue
Kansas City

Charles "Kid" Nichols and Hilton Smith
Mount Moriah & Freeman Cemetery
10507 Holmes Street
Kansas City

Cal Hubbard
Oakwood Cemetery
Cherry Street
Milan

St. Louis Metropolitan Area
George Sisler
Old Meeting House Presbyterian Church
Cemetery
2250 N. Geyer Road
Frontenac

Jim Bottomley
I. O. O. F. Community Cemetery
North Church Street
Sullivan

Joe Medwick
St. Lucas Cemetery
11735 Denny Road
Sunset Hills

Zack Wheat, Satchel Paige and Sunny Jim Bottomley (top to bottom)

Nebraska

Museum of Nebraska Major League Baseball

City: St. Paul
Location: 619 Howard Avenue
Nebraska has produced more than 100 major leaguers, and this wonderful little museum, located in Grover Cleveland Alexander's hometown, focuses primarily on the five local legends who made it to the Hall of Fame: Alexander, Dazzy Vance, Sam Crawford, Bob Gibson and Richie Ashburn. There also are displays for many other former major leaguers who have roots in the state. Opened in 1991 and moved to its current location in 2000, the exhibits include balls, jerseys, autographs, books, programs, scrapbooks and more.

Grover Cleveland Alexander historical marker

City: St. Paul
Location: Alexander Avenue (which runs north of the North Loup river through Howard County)
The marker dedicated to Alexander is near an American Legion field that also is named for him. Alexander, the outstanding righthanded pitcher who won 373 major league games over his 20-year career, died here on November 4, 1950, and he is buried at:
Elmwood Cemetery
St. Paul

Richie Ashburn was a Whiz Kid, both in Philadelphia and Tilden.

Richie Ashburn Field

City: Tilden
Location: 100 Center Street
Richie Ashburn, born in Tilden on March 19, 1927, was one of the most popular players of his era. The speedy former Philadelphia Phillies center fielder topped the .300 plateau nine times, collected 2,574 hits and won batting titles in 1955 and '58. Ashburn, a career .308 hitter, was a member of the young, ener-

getic 1950 Whiz Kids, who won the National League pennant on the last day of the season before losing to the Yankees in the World Series. After retiring as a player, Ashburn worked as a Phillies broadcaster for 35 years, many in the booth alongside legendary Harry Kalas. Ashburn was inducted into the Hall of Fame in 1995—the same day later Phillies great Mike Schmidt went in—and he died in New York in 1997. The municipal ballpark was renamed Ashburn Field in his honor and a display of Ashburn memorabilia, once located at a Tilden pharmacy, can be found at:

The Madison County Historical Society Museum

210 West 3rd Street

Madison

The museum is open weekdays from 2-5 p.m. and other times by special appointment.

Sam Crawford Field

City: Wahoo

Location: 5th & Elm St.

"Wahoo" Sam Crawford, born here on April 18, 1880, was a Cincinnati and Detroit star from baseball's dead-ball era. "Wahoo Sam" was one of the game's early sluggers, a long-ball threat and longtime outfield mate of Ty Cobb. Crawford is best remembered for the all-time record 312 triples he posted over a 19-year career. The one-two punch of Crawford and Cobb led Detroit to three consecutive American League pennants (1907-09), but the Tigers lost each year in the World Series. He wound up with 2,961 hits and a career batting average of .309. Crawford was elected to the Hall of Fame in 1957 and died in Southern California on June 15, 1968. The field named for him is used for youth baseball.

Sam Crawford was one of more than 100 former players with Nebraska roots.

North Dakota

Roger Maris Museum

The 'Roger Maris' wall sits outside Lindenwood Park, where the Roger Maris Baseball League plays.

City: Fargo
Location: West Acres Shopping Center
I-29 and 13th Avenue South

This hometown tribute to Maris—accessible to all and free at Maris' request—is a free-standing exhibit along the wall of one of the mall's corridors. Curator James R. McLaughlin has done an outstanding job paying tribute to Fargo's famous son, who died in 1985. Maris, who was born in Hibbing, Minnesota, on September 10, 1934, landed in Fargo when his father, a railroad worker, moved there in 1942. Both Roger and older brother Rudy became local legends, multi-sport athletes who starred at Fargo's Shanley High School. But Roger ended up stealing the spotlight. He returned four kickoffs for touchdowns in one high school football game and led the local American Legion baseball team to a state championship. The legend grew when Maris went on to major league success with the Cleveland Indians, Kansas City Athletics, New York Yankees and St. Louis Cardinals—most notably as a two-time American League MVP with the Yankees and the man who broke Babe Ruth's single-season home run record. When Maris hit 61 homers in 1961, he became one of the most celebrated athletes in baseball history. The mall exhibit celebrates his 12-year career through videos, photos, bats, balls, trophies and many other Maris-related artifacts.

There are Maris reminders throughout Fargo. He played American Legion baseball at Barnett Field in north Fargo, where North High School now sits. There is Roger Maris Field and Roger Maris Drive in Lindenwood Park, where the Roger Maris Baseball League now plays. There is the Roger Maris Cancer Center and Roger Maris Gardens, a shrine for the modest, underappreciated baseball hero at Fargo's Jack Williams Stadium.

Roger Maris is buried at:
Holy Cross Cemetery
Fargo

Ohio

Blue Ash Sports Center

City: Blue Ash
Location: 11540 Grooms Road

Within this multi-field sports complex, the spirit of old Crosley Field lives on. That's because the fan-friendly Cincinnati ballpark has been "reconstructed." Using original Crosley blueprints, The Crosley Field Restoration Project was dedicated to the "Youth of Baseball" in July 1988. The field includes the same dimensions, a grass infield, the infamous outfield terrace and an outfield wall with the same distances, heights and angles that were found at the original Crosley. The reconstructed scoreboard is five stories high and has the same look that was found at Crosley when the last pitch was thrown there on June 24, 1970. Many original Crosley Field items have been acquired through donation and acquisition (including more than 400 original seats) and other artifacts were salvaged from a similar Crosley Field restoration project that had taken place in Kentucky. There are several plaques, an original ticket booth and handprints in cement, left by former Cincinnati stars. This new "Crosley Field" is home for many leagues as well as high school games (Moeller High), college games and other events and activities. It also has played host to several Old-Timers games.

Thurman Munson Stadium

City: Canton
Location: 2501 Allen Ave. SE

Thurman Munson Memorial Stadium (home to the Canton Coyotes in the Frontier League) was completed in 1989, named after the late Yankees catcher who was a graduate of Canton Lehman High School. Munson, a six-time All-Star, played 11 years with the New York Yankees and was named the American League Rookie of the Year in 1970 and A.L. MVP in 1976. Over his career, Thurman hit 113 home runs, drove in 701 runs and posted a career batting average of .292. Munson died tragically in a 1979 plane crash and his uniform No. 15 is displayed on the center field wall at Munson Stadium.

Former site of League Park

City: Cleveland
Location: East 66th Street and Lexington Avenue

Baseball was played at East 66th and Lexington as far back as 1891. But the

A youth center now occupies the building that once housed League Park's ticket booth and team offices.

steel-and-concrete League Park that entertained Cleveland fans with its quirky dimensions and odd rectangular shape was erected in 1910 and remained in use through 1946. League Park, which was called Dunn Field from 1920-27, measured a whopping 375 feet down the left field line and an inviting 290 to right, where drooling hitters were frustrated by a 40-foot combination concrete-and-wire fence that knocked down potential home runs and created erratic bounces. Life was never dull in Cleveland. League Park never had a seating capacity over 22,000 and its final 14 seasons were shared with massive Municipal Stadium—home games at League during the week, at Municipal on weekends. The Indians finally moved into Municipal Stadium for good after the 1946 season. The ballpark was demolished in 1951, but remnants of the stadium remain. The two-story ticket booth, which also housed team offices, is now a youth center; a crumbling piece of the first-base grandstand still stands. The stripped-down diamond still exists at its original location. There also is an historic marker as well as rumblings about a plan to renovate the park as part of a neighborhood revitalization plan.

Some memorable moments at League Park:

- October 10, 1920: Indians second baseman Bill Wambsganss made World Series history by completing an unassisted triple play in Game 5 against Brooklyn. In the same game, Elmer Smith hit the first World Series grand slam and Jim Bagby hit the first World Series homer by a pitcher.

- August 11, 1929: Babe Ruth hit his 500th home run against the Indians.

- September 13, 1936: A 17-year-old Bob Feller struck out 17 Athletics in a two-hit victory.

- July 16, 1941: Yankees center fielder Joe DiMaggio stretched his hitting streak to 56 games.

Former site of Municipal Stadium

City: Cleveland

Location: On the shore of Lake Erie between the lake and downtown Cleveland

Built in 1931 and opened in 1932 for baseball and other events, Municipal Stadium (also called Cleveland Stadium) was a ballpark for the ages. It was cavernous, an 80,000-seat steel-and-concrete monster built with hopes of landing the 1932 Olympics, which ultimately were held at the Los Angeles Coliseum. The Indians did not move to Municipal Stadium full-time until 1947, choosing to play 14 years at smaller League Park on weekdays and at Municipal Stadium on weekends and holidays. The center field bleachers at Cleveland Stadium were 470 feet from home plate and no batted ball ever reached them.

Municipal Stadium, the massive home for Cleveland baseball and football, began its tenure as a weekend and holiday facility while weekday games were played at smaller League Park.

On September 12, 1954, the Indians and Yankees played in front of 86,563 fans, the largest crowd in baseball history until the Dodgers moved into the Los Angeles Coliseum. Municipal also was home to the National Football League's Cleveland Browns and hosted college football, boxing, track and every other imaginable event. There was nothing glitzy about Municipal Stadium, which was dubbed by visitors as "The Mistake by the Lake." But the stadium was never lacking for excitement, thanks to such players as Bob Feller, Lou Boudreau, Larry Doby, Early Wynn, Rocky Colavito and Satchel Paige. The site of the stadium, which was demolished in 1996, now is occupied by the Browns' new football stadium. But the remains of the stadium still draws crowds—of fish. The rubble from the stadium was used to construct two 600-foot artificial reefs along the Lake Erie waterfront.

Some memorable moments at Municipal Stadium:

- The All-Star Games of 1935, '54, '63 and '81.

- July 17, 1941: Joe DiMaggio's consecutive-game hitting streak ended at 56 in a 4-3 Yankees' win. Indians third baseman Ken Keltner twice robbed DiMaggio of hits.

- July 17, 1960: Boston's Ted Williams hit his 500th career home run against Indians pitcher Wynn Hawkins.

- May 15, 1981: Indians righthander Len Barker pitched a perfect game, retiring all 27 Blue Jays he faced in a 3-0 victory.

- April 12, 1992: Boston lefthander Matt Young tossed a no-hitter—and lost to the Indians, 2-1.

Former site of Crosley Field

City: Cincinnati
Location: Findlay Street and Western Avenue
Cincinnati baseball was played at this site from 1884-1970, 59 of those years in cozy, fan-friendly Redland Field/Crosley Field. League Park sat at Findlay and Western from 1884-1901 before burning down. The ornate Palace of the Fans served as home of the Reds until the more modern, steel-and-concrete Redland opened in 1912. It remained Redland Field until 1934, when the name was officially changed to Crosley Field in in honor of new owner Powel Crosley Jr. Crosley Field was known for its irregular contours and simple, intimate atmosphere. Left fielders had to negotiate a terrace that began sloping upward about 20 feet from the wall, reaching a 4-foot grade. Fans in right field enjoyed the Sun Deck and those bleachers intersected at a point with the cen-

The quirks and intimacy of Cincinnati's Crosley Field (above) have been re-created at Blue Ash, Ohio, where a replica of the old ballpark exists.

ter field wall, necessitating a while line with a hand-painted ground rule that read, "Batted Ball Hitting Concrete Wall on Fly to Right of White Line— Home Run." For many years, the tin roof of a laundry, the Superior Towel & Linen Service, provided an inviting target for home run hitters over the left field wall. Players had to walk through the third base stands to get to the field from their clubhouses. In January of 1937, Crosley Field virtually disappeared when a massive flood covered it with more than 20 feet of water. Seizing the moment, Reds pitchers Lee Grissom and Gene Schott posed for a now-famous photo rowing a boat over the center field fence. The last game at Crosley was played in 1970, when the Reds moved to Riverfront Stadium. Today, in an industrial park, an historic marker identifies the site of home plate (and some Crosley Field chairs also are on display).

Some memorable moments at Crosley Field:

- October 1, 1919: The Reds won Game 1 of the World Series here, 9-1. Cincinnati's first World Series also is remembered as the "Black Sox" classic, in which eight members of the White Sox conspired with gamblers to lose. Chicago starter Eddie Cicotte reportedly signaled that the fix was on when he hit the first Reds batter, Morrie Rath, with a pitch.

- May 24, 1935: The first night game in major league history was played here, with President Franklin Delano Roosevelt throwing a switch from the White House to turn on the lights. The Reds beat the Philadelphia Phillies, 2-1.

- June 11, 1938: Johnny Vander Meer pitched the first of two consecutive no-hitters, beating Boston 3-0. He came back on June 15 to no-hit the Dodgers at Ebbets Field.

- May 27, 1937: Giants pitcher Carl Hubbell shut down the Reds in a rare relief appearance and received credit for his 24th straight win—a still-standing major league record.

- June 10, 1944: The youngest player in major league history, 15-year-old Reds lefthander Joe Nuxhall, pitched two-thirds of an inning, giving up five runs on five walks, two singles and a wild pitch.

Historic Cooper Stadium

City: Columbus
Location: 1155 West Mound Street
"The Coop" is home to the Columbus Clippers. It was built in 1931 when Branch Rickey purchased the Columbus Red Birds. Needing a new park, Rickey bought what was then farmland for $450,000 and had Red Bird Stadium built. The Red Birds left after the 1954 season and were replaced by the Columbus Jets, who played at Jets Stadium for 15 years. By 1970, the stadium had fallen into disrepair and the Jets departed. In 1977, Franklin County commissioner Harold Cooper, who had led the drive to lure the Jets in 1955, pushed for a stadium renovation and another professional team. He got both. Columbus got the Clippers and the park, now called Franklin County Stadium, received a multi-million dollar renovation. In 1984, the stadium was renamed to honor Cooper and plaques throughout the park document its historic past.

Stephan Field

City: Indian Hill
Location: Southeastern corner of Drake and Shawnee Run
A plaque marks Stephan Field, a place of the heart that was never home to Hall of Famers, but still very much affected the lives of the people who live here. It is named for Paul Stephan, a man whose enthusiastic promotion of "knothole baseball" earned praise and whose leadership inspired hundreds of boys in the 1950s and '60s.

In 1953, Paul Jr. asked his father to manage his baseball team. Paul agreed, thus starting his legendary commitment to area baseball. Although he had never played the game, Stephan was a loyal Reds fan and he coached and managed teams here for two of his sons. He didn't stop there, dedicating his time to many other teams and players for more than 20 years. The 1950s "knothole teams" practiced wherever they could get a field and Paul was a one-man operation, doing everything from lining and dragging the fields, carpooling, scheduling, finding umpires, sponsors, uniforms and equipment, etc. His wife, Alice, helped with storing and mending uniforms as her husband preached the gospel of baseball to hundreds of youngsters—teaching them to love the game.

Local hero Paul Stephan is honored for his undying commitment to the game.

From one team in 1953 to three in 1955 to 12 in 1962, the home-grown league was designed to help kids have a good time playing while learning about values and sportsmanship. In recognition of Paul's volunteer labor, Stephan Field was dedicated in August of 1964. The ceremony included speeches by the mayor and council members, and three Cincinnati players delivered a letter of commendation from the Reds. Today's Stephan Field is used for baseball, soccer, picnics and other family-related activities. And the plaque honors the man who helped teach baseball's magical lessons to many children.

Jimmie Foxx Memorial Field

City: Lakewood
Location: Kauffman Park
Arthur Avenue (north end)

On August 8, 2000, the city of Lakewood dedicated this field to Jimmie Foxx, who made Lakewood his home after playing baseball. He raised his family here and became an integral part of the community, volunteering many hours on the town's sandlot baseball fields. Members of his family unveiled the plaque at the cere-

Hall-of-Famer Jimmie Foxx made Lakewood his home after retiring.

mony and several former players, including Herb Score and Mel Harder, took part in the event.

A park, monument and museum exhibit honor the great Cy Young.

Cy Young Park

City: Newcomerstown
Location: 591 N. College St.

Cy Young's career numbers defy logic. He won 511 games—94 more than any other pitcher—over a 22-year career that straddled the turn of the century. He also pitched 749 complete games, compiled a career 2.63 ERA and posted 15 20-win seasons, five of 30 or more. Born in this area in 1867, Young made his major league debut in 1890 with Cleveland in the National League and subsequently pitched for the St. Louis Nationals and the final 11 seasons of his career in the American League for Boston and Cleveland. Young was a two-game winner for the Red Sox in the first World Series in 1903 and he made history on May 5, 1904, when he pitched the first perfect game of the 20th century, stopping the Philadelphia Athletics, 3-0. Young, who also threw no-hitters in 1897 and 1908, is the namesake for the annual awards handed out to the A.L. and N.L. top pitchers. Young finished his career with the Boston Braves in 1911 and was voted into the Hall of Fame in 1937. He died in Newcomerstown on November 4, 1955. Young's namesake ballpark hosts youth baseball and a monument honors his memory. Exhibits and artifacts at the Newcomerstown Historical Society Museum also honor Young, as well as the town's other local sports legend, former Ohio State football coach Woody Hayes.

Cy Young exhibit

City: Newcomerstown
Location: Newcomerstown Historical Society Museum
221 West Canal Street

Cy Young is buried at:
Peoli Cemetery (in yard of United Methodist Church)
State Route 258
Peoli

Branch Rickey's boyhood home

City: Rushtown
Location: 770 Duck Run
The historic marker here bears the words, "Boyhood home of Branch Rickey—Baseball Pioneer, Innovator and Executive." It honors the former president of the Brooklyn Dodgers who signed Jackie Robinson and choreographed the breaking of baseball's color barrier. Rickey also was credited with introducing the concept of farm systems in baseball while with the St. Louis Cardinals. Rickey was raised in this house with his two brothers and is buried about a mile southeast of the marker at the Rushtown Cemetery

A boyhood home marker honors the memory of Branch Rickey, the pioneer and innovator who grew up in Rushtown.

Former site of Swayne Field

City: Toledo
Location: Monroe Street and Detroit Avenue
Swayne Field, which opened in 1909, was home to the legendary Toledo Mud Hens until it was torn down in 1956. It was named for Noah Swayne, a prominent Toledo lawyer and baseball fan. From 1926-31, Casey Stengel managed the Hens, which all but guaranteed huge crowds. Other Mud Hens stars included Bill Terry, Hack Wilson and Roger Bresnahan, a local hero. The area today is the site of the Swayne Field Shopping Center.

Former site of Wakeman Red Cap Field

City: Wakeman
Location: Intersection of U.S. 20 and Cooper Street in Fletcher Park
A marker honors the former site Wakeman's Red Cap Field, home of one of this area's best semi-pro teams during the 1930s and '40s. Lights were installed

at Wakeman Field on July 24, 1935, making it possible for night baseball to be played here just two months after Cincinnati's Crosley Field hosted the first night game in major league history. The Red Caps were part of the Wakeman Baseball Club, which existed to encourage aspiring ballplayers. Wakeman Field was visited annually by Harlem Globetrotters founder Abe Saperstein's Ethiopian Clowns, a traveling African-American team. Appearances were made by such legends as Satchel Paige, Josh Gibson, Al Schacht and Jesse Owens.

"Sad" Sam Jones/Mary Weddle-Hines historical marker

City: Woodsfield
Location: Creamery Street

A two-sided historic marker commemorates two local sports legends. Sam Jones, dubbed "Sad Sam" by a New York sportswriter who thought he always looked downcast, pitched for 22 seasons in the American League. Jones' signature season was 1923, when he finished 21-8 for the New York Yankees and threw a no-hitter against the Philadelphia Athletics. The Yankees won their first World Series that year (beating the Giants) and Jones' relief effort helped the Yanks secure their Game 6 clincher. Despite his nickname, the 229-game career winner was actually a whimsical and humorous man.

Mary Weddle-Hines played for the Fort Wayne Daisies of the All-American Girls Professional Baseball League in 1954. A trailblazer for women athletes, Weddle-Hines originally played professional softball before joining the Daisies. She was one of about 600 women to play in the league.

Keep your eyes peeled for...

- The Westville Sign at the edge of town reading "Hometown of Harvey Haddix."

- The Bob Feller statue positioned outside of Cleveland's Jacobs Field.

Hall of Famers buried in Ohio

William "Buck" Ewing
Mount Washington Cemetery,
Mount Washington

Waite Hoyt and Miller Huggins
Spring Grove Cemetery
4521 Spring Grove Avenue
Cincinnati

Walter Alston
Darrtown Cemetery
Shollenbarger Road
Darrtown

Eppa Rixey
Green Lawn Cemetery
687 U. S. Highway 50
Milford

Cleveland Metro Area

Red Ruffing
Hillcrest Memorial Park
26700 Aurora Road
Bedford Heights

Ed Delahanty
Calvary Cemetery
10000 Miles Avenue
Cleveland

Billy Evans
Knollwood Cemetery
1678 Som Center Road
Mayfield Heights

Elmer Flick
Crown Hill Cemetery
8592 Darrow Road
Twinsburg

Jesse Haines
Bethel Cemetery
Phillipsburg Road
Phillipsburg

Roger Bresnahan
Calvary Cemetery
2224 Dorr Street
Toledo

Addie Joss
Woodlawn Cemetery
1502 W. Central Avenue
Toledo

Waite Hoyt, Miller Huggins, Eppa Rixey and Jesse Haines (top to bottom).

Oklahoma

Shrine to Mickey Mantle

A video store in Grove celebrates the career of Mickey Mantle, who hailed from Commerce.

City: Grove
Location: Hollywood   at Home Video Store
536 West 3rd Street, Suite 7

Terry and Valerie Hembree were close friends of "The Mick." For 12 years, they helped coordinate his marketing and charity efforts and over the years acquired numerous artifacts from their pal. Today, this dedicated husband and wife make it possible for everyone to enjoy their one-of-a-kind collection of Mickey Mantle memorabilia at the video store they run in Grove. This exhibit features thousands of items dedicated to the memory of Mantle, including memorabilia from his younger days in Commerce and his pre-professional days with the Baxter Springs Whiz Kids. Also highlighted are details of his New York Yankees career, numerous statues and figurines, balls, bats, gloves, jerseys, collector's items, autographed items and a variety of baseball cards from every era. TV monitors play Mantle game highlights, with interviews and stories told by Mick himself. And keep your eyes open when you visit—you might see an old ballplayer or two, both former teammates and opponents who have been known to drop in unexpectedly.

Some other Mantle related sites in Oklahoma...

- Mickey Mantle's boyhood home, 316 S. Quincy Street, Commerce.

- Commerce High School at 420 D St. in Commerce. This is where Mantle attended high school. In 2000, a ceremony was held to name the baseball field "Mickey Mantle Field."

- Mickey Mantle Boulevard. This road, which passes within a few blocks of Mantle's boyhood home, is a re-named section of U.S. 69.

- Portrait of Mickey Mantle at the State Capitol Building in Oklahoma City. Several years ago, a portrait of Mickey Mantle was unveiled at the capitol on the fourth-floor rotunda of the building.

Oklahoma Sports Museum

City: Guthrie
Location: 315 West Oklahoma Avenue

Opened in 1996, this 30,000-square-foot museum has a remarkable number of items staked in the rich heritage of Oklahoma baseball. Tributes are paid to all Oklahoma-related Hall of Famers, including Mickey Mantle, Ferguson Jenkins, Paul and Lloyd Waner, Carl Hubbell, Willie Stargell and Warren Spahn. The museum gives out the "Warren Spahn Award" to the major leagues' most dominant lefthanded pitcher. Throughout the museum are historic baseball items, including Pepper Martin's 1931 World Series jacket and Bobby Murcer's rocking chair, which used to sit beside his locker at Yankee Stadium. Hundreds of jerseys, bats and balls also are on display.

The Oklahoma Sports Museum in Guthrie honors Oklahoma baseball legends, including Mickey Mantle, Carl Hubbell and Warren Spahn.

Waner Park

City: Harrah
Location: Right off 23rd Street and Peebly Road

Lloyd and Paul Waner, both Hall of Famers, hail from Harrah. It's no surprise that the Little League field, the same area where they played as kids, is named for them. Their combined total of 5,611 hits are a record for major league brothers—Paul with 3,152, Lloyd with 2,459. For a good part of their careers in the 1920s and '30s, the brothers formed two-thirds of the Pittsburgh Pirates outfield.

Lloyd Waner is buried at:
Rose Hill Burial Park
6001 NW Grand Blvd
Oklahoma City

Carl Hubbell exhibit

City: Meeker
Location: Meeker City Hall
West Main Street

Meeker, the birthplace of Carl Hubbell, honors the pitching great with a welcome sign and an exhibit at city hall.

In addition to the sign that welcomes visitors to Hubbell's hometown, there also is an exhibit for him at the local city hall. Hubbell, the Hall of Fame lefthander known for his devastating screwball, played 16 seasons for the New York Giants (1928-43), winning 253 games. Visitors to city hall can see many Hubbell artifacts, including his personal scrapbook and a collection of baseballs autographed by such contemporaries as Babe Ruth and Lou Gehrig.

Carl Hubbell is buried at:
Meeker New Hope
State Highway 18 (1 mile south of U.S. Hwy. 62)
Meeker

Mickey Mantle and Johnny Bench statues

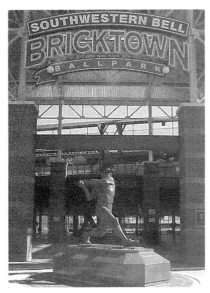

City: Oklahoma City
Location: Bricktown Ballpark
2 S. Mickey Mantle Dr.

"The Brick," as Southwestern Bell Bricktown Ballpark is informally known, opened in 1998 and is home to the Pacific Coast League's Oklahoma Redhawks. The Brick is a gorgeous, retro park where fans can get close to the action. Oklahoma legends Mantle and Bench are honored by statues outside the park. The Mantle display also includes his handprints in cement.

Statues of Mickey Mantle (above) and Johnny Bench greet visitors at 'The Brick' in Oklahoma City.

Jim Thorpe birthplace

City: Prague
Location: S. on Hwy. 99 to Moccasin Trail, 5 miles West and 1 mile South.

(Note: turn South 1 mile West after you pass the Pleasant Home Baptist Church.)

An historic marker identifies where the great Thorpe was born on May 28, 1887. The short "Jim Thorpe Road" is about a half mile from the marker, just south of Prague near State Highway 99.

Jim Thorpe monument

City: Prague
Location: Prague Historical Museum
Junction of Hwy. 62 & Hwy. 99

Outside this museum, which also sells Thorpe-related books, postcards, etc., is an historic marker identifying the area as Jim Thorpe's hometown.

Jim Thorpe's former Yale home is near his hometown of Prague.

Jim Thorpe home

City: Yale
Location: 706 E. Boston

The legendary Olympian, baseball and football star lived in this house from 1917-23. Thorpe, who is better known for his ties to college and professional football, played six years of major league baseball for the Giants, Reds and Braves. Many sports awards and family items are on display. The home, which he purchased for his family, is located near his birthplace in Prague. About 100 yards away from the home is State Highway 51, also called the "Jim Thorpe Memorial Highway."

Keep your eyes peeled for...

• A sign in Binger announcing it as hometown of Johnny Bench.

• A sign in Meeker announcing it as hometown of Carl Hubbell.

• Joe Carter Avenue in Oklahoma City.

Hall of Famers buried in Oklahoma

Joe McGinnity
Oak Hill Cemetery
1311 East Washington
McAlester

Joe McGinnity won 20 or more games seven times.

South Dakota

Babe Ruth stayed here

City: Deadwood
Location: Historic Franklin Hotel
700 Main Street
Built in 1903, the Historic Franklin Hotel has played host to thousands of famous and infamous people. It was during a 1921 barnstorming tour that Babe Ruth first stayed at the Franklin, which is located in one of the oldest active gold-mining towns in the country. Ruth played at the nearby First Ward Rodeo Grounds, where a baseball diamond still exists. To honor some of the its many famous guests, the Franklin Hotel has a number of "historic" rooms that are themed after the celebrities, both sports and otherwise, who slept there. Room 209 is the Babe Ruth room, and it comes complete with photos and other Ruth-related items. Rooms also are named after boxers Jack Dempsey and John L. Sullivan.

South Dakota Amateur Baseball Hall of Fame

City: Lake Norden
Location: 519 Main Street
605-785-3553
This small museum offers a pictorial history of the amateur game in South Dakota. It also has artifacts from about half of the 24 big leaguers who were born in the state. There also is archival material and memorabilia relating to the history of amateur baseball in South Dakota since 1900.

The birth of American Legion Baseball

City: Milbank
Location: Next to the Unity Square Athletic Complex
904 4th Avenue East (Highway 12)
American Legion Baseball was born here in 1925 and an historical marker commemorates the event near the community baseball field. A portion of the inscription reads, "In this city on July 17, 1925, by action of the South Dakota Department of the American Legion, the nationwide organization of Legion Junior Baseball was first proposed as a program of service to the youth of America." Since 1926, the league's first official year, millions of teenagers have played in the renowned national youth league, including such Hall of Famers as George Brett, Richie Ashburn, Reggie Jackson, Joe Morgan, Johnny Bench, Don Drysdale, Brooks Robinson, Ted Williams and Stan Musial.

Renovated Sioux Falls Stadium is an ideal place to go on a warm summer evening to watch the local Canaries.

Sioux Falls Stadium

City: Sioux Falls

Location: 1001 N. West Ave.

Built in 1941, Sioux Falls Stadium is nicknamed "The Birdcage" in honor of the Northern League's Canaries who play there. Baseball in Sioux Falls dates back to 1885, with the "Canaries" making their first appearance in 1889. The Sioux Falls team of that era wore bright yellow uniforms and were called the "Yellow Kids," in honor of the well-known "Yellow Kid" promoted by the William Randolph Hearst newspapers (and whose comic appeared in the *Sioux Falls Press*). When a local sportswriter suggested the team change its name to Canaries, the moniker stuck. This park was home to the Northern League Canaries in 1942 and again from 1946-53. The city went without a franchise until 1966, when the Sioux Falls Packers began play. The Packers ceased operations after the 1971 campaign and the park was used sparingly until 1993, when the independent Northern League was formed. Extensive renovations to the park began in 1999 and were completed two years later. Today, the stadium is testament to the proper blending of modern conveniences within a classic, throwback structure. Photographs throughout the park document its long and colorful history.

The Burleigh Grimes exhibit at the Clear Lake museum commemorates the 19-year career of one of baseball's last legal spitballers.

Wisconsin

Burleigh Grimes exhibit

City: Clear Lake

Location: One floor of the Clear Lake Area Historical Museum

450 Fifth Avenue

Open from Memorial Day through Labor Day, the Burleigh Grimes exhibit has been on display in his hometown for three decades. When he retired in 1934, Grimes was the last of the legal spitballers, a fiery and competitive pitcher for seven different teams. Over his 19 big-league seasons, Grimes topped the 20-win plateau five times and posted a 270-212 record. He was just 26 when the spitter, his money pitch, was banned in 1920. But he was one of 17 pitchers who were exempted from the ban because of their veteran status. Grimes relied on the pitch for the rest of his career. The museum exhibit, lovingly maintained by several of Grimes' old friends, is loaded with memorabilia. Grimes was inducted into the Hall of Fame in 1964 and died in Clear Lake on December 6, 1985, at the age of 92. He is buried at:

Clear Lake Cemetery

5th Street and South Avenue West (Veterans Memorial Drive)

Clear Lake

Baseball great Hank Aaron was on hand for the dedication of his statue in 1994, where he made his pro debut.

The professional debut of Hank Aaron

City: Eau Claire
Location: Carson Park Stadium

Carson Park is a 130.6-acre park located on Half Moon Lake with access from Lake Street or Menomonie Street.

Carson Park Stadium is where Hank Aaron began his career for minor league Eau Claire in 1952. A statue of Aaron outside the stadium commemorates this, as well as the first professional home run he hit here. Before coming to Eau Claire, Aaron played for the Negro League's Indianapolis Clowns. But he signed with the Boston Braves in June of 1952 and was assigned to Eau Claire. In his one season at Eau Claire, Aaron batted .336 and hit nine home runs in 87 games. The future Hall of Famer also was chosen to play for the Northern League's All-Star team and earned rookie of the year honors. Fittingly, Aaron returned in 1994 for the dedication of his statue. The stadium dates back to 1937 when it served the Northern League's Eau Claire Bears and, later, the Eau Claire Braves. Carson Park Stadium today hosts the amateur Eau Claire Cavaliers, American Legion baseball, Little League and several high school teams.

Addie Joss exhibit

City: Juneau
Location: Juneau City Park
Lincoln drive near Mill Street

At the Community Center in this quaint city park is a display dedicated to local legend Addie Joss, who pitched for the Cleveland Indians from 1902-11. Joss, acknowledged as one of the greatest pitchers of his era, was cut down in the prime of his career. He pitched nine seasons before dying suddenly, at age

31, of tubercular meningitis. His trademark pinwheel, sidearming delivery baffled hitters and helped Joss post four straight 20-win seasons. Included among his 160 career victories was the second perfect game of the century in 1908, another no-hitter in 1910 and 45 shutouts. Joss, who was elected to the Hall of Fame in 1978, is honored by an historic marker and a baseball field that bears his name.

The "American League" is born

City: Milwaukee
Location: Republican House Hotel (former site)
Corner of 3rd and Kilbourn
The grand Republican House Hotel stood at this location from 1885-1961. On March 5, 1900 (in room 185), it was the location for an important meeting that altered the course of baseball history. Five representatives of the former Western League (including Ban Johnson and White Sox owner Charles Comiskey) met here and finalized plans to change the name of their eight-team alignment to the "American League." After the 1900 season, the new "major league" was ready to challenge the longstanding National League for players and prestige. An historic marker was dedicated here in July, 2001, to coincide with the centennial of the A.L.

Former site of County Stadium

City: Milwaukee
Location: One Brewers Way
Helfaer Field

The former County Stadium, now the site of Helfaer Field, has become a haven for youth baseball and softball in the shadow of Miller Park.

County Stadium opened in 1953—the first ballpark built with lights and the first built entirely with public funds. Three days after opening to the public, County became a major league park when the Braves announced they would relocate there from Boston; in 1970, five years after the Braves had moved to Atlanta, the American League's Brewers relocated to Milwaukee from Seattle and played at County Stadium through 2000, at which time the aging structure was demolished.

Some of the many great moments at County Stadium:

- September 23, 1957: Hank Aaron gave Milwaukee its first pennant with an 11th-inning home run against St. Louis.

- May 26, 1959: Twelve innings of perfection went for naught when Pittsburgh's Harvey Haddix lost to the Braves in the 13th.

- April 30, 1961: Giants center fielder Willie Mays hit four home runs in a 14-4 win over the Braves.

- September 9, 1992: Robin Yount collected his 3000th career hit in a 5-4 loss to Cleveland.

Baseball is still played on the grounds where County Stadium once stood. Helfaer Field, a beautiful youth baseball and softball facility built in the shadow of new Miller Park, provides a nostalgic reminder of days gone by. Just off the concourse down the third-base line, fans can visit a memorial to the 192 men who played for the Milwaukee Braves from 1953-65. A few steps away, the exact site of home plate at County Stadium is marked. And over the outfield wall sits a monument to the Miller Park workers who died in a construction accident as well as bronze statues of Hall of Famers Hank Aaron and Robin Yount and a

Horlick Field in Racine was home for the Racine Belles of the All-American Girls Professional Baseball League.

series of tributes to other Brewers stars. Helfaer Field has 502 bleacher seats and additional concourse seating of 220. It has quickly become the premier location for youth baseball and girls softball in Milwaukee.

Horlick Field

City: Racine
Location: 1648 N. Memorial Drive, on the corner of High Street and North Memorial Drive.

Although football was played here as early as 1922 (as the home field for the Racine Horlick Legion) and is still played by several high schools, there is some great baseball history, too. In 1943, the year the All-American Girls Professional Baseball League was formed, the Racine Belles moved in. One of four charter franchises (along with the Rockford Peaches, Kenosha Comets and South Bend Blue Sox), the legendary Belles played here until 1950. Today, though the field has been modified to accommodate football, baseball is still played by various amateur leagues. If you poke around, you'll find the original left-center field distance marker still standing in the southeast corner of the park, hidden beyond the east football grandstand. A bronze plaque at the original entrance commemorates the Belles' history in the park.

Hall of Famers buried in Wisconsin

Al Simmons
St. Adalbert's Cemetery
3801 South 6th Street
Milwaukee

Dave "Beauty" Bancroft
Greenwood Cemetery
8402 Tower Avenue
Superior

Al Simmons (top) had a lifetime batting average of .334. Dave Bancroft led the league in putouts by a shortstop four straight years.

·

The West

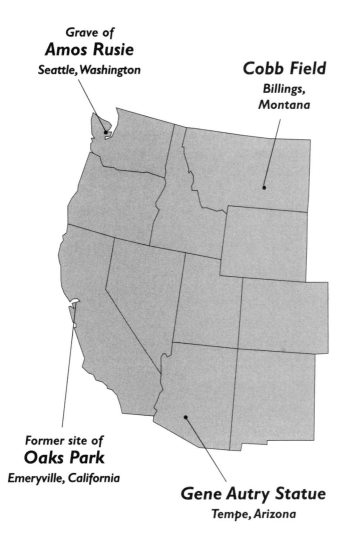

Grave of
Amos Rusie
Seattle, Washington

Cobb Field
Billings,
Montana

Former site of
Oaks Park
Emeryville, California

Gene Autry Statue
Tempe, Arizona

Arizona

Warren Ballpark

City: Bisbee
Location: Ruppe Avenue between Bisbee Road and Arizona Street
(About 10 miles north of the U.S.-Mexico border in Southeast Arizona)

The first professional ballpark in Arizona is still in use today. Warren Ballpark actually is one of the oldest professional parks in the United States, dating back to June 27, 1909, when a local Bisbee team beat a team from El Paso, 8-3. In 1913, the New York Giants and Chicago White Sox stopped there as part of their world barnstorming tour, and from 1928-55, Class C and D minor league teams played there. In 1930, the original wooden grandstand was replaced with concrete and steel. An historic plaque was placed at the ballpark in 1994 by the city of Bisbee and high school teams play there today.

Former site of Francisco Grande Baseball Complex

City: Casa Grande
Location: 26000 Gila Bend Highway

The Giants trained at Casa Grande for 23 years before moving to Scottsdale in 1984. The complex included a cloverleaf of baseball diamonds, which still are there—often covered with golf balls from a nearby driving range. The big field where Willie Mays and Willie McCovey once played now is covered with weeds. The bleachers are gone, but two concrete ramps that once led to the seating area still remain—ruins that provide a small hint of what

Willie Mays, Willie McCovey and Orlando Cepeda once graced the fields at Francisco Grande.

once was. The golf resort that occupies the nearby property keeps an autographed photo of Mays hanging in the bar, as well as a few other baseball momentos from the Francisco Grande Baseball Complex.

Former site of Rendezvous Park

City: Mesa
Location: 3rd Street and Center
The Chicago Cubs left California's Catalina Island to train in the desert back in 1952. Ernie Banks played many games here before the Cubs left in 1966. The park sat vacant until Charlie Finley moved the Oakland A's spring base to Mesa in 1969. But the A's have been gone since 1976 and the former Rendezvous Park now is the site of the Mesa Convention and Visitors Bureau.

Don & Charlie's memorabilia collection includes a Comiskey seat.

Don & Charlie's

City: Scottsdale
Location: 7501 E. Camelback Road
480-990-0900
Chicago native Don Carson opened his eatery here in 1981 and it has grown into a tourist attraction—for its great food as well as its sports memorabilia, particularly items having to do with baseball. Adorning the walls in every room of the spacious restaurant are hundreds of signed baseballs, jerseys, bats, mitts and more. There's a seat from old Comiskey Park right by the front door, signed photographs and artwork—it's as much a sports museum as a restaurant and well worth a visit after a Cactus League game. During spring training, the restaurant is a favorite haunt of players, coaches, managers and umpires. Don and Charlie's is open daily from 5-10 p.m.

Former site of Sun City Stadium

City: Sun City
Location: 111th and Grand Avenue
The Milwaukee Brewers trained here from 1973-85. Rookies Robin Yount and Paul Molitor started out here; Hank Aaron spent his last spring training here (1976). Torn down in 1996, it now is the location for an apartment complex.

Gene Autry statue

City: Tempe
Location: Tempe Diablo Stadium
2200 West Alameda Drive

Just inside the main entrance to the spring training home of the Anaheim Angels, appropriately, is a bronze bust of longtime owner Gene Autry. The popular cowboy singer and actor, who made 95 movies and recorded several hit songs, owned the Anaheim franchise for 38 years after retiring from Hollywood and he watched his Angels win three pennants, but never a World Series. Autry also is saluted at Edison International Field in Anaheim (where the Angels play their regular-season games) with a retired No. 26, symbolic of his honorary status as the team's 26th

The Cowboy still watches over spring activities in Tempe.

player. Next to the bronze bust in Tempe is a wall that displays the Gene Autry "Courage Awards."

Hi Corbett Field

City: Tucson
Location: 3400 E. Camino Campestre
Randolph Park
602-327-9467

Historic Hi Corbett Field has served as a spring training facility since 1945. Named in honor of prominent Tucson resident Hi Corbett, who was instrumental in bringing major league spring training games to Tucson and Phoenix, the park was spring home for the Cleveland Indians from 1945-92 (Corbett was a close friend of former Indians owner Bill Veeck) and the current Cactus League home of the Colorado Rockies, who moved in to the complex as a 1993 expansion team. The Class AAA Tucson Toros of the Pacific Coast League played at Hi Corbett Field from 1969-98, but now play (as the Tucson Sidewinders) at new Tucson Electric Park, which is shared by the Arizona Diamondbacks and Chicago White Sox as a spring training facility. Despite significant renovations over the years, Hi Corbett Field still maintains its "old time" flavor.

The Cactus League has been operating in Arizona long enough to have produced some of its own "Lost Ballpark" sites—places where legends of the game once roamed.

Keep your eyes peeled for ...

- The statue outside Phoenix's Bank One Ballpark on Seventh Street, the one of the Arizona ballplayer signing an autograph for a young fan. Around the corner, near the ballpark's main rotunda, are showcases displaying memorabilia from the 2001 World Series, Arizona's dramatic seven-game victory over the New York Yankees.

An autograph-signing player serves as a constant reminder and mission statement outside Bank One Ballpark in Phoenix.

- "Diamonds Back" Youth Fields are sponsored by the Arizona Diamondbacks. There are currently seven youth ball fields in the Phoenix area that have been created as part of this charitable program:

  Curt Schilling Field
  Indian Bend Elementary School
  Phoenix
  This is where the Diamondbacks' star pitcher attended school as a child.

  Brian Anderson Field
  Lions Park
  Guadalupe

  Jay Bell Field
  Gateway Elementary School
  Phoenix

  Matt Williams Field
  Simpson Elementary School
  Phoenix

Randy Johnson Field of Dreams
East Lake Park
Phoenix

Steve Finley Field
Smith Park (southeast corner of
41st Avenue and Grant Street)
Phoenix

Todd Stottlemyre Field
Guadalupe

Hall of Famers buried in Arizona

Jocko Conlan
Green Acres Cemetery
401 N. Hayden Road
Scottsdale
480-945-2654

Jocko Conlon

California

Gene Autry statue

City: Anaheim
Location: Edison International Field
2000 Gene Autry Way
714-634-2000
At the stadium's Gate 2 entrance, former Angels owner Gene Autry is immortalized with a life-size bronze statue and plaque. In front of the stadium, under the giant helmets, are the handprints of six former Angels players cemented in the stadium courtyard: Bobby Grich, Bob Boone, Reggie Jackson, Rod Carew, Don Sutton and Jim Fregosi. Just inside Gate 4 is a beautiful statue honoring Michelle Carew, Rod Carew's daughter who died in 1996.

Site where famous Japanese-American baseball team played

City: Anaheim
Location: 2179 Clement Avenue

From 1916-38, this was the location of the Alameda Japanese American ATK baseball field. Games were played on weekends against other Japanese-American and semi-pro teams, and the park served both as a recreational and social gathering place for the Japanese community. Today it's the site of the AAAAA Storage facility and the historic plaque that's here, dedicated in 1992, marks the approximate location of home plate.

La Palma Park

City: Anaheim
Location: Harbor Boulevard

Built in 1939, La Palma Park (known today as Glover Stadium/Dee Fee Field) was a spring training host for the Seattle Rainiers (of the Pacific Coast League) that year. The St. Louis Browns trained there in 1946, and Connie Mack brought his Philadelphia Athletics to La Palma in the springs of 1940, '41 and '43. During World War II, Joe DiMaggio played several games at La Palma as a member of his airbase team (he was stationed at nearby Santa Ana Army Air Base). Today the field is used for local leagues, including high school and college games.

The grandstand at Pearson Park captures the ambience of a throwback field of dreams.

Pearson Park Grandstands

City: Anaheim
Location: Lincoln and Harbor Boulevards

Since the early 1920s, locals have gathered at this park to watch amateur and semi-pro baseball. Connie Mack's Athletics also would travel down the street from La Palma Park and play here during their spring training stays in the 1940s. Although the Park's grandstand has undergone some major renovation work over the years, it remains a beautifully maintained example of an old-time baseball structure.

Babe Ruth and Walter Johnson game

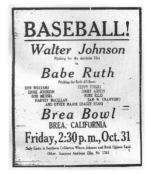

City: Brea
Location: Brea Bowl (former site)
Gateway Shopping Center
401 West Imperial Highway
On October 31, 1924, Babe Ruth and Walter Johnson played a barnstorming game that has become a part of the area's folklore. Sponsored by the Anaheim Elks Club, it was a homecoming of sorts for Johnson, who grew up in the neighboring oil town of Olinda. About 5,000 people turned out at Brea Bowl field, more than double nearby Anaheim's total population of 2,000 at that time. Ruth's team won, 12-1, and the day was capped by two Ruth home runs (one that reportedly traveled 550 feet). The game was documented, remarkably, by an 18-year old named George E. Outland, who made a hobby of photographing players and getting many of his shots autographed. A poster promoting the event (top right) touts it as the "only game in Southern California where Johnson and Ruth oppose each other." Today, the site of the Brea Bowl is the Gateway Shopping Center.

Former site of Olive Memorial Stadium

City: Burbank
Location: George Izay Park
West Olive Ave. and Mariposa Streets
818-238-5300
Olive Memorial Stadium was the spring training home of the St. Louis Browns from 1949-52. The Browns' spring games drew such celebrities as Bob Hope and Nat King Cole and featured various visiting professional stars, from Satchel Paige, Luke Appling and Nellie Fox to Ralph Kiner and Willie Mays. The ballpark, after enduring years of structural damage from earthquakes, was razed in 1994, but the diamond still remains. The war memorial plaques that once adorned the outside stadium have been remounted near where the grandstand once stood.

Big League Dreams Sportsparks

City: Cathedral City
Location: 33700 Date Palm Drive
760-324-5600

Big Dreamers can experience what it was like to play at some of baseball's most historic ballparks, including the former New York Polo Grounds.

City: Mira Loma (Riverside area)
Location: 10550 Galena Street
909-685-6900
City: Chino Hills
Location: 16333 Fairfield Ranch
909-287-6900

This recreational facility offers playing fields for everything from volleyball to flag football, but it is best known for baseball/softball fields designed as replicas of historic major league stadiums. Both youth and adults can play on a replica of Chicago's Wrigley Field, New York's Yankee Stadium, Boston's Fenway Park, New York's Polo Grounds, Pittsburgh's Forbes Field, Brooklyn's Ebbets Field, Detroit's Tiger Stadium and Cincinnati's Crosley Field. The dream of brothers Rick and Jeff Odekirk, both former players, was to create an environment that would give players the chance to experience baseball on a field of their dreams. Judging from the popularity of these fields, they succeeded.

Babe Ruth marker

City: Dunsmuir
Location: Dunsmuir City Field
Dunsmuir Avenue, toward the northern end of town

On October 22, 1924, Babe Ruth played an exhibition game in Dunsmuir, a logging town located about 98 miles south of the Oregon border. It was part of his nationwide barnstorming tour and the Bambino was joined by Yankees teammate Bob Meusel. The game was sponsored by the Dunsmuir Lions Club and drew about 900 fans. Following his appearance, Ruth wrote the town the following letter (excerpted from the Dunsmuir Centennial Book):

"To everybody (and that means everybody) in Dunsmuir, Calif. We don't know yet how to tell you what a wonderful time we had in Dunsmuir. ... When it comes to beautiful girls, wonderfully fine fellows, and the real two-fisted spirit of California—little Dunsmuir gave us more laughs, more hospitality, more thrills, and more things to remember than any place between Broadway & Shasta."

The field where the game took place still stands and today is used by the Dunsmuir High School Tigers. A commemorative marker honors Ruth at the field.

George Brett Field

City: El Segundo
Location: Recreation Park
Corner of Pine and Eucalyptus streets
Located a few blocks from where the former Kansas City Royals slugger went to high school, this field was dedicated on April 24, 1999, to Brett, who returned for the ceremony. Brett's three brothers, all of whom played professional baseball, also attended El Segundo High.

Former site of Oaks Park

City: Emeryville (between Oakland and Berkeley)
Location: 1120 Park Avenue
From 1913-57 this was the site of Oaks Park, also called Emeryville Park, the home of the Pacific Coast League's Oakland Oaks. It was torn down in 1957 to clear the way for a Pepsi-Cola bottling plant, which in time would also be torn down to make way for a Pixar Animation Studio. A plaque marks the location.

Walter Johnson's Alma Mater

City: Fullerton
Location: Fullerton Union High School
201 East Chapman Avenue
714-626-3801
Walter Johnson attended high school at Fullerton, graduating in 1905, and is represented on the school's "Wall of Fame." Other former players who attended the school and are honored on the wall are Pirates shortstop Arky

Vaughan (class of 1930) and Braves catcher Del Crandall (class of 1947). Other notable school graduates and Wall of Fame members include Richard Nixon (class of 1927-28) and guitar legend Leo Fender (class of 1932.)

Walter Johnson Athletic Field

City: Fullerton
Location: Ted Craig Regional Park
3300 State College Blvd.
714- 990-0271
This baseball complex, named for the former Washington Senators pitching great, is located near the former site of the Brea Bowl. Johnson, who spent a portion of his youth in nearby Olinda, also has a street (Walter Johnson Lane) named in his honor.

Jackie Robinson Stadium

City: Los Angeles
Location: UCLA
Constitution Avenue
From 405 South: Exit Wilshire Blvd. east. Turn left onto Sepulveda Blvd. Turn left onto Constitution Ave. The stadium is on the right.
From 405 North: Exit Montana Ave. Turn right onto Sepulveda Ave. Turn right onto Constitution Ave.
The UCLA stadium is named for alumnus Jackie Robinson, who broke baseball's color barrier when he joined the Brooklyn Dodgers in 1947. Robinson was a four-sport letterman at UCLA, an outstanding athlete who competed in football, basketball, track and baseball before beginning his pioneering social efforts and journey to the Hall of Fame. A bronze statue of Robinson is located near the concession stand on the concourse level of Jackie Robinson Stadium. The statue was dedicated on April 27, 1985, before a UCLA-Arizona State game. The statue dedication was made almost 13 years after Robinson's death.

Former site of Wrigley Field

City: Los Angeles
Location: 42nd Street and Avalon
The "other" Wrigley Field opened on April 27, 1925, at the corner of Avalon Street and 42nd Place in South Central Los Angeles. Owned by chewing gum magnate William Wrigley, it was partially modeled after Chicago's Wrigley Field, although the Los Angeles facility was called Wrigley Field first (Chicago's park got its name in 1926). Wrigley owned two minor league teams in Southern

Wrigley's former center field is still grass covered, but now it's on the grounds of a hospital.

California—the Los Angeles Angels and the Hollywood Stars—and both played at Wrigley at various times. Wrigley Field was home of the Angels from 1925-57; the Stars played here from 1926-35 and 1938. Given it's proximity to Hollywood, Wrigley Field was used for such 1940s and '50s movies as *Pride of the Yankees, The Kid From Left Field, Damn Yankees, It Happens Every Spring and The Geisha Boy.* An episode of *The Munsters* was filmed here, and millions of fans became familiar with Wrigley thanks to the 1960s television show *Home Run Derby.* The park's only brush with major league baseball came in 1961, when the expansion Angels played their games there. Friendly Wrigley yielded 248 home runs that season, more than any other ballpark in big-league history. The last game was played at Wrigley Field on October 1, 1961, and the stadium was demolished in 1966. The former site of Wrigley Field today is occupied by a public park and recreation center, a community mental health center and a senior citizens center. Although there is no plaque or marker, most of the houses beyond the left field wall, the ones so visible during *Home Run Derby,* still remain.

Former site of Gilmore Field

City: Los Angeles
Location: CBS Television City
7800 Beverly Boulevard

Gilmore Field was constructed in 1938 for the Hollywood Stars, a minor league team owned by such celebrities as Bing Crosby, Gracie Allen, William Frawley, Walt Disney and Cecil B. DeMille. Maybe the most intimate baseball venue ever designed (home plate was only 34 feet from the fans; first and third bases only 24 feet away), Gilmore Field was as much a place for star gazing as baseball. When it opened on May 2, 1939, Jack Benny, Al Jolsen, Gary Cooper, Robert Taylor and Bing Crosby were on hand for pregame festivities; starlet and co-owner Gail Patrick threw out the first pitch to comedian Joe E. Brown. A special VIP room under the stands made it easy for celebrities to socialize in private. Gilmore Field was torn down in 1958 and all that remains is a row of palm trees that traced the line beyond where the left field wall once stood. An historical marker, with some photos of old Gilmore Park, are displayed near the location of its former front entrance, on the wall of Studio 46.

Los Angeles Coliseum

City: Los Angeles
Location: 3911 South Figueroa Street

It is best remembered as the host site for two Summer Olympics (1932 and '84) and the setting for numerous college and pro football games as well as other sports and nonsports events. But the Los Angeles Coliseum also served as home for the Los Angeles Dodgers from 1958-61. After moving to Los Angeles from Brooklyn, the Dodgers played there while Dodger Stadium was being built. With the Coliseum's huge capacity (93,600) and the sudden demand for professional baseball, the Dodgers topped 2 million in attendance in 1959 and '60 while enduring criticism for playing in a football stadium that was ill-suited for baseball. The difficult proposition of fitting a diamond into a horseshoe-shaped facility resulted in a left field line that was 251 feet from the plate, a pitcher's nightmare that was only partially alleviated by a 40-foot screen. A temporary right field fence cut off fans seated at the far end of the horseshoe. A plaque mounted on the famous Coliseum arches commemorates the Dodgers' victory over the Chicago White Sox in the 1959 World Series. The Game 5 attendance of 92,706 is a still-standing postseason record. But it can't match the 93,103 who turned out on May 7, 1959, for an exhibition game between the Dodgers and Yankees to honor former catcher Roy Campanella, who was confined to a wheelchair after a paralyzing car accident. It

The massive Los Angeles Coliseum was a temporary baseball home for the Dodgers.

still ranks as the largest crowd to witness a major league game. In a pregame ceremony, Campanella was wheeled out to second base by his long-time teammate, shortstop Pee Wee Reese. College football is the primary sport played today at this venerable Los Angeles landmark.

Joe DiMaggio's boat

City: Martinez
Location: Martinez Marina Park
North of downtown Martinez at the foot of Ferry Street, near Amtrak's Martinez train station
Joe DiMaggio was born in Martinez on November 25, 1914. You can see DiMaggio's yacht, the "Joltin' Joe," on display at the Martinez Marina Park. The boat was a gift to DiMaggio from the Yankees, presented to him on Joe DiMaggio Day at the end of the 1949 season. DiMaggio, despite being ill, got two hits to help the Yankees beat Boston that afternoon, setting up New York's pennant-clinching season finale the next afternoon. DiMaggio retired to the Bay Area after his storied career and often used his boat for short trips with then-wife Marilyn Monroe. Years later, he donated the boat to the city. A plaque on the boat describes some of its history.

Joe DiMaggio exhibit

City: Martinez
Location: Martinez Museum
1005 Excobar Street
925-228-8160
Also in DiMaggio's hometown at the Martinez Museum, there is a small display of DiMaggio items, including his 1914 birth certificate.

Hans Lobert races a horse

City: Oxnard
Location: E Street and Wooley Road, near Oriffill School
On November 11, 1913, the New York Giants and Chicago White Sox played a game in this small coastal town as part of their worldwide barnstorming tour. The teams stopped at Oxnard because it was the hometown area of Giants outfielder Fred Snodgrass. Players and managers, including such greats as John McGraw, Christy Mathewson, Tris Speaker, Hal Chase, Fred Merkle and Sam Crawford, were treated like royalty when they arrived by train for the big game and, after a ceremonial barbecue, the teams made their way to a newly built grandstand where thousands of people from all over Southern California

had gathered to watch them play. The Giants won the game, 3-2, but an event that followed the game made much bigger news—a match race around the bases between Hans Lobert, a speedy third baseman playing with the Giants on the tour, and a horse. Umpire Bill Klem signaled the start and the race was on. Lobert led rounding second, but the horse bumped him near shortstop and took the lead. Lobert lost by a nose. The event was captured by newsreel cameras and shown all over the country. The field where the game and the race took place still exists, as part of the Oriffill School in Oxnard.

Jackie and Mack Robinson are memorialized by bronze sculptures in Pasadena.

Robinson memorial

City: Pasadena

Location: Located on Garfield Avenue, north of Union Street, across the street from City Hall.

Dedicated November 6, 1997, these two huge bronze sculptures commemorate the lives of brothers, Jackie and Mack Robinson, who grew up in Pasadena. Jackie, of course, went on to fame as the man who broke baseball's color barrier in 1947 when he joined the Brooklyn Dodgers. But Mack enjoyed a little athletic success of his own—a silver medal in the 200-meter race at the 1936 Olympics in Berlin.

Former site of Jackie Robinson's home

City: Pasadena

Location: 121 Pepper Street

In 1920, an uncle in Pasadena invited Mollie Robinson and her five children to leave Cairo, Georgia, and live with him. Mollie's husband had abandoned her, so she packed up Edgar, Frank, Mack, Jackie and Willa Mae and headed west to this spot, where a four-bedroom cottage once sat. The Robinson family lived at this address for 24 years. Jackie, who ran with the "Pepper Street Gang" for a time, went on to graduate from Washington Junior and Muir Technical High School. He then attended two-year Pasadena Junior College, where he starred in football, track and baseball. The next year he entered UCLA. The marker sits on the sidewalk in front of a vacant lot where the house once stood.

Jack Benny Statue

City: Rancho Cucamonga
Location: The Epicenter
Rochester Avenue off Foothill Boulevard
On the old Jack Benny television show, a train conductor routinely called out the stops of "Anaheim, Azuza and … Cucamonga." So, in tribute to the famed comedian, the Rancho Cucamonga Quakes erected a life-size bronze statue of Benny at the main entrance to their park and even named the ballpark's main street "Rochester," a tribute to Benny's sidekick. The Quakes are the Class A California League affiliate of the Anaheim Angels and this impressive minor league park opened in 1993.

The White Sox Redwood

City: Riverside
Location: Low Park near the corner of Arlington and Magnolia
On Arbor Day, 1914, members of the Chicago White Sox planted a tree in this park that still thrives. "The White Sox Redwood," as it is known today, was placed by first baseman Hal Chase and third baseman Harry Lord during a ceremony before the Sox played an exhibition game at Evans Park, which was located several blocks away. Near the base of the tree is a plaque commemorating the tree-planting ceremony. Also, a mere baseball toss from the tree, stands the first orange tree planted in California.

Jack Benny stands sentry for the Rancho Cucamonga Quakes.

Lefty Gomez Field

City: Rodeo
Location: 470 Parker Avenue
This is one of three sports-related sites that California has designated as a point of historical interest. (The other two are the Los Angeles Coliseum and the Willow Springs International Raceway in Rosamond.) Vernon "Lefty" Gomez was born in Rodeo and played briefly for the nearby San Francisco Seals. In 1929, the New York Yankees picked him up for $35,000 and two years later, the lanky southpaw with the trademark high leg kick and infectious personality won 21 games with the support of teammates like Lou Gehrig and Babe Ruth. Gomez combined with Red Ruffing to give the Yankees the top lefty-righty

pitching combination of the 1930s. In addition to posting a 189-102 career record, Gomez also was 6-0 in World Series play and twice (1934, '37) won the American League's pitching triple crown—wins, ERA and strikeouts. Gomez, inducted into the Hall of Fame in 1972, died in Greenbrae, California, on February 17, 1989.

Tony Gwynn Field

City: San Diego
Location: San Diego State University
5500 Campanile Drive
619-594-5200
Tony Gwynn Stadium became the new home of the San Diego State baseball program during the 1997 season. The $4 million facility was made possible through the generosity of San Diego Padres owner John Moores and his wife, Becky, who donated the funds to build a park named for the school's most famous player. In 2002, Tony Gwynn became coach of the Aztecs baseball team. Tony's brother, Chris, also was an All-American baseball player at San Diego State and a member of the 1984 U.S. Olympic baseball team. He went on to play parts of 10 seasons in the major leagues for the Dodgers, Royals and Padres. He works today as a Padres scout.

Stephen and Mary Birch Foundation Baseball Museum

City: San Diego
Location: San Diego State University
The museum is located on the concourse of Tony Gwynn Field behind the third base stands. Partly financed by a grant from the Stephen and Mary Birch Foundation, the free museum features displays and exhibits honoring former Aztecs teams and players who have contributed to the tradition of San Diego State baseball. Among the highlights are lockers detailing the careers of former Aztecs Tony Gwynn (San Diego Padres 1982-2000) and Travis Lee, who currently plays with the Tampa Bay Devil Rays. In addition to photographs, scrapbooks, trophies and other memorabilia, the museum also features a big-screen television that offers Aztecs highlights.

Albert Spalding Residence

City: San Diego
Location: Point Loma Nazarene College
3900 Lomaland Drive
619-849-2200

This ornate building is now part of a college campus. But from 1899-1915, it is where baseball pioneer and former pitcher Albert G. Spalding lived until his death. Spalding, retired from baseball, was introduced to an esoteric school of thought known as "theosophy" by his wife and moved his family to the Utopian community of the Theosophical Society, which was located in this building. The order left the premises in the 1950s.

The Pacific Ocean lies behind the outfield fence at Carroll B. Land Stadium.

"America's Most Scenic Ballpark"

City: San Diego
Location: Carroll B. Land Stadium
Point Loma Nazarene College
3900 Lomaland Drive
619-849-2200

Nestled on the seaside cliffs of San Diego overlooking the Pacific Ocean, no other collegiate baseball park—or perhaps no park anywhere—can match the picturesque views of Carroll B. Land Stadium. In 1998, the Crusader's home field was designated "America's Most Scenic Baseball Park" by *Baseball America*. The park was re-named in 1998 for Carroll Land, who coached collegiate ball at the school for 35 seasons.

The San Diego Hall of Champions

City: San Diego
Location: 2131 Pan American Plaza, in Balboa Park
619-234-2544

Located in beautiful Balboa Park, this renowned museum and hall of fame features a permanent baseball exhibit that occupies a large gallery on the first level of the 70,000-square-foot facility. Many exhibits and hundreds of pieces of memorabilia commemorate San Diego baseball sports history, and the museum provides opportunities for interactive, hands-on experiences for both children and adults. There also is a permanent exhibit dedicated to San Diego legend Ted Williams.

Former site of Lane Field

City: San Diego
Location: West Broadway and Pacific Coast Highway
Lane Field, built on the coast of the Pacific Ocean in 1936, was home for the Pacific Coast League's San Diego Padres from 1936-57. Hoover High School's Ted Williams played at Lane Field in 1936 and '37 and it was here that former Red Sox general manager Eddie Collins came to scout and eventually sign the promising young hitter. The location of Lane Field, which was torn down in the late 1950s, is now a parking lot. Plans are being discussed to erect an historic marker.

Lefty O'Doul Bridge

City: San Francisco
Location: Third Street, China Basin, leading into Pacific Bell Park
The bridge, visible from the stands in new Pacific Bell Park, is named in honor of one of the Bay Area's most beloved players. O'Doul, an outstanding major league hitter and legendary batting coach, still shares the National League record for hits in a season—254. The .349 career hitter batted .398 in that 1929 season with 32 home runs and 122 RBIs for the Philadelphia Phillies.

McCovey Cove

City: San Francisco
Location: Pacific Bell Park
24 Willie Mays Plaza
This is where the kayaks, canoes and other small vessels gather to await the next home run by Barry Bonds and other lefthanded sluggers—located just over the right field wall at Pac Bell Park.

McCovey Cove has provided the landing spot for many Barry Bonds home runs.

Willie Mays Statue

City: San Francisco
Location: Pacific Bell Park
24 Willie Mays Plaza
At the stadium's main entrance, surrounded by 24 palm trees, is a 9-foot sculpture of the Giants' legend.

Lefty O'Doul's

City: San Francisco
Location: 333 Geary Street
415-982-8900
This San Francisco landmark was opened in 1958 by Lefty O'Doul, who was born at San Francisco in 1897 and remains a legendary figure there more than three decades after his death. The former pitcher-turned-outfielder

Willie Mays guards the entrance to Pac Bell Park.

compiled a .349 average over 11 major league seasons, but he probably is better remembered in this area as the longtime manager of the Pacific Coast League's San Francisco Seals (1935-51), a renowned mentor and teacher of young players and a beloved local figure. O'Doul also was a baseball ambassador who made annual visits overseas in the 1930s and earned a reputation as "The Father of Baseball in Japan." The memorabilia in O'Doul's restaurant is plentiful and authentic, and the popular eatery also features one of the last Hofbrau menus in San Francisco.

Former site of Seals Stadium

City: San Francisco
Location: 16th and Bryant
From 1931-57, this quaint, single-level neighborhood ballpark served as the home to the Pacific Coast League's San Francisco Seals. This is where Joe DiMaggio played minor league ball in the 1930s and compiled his 61-game hitting streak, an amazing 1933 run that served as a preview for his 56-game streak in 1941 with the New York Yankees. The Seals' last game at the stadium was played on September 13, 1957, at which point it became the temporary home of the relocating New York Giants. The Giants played at Seals for two years while Candlestick Park was being built. Their last game there was September 20, 1959, and Seals Stadium was demolished two months later. The former location of Seals' home plate is buried beneath an Old Navy clothing store. First base is occupied by a Petco store and the center field once manned by Willie Mays is

now a parking lot. There is no historical plaque or marker to identify the former landmark. But the Hamm's brewery building, which stood behind the home plate area, is still there.

Double Play Bar & Grill

City: San Francisco
Location: 2401 16th Street (at Bryant)
415-621-9859

Located directly across from where Seals Stadium once stood is the historic Double Play, a bar and grill that has been in business at this site since 1909. Once a famous hangout before and after games at Seals Stadium, it is now a shrine to the memory of the long-gone minor and major league park. You'll find

photographs, caps, jerseys and mitts covering the walls as well as seats from Seals Stadium and, above the bar next to a 1939 Seals jersey, the round, gold top of the stadium's longtime flagpole. In the back dining room, all four walls are part of a Seals Stadium mural, painted in exquisite detail.

The Double Play Bar & Grill revives the memory and baseball atmosphere of Seals Stadium.

Former site of Recreation Park

City: San Francisco
Location: 15th and Valencia

Pre-Seals Stadium, this was home of the Seals from 1906-30 and the Mission Reds from 1926-30. During a 1920s barnstorming tour, Babe Ruth's Bustin' Babes played Lou Gehrig's Larrupin' Lous here.

Former site of Ewing Field

City: San Francisco
Location: Turk and Masonic

Ewing Field, home to the San Francisco Seals in 1914, was quickly abandoned because of dense fog that blanketed the park. The team returned to Recreation Park.

"The Ball Player" statue

City: San Francisco
Location: Golden Gate Park
This popular statue of a baseball player was created by Douglas Tilden, a Chico, California, product who lost his hearing at age 5 after a bout with scarlet fever. Tilden studied his craft in Paris under renowned sculptor Paul Chopin, who also was deaf. The Ball Player statue was Tilden's first work, accepted upon completion by the Salon des Artistes Francais on the Champs Elysees in 1889.

Bay Area Sports Hall of Fame

City: San Francisco
Location: Six sites (listed below) throughout the Bay Area that exhibit a series of inductee plaques.
415-352-8835
This non-profit organization was conceived and founded by the San Francisco Chamber of Commerce in 1979. Annual contributions aid in the development of Bay Area youth through The Youth Fund. The organization's work funds many projects in the city, and inductees are visible throughout the Bay Area, presented as a series of plaques in public areas. Here are the six locations:

- Network Associates Coliseum
  7000 Coliseum Way
  Oakland
  510-569-2121
  Dick, Bartell, Rollie Fingers, Curt Flood, Catfish Hunter, Reggie Jackson, Ernie Lombardi, Billy Martin, Joe Morgan, Vada Pinson, Bill Rigney, Frank Robinson and Willie Stargell

- Pac Bell Park
  24 Willie Mays Plaza
  San Francisco
  Vida Blue, Orlando Cepeda, Juan Marichal, Willie Mays, Willie McCovey and Lefty O'Doul.

- Sacred Heart Cathedral Prep School
  Sacred Heart Cathedral Preparatory
  1055 Ellis Street
  San Francisco
  415-775-6626
  Dolph Camilli, Joe Cronin and Harry Heilmann

- University of California, Berkeley
  510-642-6000
  Sam Chapman

- San Francisco International Airport (Domestic terminal)
  650-624-7200
  Dominic DiMaggio—Gate 80
  Joe DiMaggio—Gate 81
  Dennis Eckersley—Gate 80
  Lefty Gomez—Gate 90
  Eddie Joost—Gate 83
  Dave Stewart—Gate 87

- Jackson Playground
  Arkansas (between 17th and Mariposa Streets)
  San Francisco
  Tony Lazzeri

Historic Municipal Stadium

City: San Jose
Location: 588 E. Alma Avenue
408-297-1435
Built as part of Franklin Roosevelt's Works Progress Administration (WPA),

Municipal Stadium opened on March 8, 1942, when the San Francisco Seals defeated the Portland Beavers, 15-8. Now home for the San Francisco Giants Class A California League affiliate, the San Jose Giants, old-time Municipal Stadium celebrates local baseball history with a series of painted murals located around the stadium. Included

Historic Municipal Stadium has been fulfilling San Jose baseball dreams since 1942.

is a timeline of baseball in San Jose, which traces every former San Jose alumnus who makes it to the major leagues.

Chicago Cubs spring training field

City: Santa Catalina Island
Location: Country Club Road in Avalon
From 1921-51, this was a spring training facility for the Chicago Cubs. Cubs owner William Wrigley built a diamond and a practice field in Avalon, with the ballfield's dimensions matching those of Wrigley Field in Chicago. Surrounded by eucalyptus trees, the field was located below Wrigley's mountainside country club, which housed the players' locker rooms. (Wrigley, in fact, owned the island.) Wrigley himself was a familiar face at the field, usually sit-

The plaque documents the Cubs' Catalina past.

ting in the bleachers to watch workouts. Typically, Cubs pitchers, catchers and rookies arrived in mid-February and the rest of the team followed a week later. By mid-March, the team would break camp and sail for Los Angeles and two weeks of exhibition games in California. Then the Cubs would slowly work their way across the Southwest, playing games in towns along the way. Today, at the site where a ballfield still sits, are three plaques, including one that once adorned the tower of Los Angeles' Wrigley Field and marked the dedication of that stadium in 1926 by Judge Kenesaw Mountain Landis. It reads: "This tower was erected by Wm. Wrigley, Jr., in honor of the baseball players who gave or risked their lives in the defense of their country in the great World War. Jan. 15, 1926." Another plaque was placed by the Avalon Men's Softball League and the third carries the inscription, "Los Angeles was the home of the Los Angeles Angels, Pacific Coast League AAA ball club. William Wrigley, Jr. bought the Angels in 1921. Ownership was transferred to the Santa Catalina Island Company in 1932. From 1941 to 1957 the club was owned by the Chicago National League ball club, the Chicago Cubs. For 26 years between 1921 and 1951, the Chicago Cubs held their annual spring training at this field in Catalina."

Lenny's Dykstra's car wash

City: Simi Valley
Location: 1144 Los Angeles Avenue
805-581-9300
Former Philadelphia and New York Mets outfielder Lenny Dykstra has been "cleaning up" since retiring in 1996 with a chain of successful car washes. He has a second location in Corona and a third opening shortly. Dykstra, making

sure his customers have plenty to see as their vehicles are scrubbed, has installed an impressive showcase with lots of memorabilia from all sports.

Historic Recreation Park

City: Visalia
Location: 440 North Giddings Street
559-625-0480

Recreation Park, the home of professional baseball in Visalia since 1946, is the name of a city park that includes a skate park, basketball courts and picnic areas. The stadium itself does not have a name. The ballpark was preceded by an all-wood structure that stood on the current site before the existing stadium was built in 1967. The concrete exterior of the main grandstand covers soil removed from the trench used to build Highway 198 through central Visalia. With a capacity of 1,647, the stadium remains the second smallest in the minor leagues. The front row of backstop seats is a cozy 28 feet from home plate, providing what might be the closest view of game action in professional baseball. Dozens of major league stars—Barry Zito, Mark McGwire, Ken Griffey Jr., Don Drysdale, Kirby Puckett—have played at the stadium, which currently is the home of the Visalia Oaks, a Class A California League affiliate of the Colorado Rockies.

Keep your eyes peeled for...

Stengel Field
Verdugo Park across the street from Glendale Community College
Glendale
This field, named for Stengel, the "Old Professor" (and longtime Glendale resident), serves as home of the Cresenta Valley (high school) Falcons.

Ted Williams Parkway
Poway
In 1992, a section of State Route 56 in North San Diego County was re-christened the "Ted Williams Parkway" in honor of its local hero.

Plaque at Dodger Stadium
1000 Elysian Park Avenue
Los Angeles
213-224-1400
It remains one of the crown jewels in professional sports and a landmark. The plaque was unveiled in 1962 when the stadium opened and can be found on the upper level, just inside the gate near the gift shop.

Fiscalini Field
1103 E Highland Avenue
San Bernardino
The Pittsburgh Pirates used this site for spring training in the 1940.

Brookside Park
Pasadena
The White Sox trained here in the 1930s and '40s and it is now the location of 4,500-seat Jackie Robinson Stadium.

John Berardino's star on the Hollywood Walk of Fame
Berardino started in the major leagues with the St. Louis Browns in 1939 and went on to play for the Pirates and Indians (he was on the 1948 World Series champion Indians team). But he probably is best remembered as *General Hospital's* Dr. Steve Hardy, a role he played for 33 years until his death in 1996.

Hall of Famers buried in California

Harry Hooper
Aptos Cemetery
7600 Soquel Drive
Aptos

Joseph "Arky" Vaughan
Eagleville Cemetery
West side of Main Street north of town
Eagleville

Los Angeles Metropolitan Area
Casey Stengel
Forest Lawn Cemetery
1712 S. Glendale Avenue
Glendale
800-204-3131

Bobby Wallace and Sam Crawford
Inglewood Park Cemetery
3803 West Manchester Boulevard
Inglewood
310-412-6500

Leo Durocher
Forest Lawn Cemetery
Hollywood Hills

Harry Hooper (top) and
Arky Vaughan.

6300 Forest Lawn Drive
Los Angeles
323-254-7251

Hank Greenberg
Hillside Memorial Park & Mortuary
6001 West Centinela Avenue
Los Angeles
310-641-0707

Frank Chance
Rosedale Cemetery
1831 W. Washington Boulevard
Los Angeles
323-734-3155

Chick Hafey
Holy Cross Cemetery
2121 Spring Street
St. Helena
707-963-1703

Bid McPhee
Cypress View Mausoleum
3953 Imperial Avenue
San Diego
619-263-3151

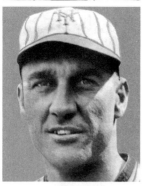

San Francisco-Oakland Metropolitan Area
George Kelly and Joe DiMaggio
Holy Cross Cemetery
1500 Old Mission Road
Colma
650-756-2060

Tony Lazzeri
Sunset View Cemetery
101 Colusa Avenue
El Cerrito
510-526-6212

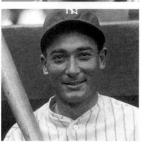

(From top) Hank
Greenberg, Chick Hafey,
George Kelly and Tony
Lazzeri.

Ernie Lombardi
Mountain View Cemetery
5000 Piedmont

Oakland
510-658-2588

Vernon "Lefty" Gomez
Mount Tamalpais Cemetery
2500 5th Avenue
San Rafael
415-459-2500

Eddie Mathews
Santa Barbara Cemetery
901 Channel Drive
Santa Barbara
805-969-3231

Ernie Lombardi (top) and
Lefty Gomez.

Colorado

Coors Field

City: Denver
Location: 2001 Blake Street (At 20th Street)
800-388-ROCK

Balls just seem to travel a little further at 5,280 feet above sea level, and that's what gives Coors its distinctive flavor. It's also gorgeous, the fan-friendly home of the Colorado Rockies. Just so you know where you are, the

Coors Field is one of baseball's most scenic ballparks.

upper deck's 20th row is painted purple, signifying exactly one mile above sea level. The rest of the park's seats are green.

Colorado Sports Hall of Fame

City: Denver
Location: INVESCO Field at Mile High
303-839-8735
www.coloradosports.org

The Colorado Sports Hall of Fame Museum (presented by Coors Brewing Company) is located on the west side of INVESCO Field, home of the NFL's Denver Broncos. Inductees to the Colorado Sports Hall of Fame are chosen by an independent selection committee composed of media representatives from throughout the state. Baseball players and coaches inducted since 1960 include Goose Gossage, Bill Fanning, L.C. Butler and Robert "Bus" Campbell, all of whom have ties to Colorado. Tours of INVESCO Field are offered through the museum, and the tour includes a view of Mile High Stadium's former site (now the INVESCO Field parking lot). Mile High, built in 1948, was originally home to the Bears, Denver's minor league baseball team. When the American Football League was launched in 1960, Mile High became home to a second sports team— the Broncos. It continued as a baseball and football venue for almost 40 years. In 1985, a then-minor league affiliate of the Cincinnati Reds moved to Denver and the expansion Colorado Rockies arrived in 1993 as Denver's first major league baseball team, playing their games at Mile High. The Rockies moved to their new Coors Field home in 1995 and Mile High was demolished after the 2001 football season.

Idaho

McDermott Field

City: Idaho Falls
Location: Elva Street at Blaine Avenue in Highland Park
208-522-8363

Idaho Falls has the longest continuous membership in the Pioneer League, dating back to 1940, the year after its formation. Historic McDermott Field, opened in 1940 as Highland Park, has seen all of the action over the years. Most of the main grandstand was rebuilt in 1976 after arsonists set fire to the park, and the name was changed to honor E.F. McDermott, a local newspaper publisher. The park, the current home of the Class A Idaho Falls Padres, still has plenty of nostalgic charm.

Harmon Killebrew Field

City: Payette
Location: Payette High school
1500 6th Avenue South
208-642-3327
Harmon Killebrew, born in Payette on June 29, 1936, attended Payette High and is the namesake for the school's sports field. Killebrew, one of the game's most feared sluggers in the 1950s and '60s, pounded out 573 home runs over 22 seasons with the Washington Senators, Minnesota Twins and Kansas City Royals. He won six American League home run titles, topping the 40 plateau eight times and drove in 100 or more runs on nine occasions. Killebrew, who was inducted into the Hall of Fame in 1984, also is honored with a display inside the school.

Walter Johnson Memorial Park

City: Weiser
Location: Corner of Hanthorn and East 3rd Street
This is the town where the great Walter Johnson was playing semi-pro ball and digging holes for the local telephone company when he was signed to his first major league contract. Johnson, who was born in Kansas in 1887, moved to California with his family soon after birth. But he found himself in Idaho in 1907, a young pitching prodigy looking for a break. It came when Washington manager Joe Cantillon, who was interested in a local outfielder named Clyde Milan,

This Idaho park was where Walter Johnson was 'discovered.'

sent an injured catcher to Idaho to scout the player. He signed both Milan and Johnson, who immediately embarked on his Hall of Fame career. In addition to the baseball field, another local Johnson landmark is the train station where the Big Train bid farewell to his Weiser teammates in 1907.

Walter Johnson Display

City: Weiser
Location: Snake River Heritage Center
2295 Paddock Avenue
208-549-0205
You'll find a Walter Johnson display at this small museum, including photos, artifacts and even one of Johnson's uniforms.

Montana

Cobb Field

City: Billings
Location: 901 N. 27th Street
406-252-1241.
Cobb Field is not named for Ty Cobb, as one might suspect. It is named as a tribute to Robert Cobb, who was owner of the Pacific Coast League's Hollywood Stars in the 1940s. It was because of Cobb that professional baseball found its way to Billings. Although he played a big role in the success of the PCL on the west coast, he is probably best remembered as the founder and owner of the legendary Brown Derby restaurant in Hollywood. In fact, the Cobb Salad was named for him (an accidental creation that was a result of Cobb asking that a salad be thrown together for him with whatever scraps were left lying around the kitchen). Home to minor league baseball since 1948, Cobb Field serves as home for the Mustangs in the Summer Class A Pioneer League, a team affiliated with the Cincinnati Reds.

Nevada

Las Vegas Club

The Las Vegas Club is filled with memorabilia from Dodgers greats such as Duke Snider.

City: Las Vegas
Location: 18 E. Fremont Street
702-385-1664

The idea for this club came in 1962, when "Marvelous" Mel Exber asked Los Angeles Dodgers basestealing sensation Maury Wills for an autograph. Wills signed for the Brooklyn-born Exber and a relationship was born. After the 1962 season, when Wills and such teammates as Duke Snider, Sandy Koufax and Don Drysdale rolled into Vegas for some vacation time, Exber invited them to his club, which soon transformed into a memorabilia shrine for Dodgers fans. With its Ebbets Field facade, free sports museum and "Dugout Restaurant," the Las Vegas Club's classic sports theme remains unique in a town where pyramids, palaces and volcanoes dominate the strip.

The Nevada Griffons

City: West Highland
Location: Lyons Field
www.nevadagriffons.org
The Nevada Griffons, a team of collegiate athletes, play at Lyons Stadium in June and July. Over the 15 years that the Griffons have played in Nevada, many of their players have gone on to professional careers.

Oregon

Historic Civic Stadium

City: Eugene
Location: 20th and Williamette
Built in 1938, Civic Stadium was originally designed as both a football and baseball facility. It was part of a Works Progress Administration project that was designed to develop an entire area. The Depression-era wooden stadium now is one of the oldest in the minor leagues. Originally home to semi-pro baseball, it later became home to the Pacific Coast League's Emeralds and now serves as the Padres' Class A affiliate in the Northwest League. Over the years, Civic Stadium has been used for everything from high school football and soccer to a rodeo in the mid-1980s. The women's Little League Softball World Series also is held here every August.

Oregon Sports Hall of Fame

City: Portland
Location: 21 SW Salmon

503-227-7466

Since 1980, the Oregon Sports Hall of Fame has inducted the best of Oregon athletes, teams and coaches as well as those who have made a special contribution to sports. Twenty-seven baseball players have been inducted into the Oregon Sports Hall of Fame, including Johnny Pesky, Bobby Doerr, Artie Wilson, Dale Murphy, Wally Backman, Mickey Lolich and Rick Wise. The highlights of the baseball exhibit include a "Dugout Display" and a virtual demonstration that lets visitors catch a simulated 90-mph baseball. Players are inducted by members of the public ($25 a year to become a voting member) and artifacts include Portland Beavers memorabilia and even a pair of seats from long-gone Vaughn Street Ballpark.

Sckavone Stadium

City: Portland
Location: SE McLoughlin & Spokane (Located in Westmoreland Park)
503-823-PLAY

This neighborhood stadium has been the launching ground for several professional careers and local championship teams. The park, named for Nick Sckavone, the man who spearheaded the efforts to get it built in 1940, was rebuilt in 1992.

Sckavone Stadium, a neighborhood facility built in 1940, has been the launching ground for several professional careers.

PGE Park

City: Portland
Location: 1844 SW Morrison
503-553-5400

PGE Park, home of the Pacific Coast League's Portland Beavers, has a rich and storied history that dates back to 1926. Multnomah Stadium, as it was known when it opened on October 9, 1926, with a University of Washington football victory over Oregon, played host to its first baseball game in 1956, when the Beavers left the notoriously fire-prone Vaughn Street Ballpark. In 1967, Multnomah Stadium was purchased by the City of Portland and renamed Civic Stadium. The Beavers and Portland Timbers played at Civic Stadium in the 1960s and '70s and, more recently, it has hosted a wide array of speakers, performers and international sporting events, from the Billy Graham Crusade to the women's World Cup soccer events of 1998 and '99. Other sports figures and entertainers who have appeared at the stadium over the years include Joe DiMaggio, Pete Rose, Norm Van Brocklin, Elvis Presley, Bob Hope, David Bowie, Tom Petty and Bob Dylan. Soccer great Pele even played his last game here. After a $38.5-million overhaul completed in April of 2001, Portland's PGE Park is now poised to attract a major league franchise. But great efforts have been taken to retain the historic charm of the park that dates back more than 75 years.

Former site of Vaughn Street Ballpark

City: Portland
Location: 2409 NW Vaughn Street

Built in 1901, Vaughn Street Ballpark (also called Lucky Beavers Stadium) was home to the Portland Beavers of the Pacific Coast League. They won four pennants from 1910-14 and this is also where future Hall of Famer Bobby Doerr was signed by the Red Sox. The rickety wooden park caught fire many times and was torn down a year after the Beavers moved to Multnomah Stadium in 1955. Today, a marker at the site now occupied by industrial buildings tells visitors that a stadium once stood there.

Utah

Franklin Covey Field

City: Salt Lake City
Location: 77 West 1300 South
801-485-3800

Opened in 1994, this stadium boasts top-notch Pacific Coast League baseball as well as one of the most scenic atmospheres in the professional ranks. First-time visitors to Franklin Covey Field are mesmerized by the exquisite, panoramic views of the Wasatch Mountains beyond the outfield wall. The stadium was specifically designed to reflect the natural beauty of the mountain range, and the architects hit this one out of the park. The Salt Lake Stingers, a Class AAA affiliate of the Anaheim Angels, play here and they were the 2002 Central Division champs. For its first seven years, Franklin Covey was occupied by the Salt Lake Buzz. Fans fondly recall the stadium's first season, when the Buzz set an all-time Pacific Coast League attendance record and Salt Lake's Marty Cordova ate up the league with a .358 average—the year before he claimed American League Rookie of the Year honors with the Minnesota Twins. Affordable, comfortable and aesthetically unique, this is a wonderful place to enjoy a game.

Washington

Former site of Sick's Stadium

Sick's Stadium, longtime home of the Rainiers, had a short-lived brush with big-league baseball.

City: Seattle
Location: Lowe's of Rainier
2700 Rainier Avenue South
206-760-0832

Sick's Stadium, which opened in 1938, was the second ballpark built on this site. Before that, Dugdale Park served as home to the Pacific Coast League's Seattle Indians. When Dugdale burned down after a July 4 fireworks celebration in 1932, the team moved to Civic Field for six years while a steel-and-concrete facility was built at the former Dugdale site. New Sick's Stadium was named after Raniers owner Emil Sick and the 12,000-seat park hosted minor league baseball until the early 1960s. When a major league franchise was awarded to Seattle in 1967, Sick's capacity was increased to 25,000. But the Seattle Pilots played there just one season, a franchise beset by financial difficulties that eventually forced its move under new ownership (Bud Selig) to Milwaukee. After the Pilots left, Sick's Stadium was used as a minor league ballpark again until 1976 and then sat empty while the expansion Mariners, another Seattle major league experiment, played in the Kingdome. In 1979, Sick's Stadium was demolished. The former site of Sick's Stadium is now occupied by a Lowe's Home Improvement Warehouse. Look for a glass display case inside the store with memorabilia from both the Rainiers and Pilots; just outside the front door is a bronze home plate with a metal statue of a player holding a bat. Its inscription reads: "BATTER UP! You are standing on the former site of Sick's Seattle Stadium, home of the Seattle Rainiers and Seattle Pilots. If the year were 1942, you'd be in perfect position to knock one out of the park."

Historic Cheney Stadium

City: Tacoma

Location: 2502 South Tyler (Intersection of Tyler and 19th street in Tacoma just off of Highway 16)

253-752-7707

Built in 1960, Cheney Stadium is the oldest baseball facility in the Pacific Coast League. Home to the Mariners' Class AAA Tacoma Rainiers, Cheney has been the stomping grounds of such future stars as Willie McCovey, Alex Rodriguez and Mark McGwire. But what makes the park special is the tradition that oozes from every nook and cranny. Especially notable are the pieces that were transplanted from San Francisco's Seals Stadium—the light standards and blue reserved bleacher benches that moved north when the Bay Area park was demolished. The origin of Cheney Stadium dates back to 1957 when local businessmen Ben

A bronze tribute to Ben Cheney is a constant at the ballpark that bears his name.

Cheney (a statue of him now sits in a box seat at the ballpark) and Clay Huntington worked to bring Pacific Coast League baseball to Tacoma. In the fall of 1959, the San Francisco Giants met with Tacoma officials to discuss moving their Class AAA Phoenix club to Tacoma. The Giants committed to the move, provided Tacoma would construct a stadium by April 1960. The deal went through and in less than four months, the stadium was built, including the parts from Seals Stadium. The first scheduled game was rained out on April 14, 1960. When the game was played as part of a day/night doubleheader on April 16, the Tacoma Giants lost their inaugural Cheney Stadium game, 7-2, to the Portland Beavers. Tacoma took the nightcap, 11-0—thanks to the pitching of future Hall of Famer Juan Marichal.

Hall of Famers buried in Washington

Amos Rusie had 246 career wins and 1,950 strikeouts.

Amos Rusie
Acacia Cemetery
14951 Bothell Way NE
Seattle
206-362-5525

Earl Averill
Grand Army of the Republic Cemetery
8601 Riverview Road
Snohomish
360-568-4090

Wyoming

Burial site of Benjamin Franklin Hunt

City: Greybull
Location: Hillside Cemetery
Ben Hunt, a 6-foot-5 lefthander, compiled a 2-4 record in 1910 and '13 with the Boston Red Sox and St. Louis Cardinals. Hunt, a native Oklahoman, died in 1927 at Greybull.

Outside the Lines

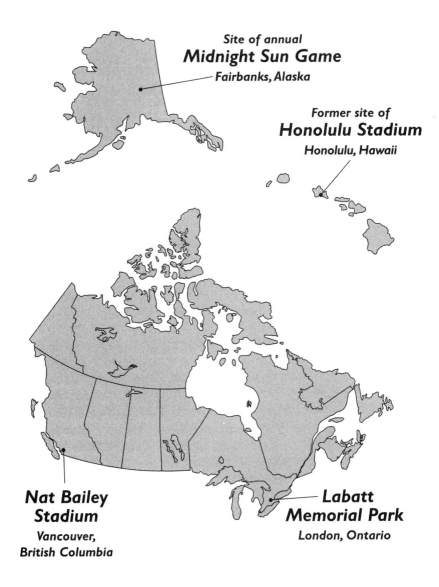

Site of annual
Midnight Sun Game
Fairbanks, Alaska

Former site of
Honolulu Stadium
Honolulu, Hawaii

**Nat Bailey
Stadium**
**Vancouver,
British Columbia**

**Labatt
Memorial Park**
London, Ontario

Alaska

The Midnight Sun Game

City: Fairbanks
Location: Growden Memorial Park
Located near the intersection of Wilbur and Airport Rd.

"What began nearly 100 years ago on a bet between two local bars has evolved into one of baseball's unique natural events. The Midnight Sun Game, played in Fairbanks on the summer solstice every year since 1906, is played in the middle of the night with only natural light."

—Baseball America's 12 must-see events

Growden Park is home for the Fairbanks Alaska Goldpanners, one of six teams in the Alaska Baseball League, a premier wooden-bat collegiate summer circuit. The Goldpanners have been the starting point for many major leaguers, including Barry Bonds, Jason Giambi, Dave Winfield and Graig Nettles, since forming in 1960. That year, the Goldpanners adopted one of baseball's most charming traditions—"The Midnight Sun Game." A Fairbanks landmark event since 1906, the annual game takes place on June 21, the longest day of the year when the area experiences almost 24 hours of daylight. The game begins at 10:30 p.m. and often lasts until 2 a.m. Since Fairbanks is only 160 miles south of the Arctic Circle, the sun is just beginning to set in the north as the game gets under way. At its conclusion, the sun is beginning to rise in the north—

In 1908, the Midnight Sun Game, which has become a Growden Park tradition, was being played for only the third time.

one of the world's natural phenomenons. (The light fades toward the middle of the game, but returns by its end.) Never has artificial lighting been used for this unique event, and never has the game been postponed or delayed because of darkness. According to custom, the game is stopped at midnight for the singing of the Alaska Flag Song. Through 1962, the Goldpanners played the Range All-Stars in the annual event, but since 1963, they have matched up against a different opponent, usually a team from out of state. Before the Goldpanners took control of the event, various local and military teams played against each other. The game is traditionally a celebration of the summer solstice and is treated as a holiday in Fairbanks, with shops and businesses closing early.

About Growden Park: Originally named Memorial Park, Growden was renamed in 1964 in honor of James Growden, who, along with his two sons, was killed in a tidal wave created by the Good Friday Earthquake of 1964. Growden had been heavily involved in Fairbanks youth activities for years. In 1964, it became the first outdoor lighted facility in Alaska, and though the seating capacity is about 3,500, more than 5,000 fans jammed the park in 1967 for the Midnight Sun Game when the Goldpanners played Kumagai-Gumi of Japan. The park has box seats and grandstand benches from old Sick's Stadium in Seattle, which was home of the Seattle Rainiers minor league team and the 1969 Seattle Pilots major league team.

Hawaii

The Babe Ruth Banyan Tree

City: Hilo
Location: In front of the Hilo Hawaiian Hotel
71 Banyan Drive
702-438-1166

Before Babe Ruth led a team of all-stars to Japan in 1934, he brought his wife and daughter to Hawaii in 1933, combining a little business with pleasure. Ruth took time to play in two exhibition games while in Honolulu and spent the rest of his time playing golf, eating at all the best places and soaking up the local culture. After hitting two home runs in one of the exhibitions, the Babe took time to plant a banyan tree on Banyan Drive, an idyllic piece of land facing Hilo Bay. This was a custom performed over the years by many visiting celebrities, including Cecil B. DeMille, Amelia Earhart, Franklin D. Roosevelt and Richard Nixon. Ruth's Banyan tree has continued to thrive in front of the popular Hilo Hawaiian Hotel. It is surrounded by a swatch of red ginger and a plaque with "Babe Ruth" on it.

Former site of Honolulu Stadium

City: Honolulu
Location: Corners of King and Isenberg
The old Honolulu Stadium where Ruth played his exhibition games was torn down in 1976. The legendary ballpark, which opened in 1926, also played host to Elvis Presley, Jesse Owens and many sports and entertainment events. Located on the two-acre site today is Stadium Park.

Hall of Famers buried in Hawaii

Alexander Cartwright
Oahu Cemetery, 2162 Nuuana Avenue
Honolulu
808-538-1538

Alexander Cartwright

Canada

The first baseball game in North America

City: Beachville, Ontario
Location: On King Street west of Zorraline behind Baptist Church, in the subdivided lots
Signs at both ends of town proclaim Beachville as the site of the first record-ed baseball game in North America. While that claim has never been recognized as valid by the Hall of Fame at Cooperstown, it is clear that something resem-bling a baseball game did happen there on June 4, 1838—a year earlier than Abner Doubleday's now-controversial "Cooperstown game."

The claim is based on a letter from Dr. Adam E. Ford to a pre-19th century magazine called *Sporting Life*. In his letter, Ford details the rules of a game played in a Beachville pasture and recalls the names of various players. The let-ter, published May 5, 1886, was titled, "A Game of Long Ago Which Closely Resembled Our Present National Game." Ford had grown up in Beachville and what set his letter apart from other remembrances of early baseball was the detail he provided on how the game was played, the players, the rules, the dia-grams—clearly something organized had happened in this small Canadian town almost 50 years earlier. Ford's original letter is on display at the Hall of Fame.

Beachville District Museum

City: Beachville, Ontario
Location: 584371 Beachville Road
519-423-6497
A diorama of the historic game played at Beachville is on display at this small museum, as is a plaque placed here in honor of the game.

The oldest active baseball facility in North America

City: London, Ontario
Location: Labatt Memorial Park
Riverside Drive & Wilson Avenue
This Canadian ballfield is the world's oldest site continually used for baseball. It opened in 1876 as Tecumseh Park and, after the original grandstand was destroyed by flood in 1937, the Labatt family (Labatt Breweries) refurbished the park and donated it to their home city. It was most recently used as a facility by the Frontier League's London Werewolves, who left in 2001. It is home today for the London Majors, a member of the Intercounty Baseball League in southwestern Ontario, as well as several London-area teams.

Montreal honors Jackie Robinson with this statue at Olympic Stadium.

Jackie Robinson statue

City: Montreal
Location: Olympic Stadium
4549 Pierre-de-Coubertin Avenue
514-8GO-EXPOS
The statue outside Olympic Stadium honors Jackie Robinson, who made his Organized Baseball debut in 1946 as a member of the Class AAA Montreal Royals.

Jarry Park

City: Montreal
Location: 285 Faillon W
514-273-1234
Jarry Park was site of the first major league game played outside the continental United States. The historic first came on April 14, 1969, when the expansion Montreal Expos

opened their first season with an 8-7 victory over the St. Louis Cardinals. The Expos played at cozy Jarry through the 1976 season, at which point they moved into Olympic Stadium, a multi-sports facility built for the 1976 Olympic Games. Jarry Park with its capacity of 28,000 featured baseball's first bilingual public address announcements. Long home runs to right field had a good chance of landing in a public swimming pool. Jarry Park, still standing, is used regularly for social and civic events, professional tennis and other large outdoor gatherings.

Phil "Babe" Marchildon plaque

City: Penetanguishene, Ontario
Location: Phil Marchildon Memorial Park
A plaque honors local pitching hero Phil "Babe" Marchildon, who compiled a nine-year major league record of 68-75 for the Philadelphia Athletics and Boston Red Sox from 1940-50. Marchildon, a righthander, was inducted into the Canadian Sports Hall of Fame in 1976. The plaque bearing Marchildon's name was dedicated by the Penetanguishene Sports Hall of Fame in 1997.

The Canadian Baseball Hall of Fame & Museum

City: St. Mary's, Ontario
Location: 386 Church St. South
519-284-1838
The original dream of a Canadian Baseball Hall of Fame began in 1983 in Toronto. The idea was to preserve Canada's baseball heritage and help promote the sport's growth in Canada at every level. The dream has now grown into a major annual event that includes induction ceremonies, an outstanding museum and hopes of St. Mary's, a southwestern Ontario town, becoming "Canada's Cooperstown." St. Mary's, now the permanent home of the Canadian Baseball Hall of Fame, opened its museum on June 4, 1998, in an historic stone home on its 32-acre site. In addition to its state-of-the-art, interactive museum, "Stonetown" now includes a spring training-type complex that rivals many found in Florida and Arizona—three baseball diamonds, lodging, a conference services center, an auditorium, walking trails, picnic grounds and an amphitheater. Stonetown soon will become the permanent training center for Canada's Olympic Baseball Team and the country's premier venue for camps, tournaments and championships for all ages. Fans can watch their baseball while sitting in 70 chairs from Exhibition Stadium, the former home of the Toronto Blue Jays, and many more will be used for a new stadium being built. The historic building that houses the museum was built in 1886.

Babe Ruth's first "professional" home run

City: Toronto
Location: Hanlan's Point
Take ferry from the mainland; ferry docks are located at the south end of Bay Street, on Queens Quay West.

Babe Ruth hit his first home run as a professional in 1914 for Baltimore during an exhibition game at Fayetteville, North Carolina. But the Bambino hit his first live game professional home run later that year in Toronto. Ruth's Toronto blast happened shortly after he had been traded by his Baltimore minor league club to the Boston Red Sox, who assigned him to the Providence Grays of the International League. Ruth hit his only minor league homer on September 5, 1914, at Toronto's Hanlan's Point Stadium in a game against the Maple Leafs. Ruth, who played only 46 minor league games, was pitching for the Red Sox by the end of the season. The stadium was torn down in the 1930s, but a plaque marks the location of Ruth's home run.

Nat Bailey Stadium

City: Vancouver, British Columbia
Location: 33rd & Ontario Street
Built in 1951, Nat Bailey Stadium is one of the oldest structures still used by minor league teams. Originally named Capilano Stadium after a local brewery, the park was renamed in 1978 when the Class AAA Vancouver Canadians entered their inaugural season in the Pacific Coast League. The park was named for Nat Bailey, a longtime supporter of baseball in the Vancouver area and the first owner of the popular White Spot restaurant chain.